STEAM DAYS AT HAYMARKET

The Collected Reminiscences of Shed Life both on and off the Footplate

BY HARRY KNOX

Copyright IRWELL PRESS LIMITED
ISBN-10 1-903266-77-7
ISBN-978 1-903266-77-9

First published in the United Kingdom in 2007
by Irwell Press Limited, 59A, High Street, Clophill,
Bedfordshire MK45 4BE
Printed by Newton Printing, London

CONTENTS

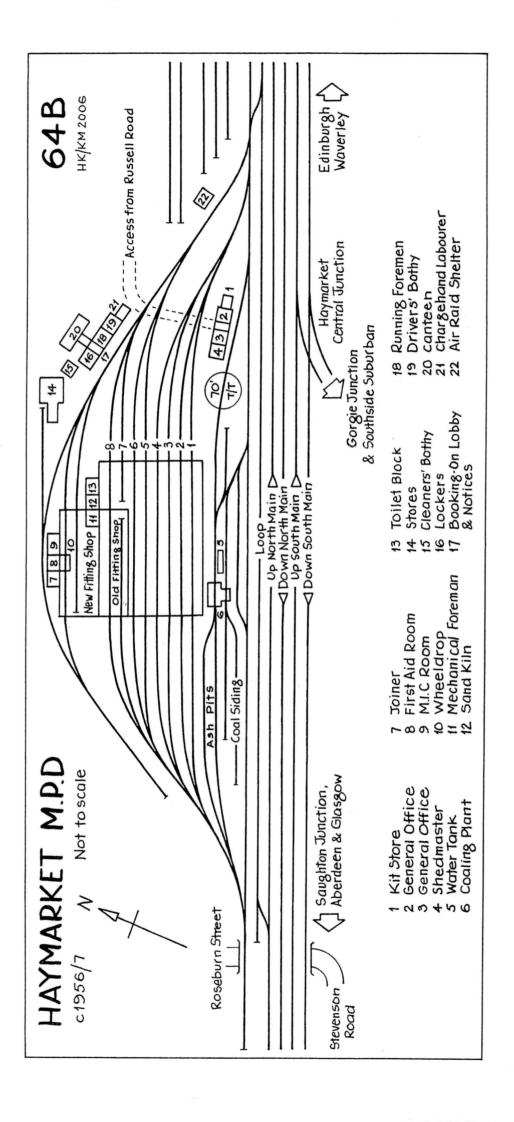

HAYMARKET M.P.D.

c 1956/7   Not to scale

64B

HK/KM 2006

N

Roseburn Street

Saughton Junction, Aberdeen & Glasgow

Stevenson Road

Access from Russell Road

Edinburgh Waverley

Haymarket Central Junction

Gorgie Junction & Southside Suburban

New Fitting Shop
Old Fitting Shop

Ash Pits
Coal Siding

Loop
Up North Main
Down North Main
Up South Main
Down South Main

70' T/T

1 Kit Store
2 General Office
3 General Office
4 Shedmaster
5 Water Tank
6 Coaling Plant

7 Joiner
8 First Aid Room
9 M.I.C Room
10 Wheeldrop
11 Mechanical Foreman
12 Sand Kiln

13 Toilet Block
14 Stores
15 Cleaners' Bothy
16 Lockers
17 Booking-On Lobby
   & Notices

18 Running Foremen
19 Drivers' Bothy
20 Canteen
21 Chargehand Labourer
22 Air Raid Shelter

Introduction

This is the story of life in the closing days of steam at one of the 'glamorous' and well-known locomotive depots in Edinburgh, Haymarket Motive Power Depot ('MPD') or, in British Railways classification, just plain 64B. Edinburgh, in the heyday of steam had three main MPDs, all within a radius of about three miles of each other, but each was as different as chalk and cheese. Firstly, there was Dalry Road, 64C, a mere stone's throw from Haymarket, but that was the 'Caley' and definitely foreign territory. However, it was not unknown for a Haymarket Cleaner to be dispatched post-haste across to Dalry Road for a firing turn, especially on the nightshift.

The other shed was St. Margaret's, 64A, which lay to the east side of Waverley station and of course, was the 'NB', and therefore one of us. The reality was that, whilst the depots were close in proximity, they were light years apart both in work and social activity. St. Margaret's had an allocation in excess of 200 locomotives whilst Haymarket had but 80. St. Margaret's covered the bulk of the freight work in and around Edinburgh, and there was a great deal of that, whilst Haymarket had the cream of the passenger work to 'a the airts', north, south east and west. Dalry Road enjoyed both freight and passenger work, but served different stations and different yards, and thus was a different world of railway entirely. So these sheds, and the great number of men employed at each, were segregated to a large extent and each had their own Social Clubs under the auspices of the Railway Staff Association, Bowling Clubs and favourite Pubs, and seldom the three did meet.

At Haymarket, with the best of the passenger work, and with an allocation of 46 Pacifics and V2s, this is where the 'glamour' came in, and indeed Haymarket engine crews were widely referred to as the 'Glamour Boys'. But was it really glamorous? The reality of the situation was that whilst the depots were separated by either old Company loyalties, routes worked over or the allocation of work, the locomotive men had much in common, the same ambitions and concerns, the same anti-social hours of work and most of all, the same drudgery. No, there was little glamour in steam engine work and the commonly perceived world of the top link crews sitting on comfortable bucket seats as, arguably, the finest locomotives in the world rushed along at high speed with long trains, represented a mere fraction of the total work load of a steam depot. The bulk of the work was hard, dirty, very dirty, and often dangerous. It was undertaken in conditions, and in a fashion, which would have the present Health & Safety Inspectors tearing their hair out. The rostered diagrams were, to say the least, unsocial in the extreme, requiring men to book on at all the hours of both day and night.

So why did men do it? What took me to Haymarket? The answer is short and simple. A fascination with steam locomotives, an enthusiasm to experience, and the opportunity to be involved in, steam locomotives performing at the extent of their power, and a sense of comradeship and pride in the job. I think for most, but certainly not all, for every shed had its discords, this was a greater motivation rather than just the basic need to earn a living. There were many easier ways of doing that.

Haymarket, like all the depots, had real characters, many built in with the brickwork, some of whom had already passed into the annals of railway history by my time and some who are mentioned in this book. They, and the many more unrecorded men, helped lay the foundation for my future railway career, a career which, I am happy to say, which sees me now having entered my 50th year in the service. Many have now passed on, whilst others, like myself, are in the sere and yellow, but I would hazard a guess that all who experienced the great days of steam, as I was privileged to do, now remember them with a great sense of nostalgia. To them all then, this book is dedicated. I hope it does, in some small way, stir happy memories. The book is just a turning back of the clock to give a mere glimpse, through my own personal experiences, of a vanished way of life. Like the many Locomotive Depots, the engines and men who inhabited them are now nothing more than a memory. It is a book which could have been written by many, who like me, worked at Haymarket, and most with footplate experience which considerably exceeded mine. However, when the opportunity arose, I thought it right and proper to record what life was really like in the latter days of steam, at a time which has now passed into history, for future generations, including my own grandchildren.

Haymarket remains to this day a Traction Maintenance Depot, housing and maintaining the large fleet of diesel multiple units which now operate 99% of all passenger train working in Scotland. The depot bears little resemblance to the Haymarket I write about, and the trains, well, enough said!

I would like to take the opportunity to thank all the many railway colleagues, far, far too many to name, and other, special friends, who have both encouraged me not only to put pen to paper but provided loyal support in my wider railway career. I have set out to use photographs which illustrate the locomotives allocated to Haymarket, locomotives I have fired and scenes of the shed generally. The photographs used are mainly from the Transport Treasury collection and I must express my sincere thanks to Barry Hoper for the use of these splendid images. I am also grateful to Bill Rhind Brown, Dugald Cameron, Stuart Sellar and A.A. (Sandy) McLean for their photographic contributions.

Not least, a special thanks to my wife Heather, who has lived with the railway as part of everyday life for many years, who has accompanied me, uncomplainingly, around the world in my railway consultancy work, and who has now further endured the long hours of solitude when I secreted myself away in my office, tapping away, and trying to put my old diary entries into some form of coherent English.

Harry Knox,
Linlithgow, 2006.

The last remaining NB 'Atlantic', 9875 MIDLOTHIAN working the 4.10pm to Perth past Haymarket shed in September 1938. The mixed rake of coaches can clearly be seen, with a Pullman car second from the locomotive. It was scheduled for preservation at the last moment and literally had to be resurrected from the dead, being rebuilt with spare parts from other scrapped Atlantics at Cowlairs Works. It was returned to service in June 1938 and based at St. Margaret's shed. From there she was regularly employed on Perth workings. However, owing to wartime conditions, preservation was quietly forgotten and 9875 was finally withdrawn in November 1939, and cut up. (Bill Brown collection)

1. THE BEGINNING

I commenced my railway career on the 15th October 1956 and although I intend this to be my recollections of footplate and shed days, it is I think, worth recalling the railway I joined away back then. It is also, I think, important to clarify how and why I went to the footplate.

I had, from the earliest age, been passionate about railways, and steam locomotives in particular. This was not at all unusual in those days, amongst small boys, but with me, the desire never lessened as the years advanced. My one over-riding ambition was to work on the railway although, academically, I was considered to be more able than average and on course for University entrance had I so desired. This I did not particularly want. Instead I joined the railway, and then transferred to the locomotive department, partly to satisfy my childhood ambition, but secondly as a planned stepping stone in my own ambitions for my railway career. I was never a registered Fireman and I certainly did much more cleaning than firing, but at Haymarket, being such a busy depot, there was, from late April to early October, considerable opportunity for young Passed Cleaners to obtain firing experience. So this account of my life on the footplate is written by someone who did not progress through the links, nor put in the long years of firing that many of the generation of men immediately senior to me did, but one who, for three glorious years, had a very close, and thoroughly enjoyable, relationship with some of the finest steam locomotives ever designed and built, anywhere in the world.

I actually started my railway career as a Junior Clerk at Shotts Central station. Now Shotts, at that time, was a busy mining town with five working collieries. It was situated on the former Caledonian Railway line between Edinburgh Princes Street and Glasgow Central, in north Lanarkshire. It was a busy station, where a Class 1 Station Master oversaw the work carried out by some 26 members of staff ranging from the Clerks through to Porters, Numbertakers and Signalmen. He supervised the signal boxes at Benhar Junction, Shotts Iron Works, Shotts Station and Blackhall Junction, the latter being at this time an 'open as required' signal box on the NB road to Morningside. There was a considerable amount of both passenger and goods business, and the Station Master was also in charge of Shotts East on the former NB line from Bathgate to Morningside. Coal was the principal outwards traffic and part of my job each morning, under the watchful eye of the

Goods Clerk, was to prepare coal waybills for the daily output from the five collieries and then assist with the sheeting (i.e. the recording on delivery sheets) of the inwards goods sundries traffic. In the afternoon I then covered the booking office duties between the two regular shift Clerks, but again under the scrutiny of the Chief Booking Clerk. I did not particularly enjoy the work but the members of staff were, by and large, real characters and worthy of a book in their own right. I did learn a lot and indeed my interest in railway signalling was fostered by many of the Signalmen and Relief Signalmen who were on the complement at Shotts.

The saving grace for me, however, was the daily visit of Mossend Trip working, M23, which shunted the goods yard, arriving around lunchtime each day. This timing was particularly fortuitous, since the Station Master, John Dyer, one of the old school and a dyed-in-the-wool Caledonian man who brooked little or no nonsense from his staff, went home for lunch. This trip, M23, was worked by Hamilton loco-men and I soon made friends with the Drivers and Firemen. A variety of locomotives turned up on this working, ranging from the ex-Caley Jumbos through to Black Fives, Crabs, and the ex-WD 2-8-0s and 2-10-0s. On one occasion, I recall a B1 turning up, No.61246.

Within a short time, having hurried to finish my real work, I joined the crews on the footplate whilst they shunted, and it has to be acknowledged here that I owe these Hamilton men much, for they encouraged my love of engines and soon I was being taught the rudiments of firing and, on odd occasions, driving. Some days, the trip would be required to shunt the hospital

siding at Hartwood, a mile or so to the west of Shotts, and this would be done by running down to Hartwood, carrying out the shunt, and returning to Shotts. It goes without saying that I went as often as was possible. The then Chief Clerk at Shotts, Tom Kerr, turned a blind eye to these stolen trips and indeed covered for me on one or two occasions. I repaid him by never letting him down in terms of my own station duties.

And so I fired engines to my heart's content, worked the injectors and generally received a good basic schooling in steam engine management and working, an experience which was to stand me in good stead some time later. The Hamilton men put up with me, displaying great patience and long-suffering, even on the day, when, during a vigorous bout of firing on a WD 2-10-0, both the coal and the shovel went to the fore-end of the firebox. My ears still burn at the thought.

This contact daily contact with steam engines only served to fan the flames of discontent I felt for clerical duties and so, early in the New Year, I handed over an application for transfer to the Motive Power Department as an Engine Cleaner, specifying Haymarket as my preference. John Dyer called me in to his office and suggested that I had made a mistake. 'Surely you mean Edinburgh Dalry Road' he said. 'No, its Haymarket I want' I replied. 'But that's an NB depot, son, surely you want to go to the Caley'. No, I was adamant, Haymarket it was. He never spoke another word to me, not even on my last day. That was an indication of just how strong old Company attitudes persisted well into the 1950s and beyond. I was to meet this attitude time and time again over many years to come.

NB Atlantic 9902 **HIGHLAND CHIEF** allocated to Dundee Tay Bridge, at Haymarket in the mid-1930s. **This engine was withdrawn from service in October 1936. Strangely, it has not been turned to face home. (Bill Brown collection)**

The final days of steam at Haymarket shed in 1963, with A1 60159 BONNIE DUNDEE, in filthy condition, standing in the shed with an unidentified B1 and A4. Also sharing the shed is a Sulzer Type 2 diesel with an EE Type 4 lurking in the rear. (Dugald Cameron collection)

2. THE DEPOT

In February 1957, on my 17th birthday, I reported to the Shed Office at Haymarket to be 'processed'. Now the Locomotive Depot at Haymarket, by this time, was not the original shed. This had been a small two road affair much nearer Haymarket Station, on the north side of the line, and at that time was the depot for the original Edinburgh and Glasgow Railway Company, soon to be swallowed up by the North British railway, or the NB as it was more commonly known.

When the tracks leading to the west and north out of Waverley were quadrupled in the mid-1890s as a result of the huge (and embarrassing) increase in traffic after the Forth Bridge opened in 1890, the opportunity was taken to build a bigger and more spacious depot to accommodate the increased number of locomotives now requiring a home. Vacant ground existed to the north-west of the original site, about half a mile further on from Haymarket Station, at Murrayfield, or to be more precise, Roseburn. On this large site, a new shed was built consisting of eight through roads, together with 50ft turntable and a large coaling stage (or coal 'bench') at the south side. Construction started in 1892 but, due to unstable foundations, work had to stop and be started afresh; finally, in 1894, the new depot, which was still to the north of the main lines, was opened. The site was, and still is, above the normal ground level and the main lines run on a low embankment at this point. This suggests that there had been a fair degree of infill when the original line was being constructed and may give some clue as to why the original foundations became unstable. The depot itself was eventually bounded to the west by Roseburn Street and to the east by Russell Road.

Over the years it changed little. The allocation increased, locomotives grew larger and the famous Reid Atlantics, as well as the NE Atlantics now stabled there, could not be accommodated on the 50ft turntable. This was no great inconvenience, since they could easily be turned by running round the Gorgie triangle formed by the chord lines of the suburban route from Haymarket Central Junction and Haymarket West Junction respectively, converging at Gorgie East Junction. Thus engines running to the shed from the Waverley were merely routed via Gorgie if required.

With the coming of the Gresley Pacifics in 1924, it was a different story. Yes, they too could be turned via Gorgie, and I will return to this particular aspect of shed working later in this narrative, but on-shed proper, problems were being experienced, and these were many. The wooden hand-coaling stage was life expired and in need of renewal and a new mechanical coaling plant was built by the firm of Henry Lees & Co. Ltd at a cost of around £15,000, to a design adopted by the LNER elsewhere. At the same time, the opportunity was taken to replace the 50ft turntable with a new 70ft example at a further cost of £1,481. The new facilities were brought into use in 1930 and proved to be of immense value in the years to come. The Haymarket 'cenotaph' concrete coaling plant was a familiar landmark on the Edinburgh skyline for many years.

Before the advent of the Gresleys, Haymarket served the north and east of the NB system with a mix of passenger and freight trains. There was also some work over the Waverley route. However, St Margaret's had a significant share of the express passenger work from Edinburgh and the East Coast route to Newcastle had been, up to the Grouping, the preserve of the NER which, by virtue of the running powers obtained over NB metals between Edinburgh and Berwick-on-Tweed, had Atlantics and staff based at Haymarket solely for this work. In 1923, former NB Drivers were integrated into the NER link, initially with their NB Atlantics, and worked through to Newcastle. The first A1s (five of them) were allocated to Haymarket in 1924 to take over these Newcastle diagrams and in 1928 Haymarket men and engines shared in the non-stop running of the Flying Scotsman. As the new A3s were subsequently allocated they gradually displaced the A1s at Haymarket, the latter being transferred over a period to Dundee Tay Bridge, Aberdeen Ferryhill, Eastfield and St Margaret's. The P2s followed from 1934 onwards and the allocation of A4s commenced in 1936. However, by the early 1940s, with the P2s withdrawn for rebuilding, all remaining Scottish Gresleys were concentrated at Haymarket and with a major re-adjustment of engine diagrams, Haymarket men eventually took over the cream of the passenger workings out of Waverley, gaining the nick-name 'Glamour Boys'.

The depot had a complement of just over 500 Drivers, Firemen and Cleaners to work the engine diagrams, supported by some 80/90 Fitters, Boilersmiths and other Craftsmen. A further 50 or so Labourers covered firedropping, steam raising, the coaling plant, stores issuing and general shed cleaning duties. Supervision and administration of this empire was covered by a mere handful of Managers, Clerical staff and Foremen, around 25 in all.

Over the years, some further improvements were effected and the Haymarket I joined in 1957 still had eight roads but only six were through shed running roads. Number seven road was buffer-ended just inside the east end of the shed and would hold only one Pacific inside the shed. The remainder of number of seven and number eight roads formed the old fitting shop and were used solely for examination and repair and were partly screened off from the main running shed. A newer fitting shed had been added to the north side of the shed with an additional two roads. This was a spacious modern shed with facilities for a Blacksmith, Turners, and a Joiner as well as the usual fitting shed staff. The northernmost road in this shed was equipped with a Ransomes & Rapier electric wheel drop pit. Modern turning lathes and lifting and weighing equipment were provided. The Mechanical Foreman's Office was located upstairs and inside the south-east corner of this shed, enjoying a panoramic view over this maintenance empire. A further single road ran round the outside of the shed to the north and was used, during my time, to stable dead locomotives, many of our 'Director' 4-4-0s spending some of their last days there.

On the north wall of the shed, at the eastern end, was the sand kiln where sand was dried and stored for use on the locomotives. The dry sand was collected, in pails, as required, from the inside wall of the shed.

So, from east to west, locomotives coming on-shed ran to the turntable, stopping to drop off the 'kit' to the 'kit store', or at least that was the idea. The reality was that the kit store was the last place any Fireman would go seeking items of kit. The kit store was where the turntable crew were installed, and sometimes incoming crew would be relieved there, but more often than not, the incoming crew ran the locomotive right on to the turntable if they could. This store did, however, hold supplies of paraffin and rape oil and was where all lamps were filled and trimmed, in big metal trays to collect any spillage. Head/tail lamps were filled with paraffin and gauge glass lamps with rape oil. In short, the kit store was a dark, dreary, malodorous 'howf' (*a rough meeting place*), inhabited by the troglodytes of 64B. It was also the source of the 'tea water' for the General Office next door, a large, black, iron kettle sitting, permanently steaming, on the open coal fire set in one wall. It was, especially at night, a Dickensian scene straight out of *Oliver Twist* with the resident storekeepers, positive caricatures of

A3 60096 PAPYRUS in its final form with double chimney and German-style 'trough' smoke deflectors. The A3s in this final condition were given a new lease of life and carried out sterling work into the early 1960s. Again, the classic 'Haymarket pose' on the turntable. The black, corrugated-iron stores building can be seen in the right background. (J. Robertson/Transport Treasury)

Fagin, with the turntable men seated round the open fire. I am also sure it saw its fair share of juvenile delinquents over the years.

Next door was the General Office consisting of a small office, housing three clerks to the left of the entrance door, a toilet (unisex) to the west side, and then a bigger office for the Chief Clerk, the Staff Clerk, and two other clerks plus the typist. A door at the west side within this inner office was the only entrance to the Shed Master's Office. A glass veranda fronted the office to the north side, and it was to here, and the Enquiry window, staff came to be paid or to see 'the Clerks' with any queries, mainly pay related, travel facilities or for discipline. I will return to the offices and incumbents at a later stage.

With the engine turned, or not, as required, it was taken up alongside the south wall of the shed, past the big water tower, to the coaling plant, where it was coaled and then placed on one of the two sets of adjacent ashpits at the west end of the shed. The turntable crew then secured and left the engine here.

The coaling plant was looked after on three shifts, by a Coaling Plant Attendant and it was he who was responsible for keeping the hoppers filled. There were two hoppers, the smaller being reserved for the Grade 'A' coal used by the 'Non-Stop' – 'The Elizabethan' – locomotives in the summer. The plant had a capacity of 500 tons and, night and day, wagons could be seen being hoisted up the sloping sides and tipped, to keep the

hoppers charged. There was a J83 allocated as coal pilot and manned on dayshift and backshift only. This pilot, with an attendant Shunter, removed the empty wagons to Haymarket yard and brought up loaded wagons as required, always ensuring the headshunt was filled with loaded wagons for the nightshift. Wagons were then run down to the tippler platform by gravity. In my time, at least one wagon of sand and one of brake blocks were inadvertently tipped into the hopper. The sand, in particular, proved a headache to Firemen out on the road, when it started appearing with the coal in the tender. Since Haymarket was basically a passenger depot, there was no grading of coal (other than that used by the Non-Stop) and goods, passenger and pilot engines alike were all coaled with the same, high quality steam coal, generally from Scottish pits. Sometimes, coal would be received from the Yorkshire pits and this was generally of a higher calorific value than the softer Scottish coal.

The coal was fed via a chute which could be swung to discharge either forwards or backwards, and by the mere pressing of a button, tons of coal could be supplied to the tender in a very short time. It was always necessary to check the lie of the chute and ascertain that no large lumps were lying in it before operating the button, since the lie could be altered by the sheer weight of such lumps as coal started dropping, resulting in the cab, instead of tender, being filled with coal. The Fireman, who generally did the button pressing, was protected

in a concrete shelter about the size of a phone box. This was necessary since, during coaling, splintered coal flew around like shrapnel and sometimes large lumps came down and bounced around, and Firemen had suffered head injuries in the past before any protective shelter had been provided. Indeed, the wearing of the 'British Railways' totem type cap badge by locomotive men was discouraged simply because there had a been an accident where the pins which secured the badge to the cap had been driven into a man's skull when a large lump of coal struck the front of his head during coaling, compounding the seriousness of the accident.

At Haymarket, as at many LNER depots, Drivers and Firemen did not, other on the out-based Pilots, become involved in the everyday fire dropping, ashpan and smokebox cleaning. This was done by the Shed Labourers, graded Firedroppers, who were given a differential payment, a mere pittance it has to be said, to carry out this incredibly dirty, hot and often dangerous work. They worked amongst heaps of shimmering hot ashes and smoke box char, with choking dust ever present, and seldom got any respite from the continual procession of engines coming on shed. Water was played in the pits and on the ever growing piles of ashes, but this only had the effect of creating clouds of steaming dilute sulphuric acid.

The ash lyes were cleared on a daily basis around 10.00 each morning, when there was a brief respite in firedropping. All the engines which had been out on night duties were back on shed and the returning day shift engines had still to return. During this lull, empty three plank and five plank open wagons were brought up from Haymarket Yard by the coal pilot and a veritable army of Labourers took up square mouth shovels and piled tons of ashes, clinker and smokebox char into these wagons. When the area was cleared to the Chargehand's satisfaction and the wagons full, they were removed back to the yard to be worked onwards to Borthwick Bank Coup for emptying. The battle of the ash lyes was never-ending. After the fires were cleaned, the disposal crews collected the engines, filled the tanks and set them in the required shed road, ready for preparation and the next turn of duty. A one way traffic system was the order of the day, which, as will be revealed later, could cause problems.

To the north-east side of the shed sat the material and oil store, a long low, black wooden building dating back to NB days. The building had been enlarged at some point, by the addition of a corrugated iron extension. It was here that all the lubricating (engine) oil and steam oil was stored in large metal oil tanks and issued to preparation Drivers. It was also here that the cleaning 'mickey' and paraffin was issued to the shift chargehand Cleaner. The store also held a massive stock of locomotive spares – running into the thousands in terms of separate items. There was a small serving area with a counter covered in sheet metal to withstand the pounding of oil cans being set down for filling and other sundry items which could cause damage. It was also here that one could obtain a supply of washed sweat rags for preparation duties, and cotton waste for cleaning. At the end of each shift, each man was allowed one new, clean sweat rag for washing up purposes although, truth to tell, these did not, when new, absorb water well and contained what I could only describe as wood shavings and thus were rough on the skin. Only after they had been taken home and washed once or twice, did they become soft and useful as a makeshift towel. Dirty sweat rags were returned for industrial washing and recycling. I believe that in early days, one could draw a full locomotive kit i.e. pail, spanners (various), detonators, coal hammer, brush, two firing shovels and lamps for each engine. In my time, in preparation, you had just to go around and 'thieve' all these items.

This empire was managed by Tommy Hanratty, the head Storeman, who worked an 8.00 to 17.00 shift. Tommy was responsible for recording issues and re-ordering and maintaining the stock, and he had an encyclopaedic knowledge of everything held. During my sojourn at Haymarket, I saw a Fitter go with a stores demand 'chit` seeking a new chime whistle for an A4 and actually being issued with it! Now that was a real store. The issuing of all stores was undertaken by shift Storemen. Next door to the store, on the eastern side, was the Cleaners bothy; again, more of this later. Still further to the east was the shed lobby and booking on point, the Running Foreman's Office with Timekeepers and Roster Clerk ensconced therein, and the Drivers bothy. The official route into the depot came off Russell Road, opposite the then Jeffrey's Brewery, and to access the General Offices and the Shed Master's Office, one had to cross the front of the shed by a sleepered crossing, giving right of way to engines going off-shed (if one had any sense, that is). Through the booking-on lobby and behind the Running Foreman's Office was the canteen, a long, low building where, between the hours of 07.00 and 18.00 one could obtain tea, bacon or sausage rolls, scones and a limited menu of chips-with-everything hot meals. If I recall correctly, a cup of tea and a bran scone with jam cost a mere 3d (in old money) in 1956/7.

This canteen was run entirely by four ladies, supervised by a Driver, Jimmy Donald, who never drove and indeed was seldom seen in overalls. He was the 'Maitre D' of this establishment, but I never really found out what his official standing was. The canteen was a popular haunt of preparation crews waiting their next charge, and also a place of rest for the Fitters. Indeed, at lunchtime every weekday, there was a fleeting moment of light entertainment, when girls from the Fergusson Confectionery factory in Roseburn Street came to lunch in the canteen. There inevitably ensued the barrage of wolf-whistles and suggestive banter between the young bloods and the girls and, believe me, those girls could hold their own with navvies when it came to swearing. I have never been tempted, since those days, to purchase any of the Fergusson products, which included their famous 'Edinburgh Rock'!

The general cleanliness of the shed area depended on the Shed Labourers, several of whom were charged with sweeping the running shed pits and walkways, the turntable pit and the front of the shed on a daily basis. Others, as previously described, had the less enviable task of clearing the ash pits and lyes, shovelling steaming ashes into wooden sided wagons. Clearing up the coal spillage in the area around the coaling plant was also a mammoth task and it was not at all unusual to have one or two tons (and sometimes even more) collected, such was the precision coaling practised by the Haymarket Firemen!

Other Labourers were designated Steam Raisers who, as the name implied, kindled dead locomotives fresh from wash out or the fitting shed. They also tended locomotives standing waiting preparation in the shed, to ensure enough fire was kept in them without raising steam pressure too high, and that boiler levels were maintained at a safe level. I was not the only preparation Fireman who had reason to swear at the Steam Raiser who had filled an engine boiler so full that the water level was out of sight. All Labourers could volunteer to work overtime and most did so on a daily basis in the summer months, cleaning engines when all the Cleaners, or most of them, were out firing. The Labourers inhabited a bothy on the south side of the ash pits, another less than salubrious establishment, shunned by even the disposal crews.

The Labourers were overseen by a Chargeman Labourer, one Peter Gibson, again a real character, and one who will appear in these pages at a later point. His brother Frank, almost as notable, was a Driver in No.2 link, running 60162 SAINT JOHNSTOUN with Driver Burrows.

In the running shed, at the west end of No.4 road, was the washout area where the Washers-out and Boilersmiths held sway. This area was always wreathed in steam and running with water and again, was to be avoided as far as possible unless one was scavenging kit during preparation. The shift Boiler Washers wore clogs, as did most of the Labourers, since any other form of footwear just would not last any time in the extreme wet and sulphurous heat under which they worked.

Although the depot, when newly constructed, had originally provided considerably more accommodation for the servicing, stabling and maintenance of the locomotive allocation, during my time, space was always at a premium. Thus, it was not at all unusual for the Fitters to have to undertake maintenance, including valve and piston overhauls, outside the shed at the foot of either No.7 or No.8 roads. Cleaners in turn worked on engines in the open and preparation too, had to be done outside, at the mercy of the Scottish weather – in particular the biting easterly winds which blow in from Scandinavia. However, to be absolutely accurate, it mattered little since, even inside the shed, because the roof was in such poor condition, when it rained, we worked in a deluge of water anyway.

And so this great depot dealt with engines night and day and all the varied grades worked together to keep the job going. The work was hard, dirty, unrelenting and sometimes dangerous, but in all the time I spent there, both on the footplate and later as a Clerk, there was never any significant disputes which stopped the job, at least not until the diesels started arriving, but more of that anon. Yes, there was a lot of grumbling sometimes, and conditions were poor, especially messing, but there was also much fun and laughter and an underlying pride in being part of 64B, a pride that was displayed for all to see in the condition in which Haymarket engines entered traffic. I, for one, am proud to have been a part of the final steam days there.

Standing in front of A4 KINGFISHER on 16th September 1960 is Driver Peter B. Robertson with his Fireman, name regrettably not remembered, prior to working what is likely to be the 4.00pm *TALISMAN* from Edinburgh to Kings Cross, as far as Newcastle. Peter was in No.3 link and this turn was one of the three Newcastle turns allocated to that link. The headlamps are not yet in place and these, along with the headboard, will be collected from the 'kit store' as the engine moves out to the shed exit signal. The changing order is typified by the two EE Type 4s in the right background; one of them, D260, was the first of the class to be allocated to 64B. As a class, they proved to be somewhat erratic and unreliable performers. (W. Hermiston/Transport Treasury)

3. THE LINK STRUCTURE

The links at Haymarket were structured on a strict seniority basis with the diagrams involving the highest mileage and earning potential allocated to the top links. Haymarket was primarily responsible for all express passenger train workings out of Edinburgh, to the south, west and north, and the link workings were altered twice every year, to reflect the changes from winter to summer timetable and vice versa. Engine diagrams were prepared centrally at York and distributed to all the East Coast depots. Twice a year, all diagrams went into the melting pot and were re-allocated to the links, but on the basis described above. This involved the Roster Clerk, Running Foremen, the Shed Master and the Trade Union Representative (ASLEF) sitting down together and thrashing out the details. At this point it must be said that Angus Gilchrist, a Driver who was also the ASLEF rep. and a member of Sectional Council B (representing the footplate grades) was an extremely fair and honourable man who represented the interests of his members absolutely, but never indulged in 'boss bashing'. Accordingly, the link workings were arranged with complete harmony each time.

However, the engine diagrams were not tablets of stone and it did mean that turns which had perhaps been in No.1 link at one point, later went to No.2 or No.3 Link. Moreover, it happened that some turns which had been worked by Haymarket at one point of the year then went to Gateshead or Eastfield or other depots. Changes in the depot allocation of turns became more prevalent as dieselisation came in

No.1 Link, the top link had, by 1957, 14 diagrammed turns of duty with 14 Drivers allocated to it. Two Drivers were paired with an engine, an A4, and the seven A4s at Haymarket were the top link engines. The roster they worked rotated not weekly, but on a fortnightly basis and each engine worked the same early and late diagrams for two weeks. The complete link, as all train running links, was structured on a rotating early turn, late turn throughout, in keeping with the National Agreements, although 'early' meant any turn commencing between 00.01 and 11.59, and 'late' 12.01 to 23.59. The two Drivers rotated through early and late, so, for example, if locomotive 60004 was allocated to the first two turns in the link, it would work the early Glasgow turn and a late Newcastle for two weeks with Driver Proudfoot early and Driver Nairn late the first week, and Driver Nairn early and Driver Proudfoot late the second week. The locomotive and Drivers would then move to the next two jobs

in the link, and so on. It sounds complicated, but worked very well, and of course, every effort was made to ensure that the Drivers always had their own engine, except when General Repairs at Doncaster were called for, or, as will be revealed, during the summer timetable.

Each top link (and No.2 link) engine had its own kit consisting of a full set of spanners, a steam oil can and a lubricating oil can, detonators, red flag, pail, footplate brush, spare gauge glasses, two firing shovels and two headlamps and a gauge glass lamp, all kept in pristine condition. The kit was kept in a padlocked locker on the tender-end and preparation of these engines was simplified in that Firemen did not have to rake around the shed trying to put a kit together. The only items of essential kit which did go 'walkabouts' on any regular basis were fire irons, which could not be easily secured or locked up. Each A4 also had a handle allocated, for opening the 'sharks jaws' front, permitting access to the smokebox.

No.1 link was allotted the highest paying mileage turns, which were not always the most socially acceptable, and it is true to say that No.1 Link had some real anti-social turns, such as the 03.57 'early Aberdeen', or the 20.00 'Mail' with just about every stop to Newcastle and a 04.00 finish.

In all, the link worked to Newcastle (mileage turns of 256 miles), Perth, Glasgow and Dundee. In the summer months, they also worked the 'Non-Stop' lodging in London on alternate days. The structure of No.1 link in terms of locomotives, Drivers and rostered turns in 1957 (winter timetable) was as below.

During the summer timetable, Haymarket crews worked the northern half of the 'Non-Stop' as it was known in railway circles, or 'The Elizabethan', to give it the proper title. This they worked to and from York, changing footplates with the Kings Cross crew via the corridor tender. This working fell to No.1 link and it was the only turn where the regular rostered Firemen, who were all Passed Firemen, worked the diagram irrespective of whether or not they might be required for driving turns. They fired on the Non-Stop and were credited with any driving turns lost because of this duty. It is, I think, fair to say that Haymarket placed more importance on the working of this train than did Kings Cross Top Shed, since this was the 'crème de la crème' turn at 64B. Kings Cross worked lodging turns right through to Newcastle on a regular basis!

It was during this time that the manning and dedicated engine rostering in No.1 link went to pigs and whistles. The engine chosen to work the Non-Stop was generally the A4 which had been shopped last and had run enough miles to be nicely run in. This then meant that the locomotive chosen was the luck

Turns	Loco.	Driver
1. 05.47 Glasgow Pcls/09.00 ex-Glasgow	60004	Proudfoot
2. 16.00 Newcastle/16.00KX		Nairn
3. 08.12 Glasgow/12.00 ex-Glasgow	60024	Redpath
4. 16.00 Glasgow/20.00 ex-Glasgow		Bee
5. 10.10 Newcastle/10.00 KX	60027	Bell
6. 22.40 Newcastle/20.20 KX		Fell
7. 7.30 Glasgow/11.00 ex-Glasgow	60009	Gemmell
8. 16.15 Dundee/20.35 ex-Dundee		Laird
9. 03.57 Dundee/05.47 Aberdeen	60011	Porteous
10. 14.15 Dundee/15.40 Aberdeen		Kennedy
11. 07.30 Dundee/09.50 Aberdeen	60012	Spilsbury
12. 20.00 Newcastle/19.00 KX		Bain
13. 07.40 Perth/12.05 ex-Perth	60031	Smith
14. 16.30 Glasgow/21.15 ex-Glasgow		Robertson

of the draw. Now, say 60027 was the chosen steed. It would be taken out of traffic a few days before the summer timetable kicked in and given a thorough going over by Fitters, Boilersmiths and the Cleaners, so that come the day it was prepared, and entered service, in a state of absolute perfection. But two Drivers in No.1 link had lost their regular 'horse'.

However, to complicate things further, there was always a 'stand by' engine for the Non-Stop, so another suitable A4 would also be taken out of traffic and given the same treatment, and yet another 'horse' was lost to the link. Bad enough but then, of the crews working the Non-Stop (two crews each week) one would have the Haymarket A4 along with a Kings Cross crew, whilst the other would work the Kings Cross engine, again with a Kings Cross crew. The stand-by engine always worked the 10.10 'Junior Scotsman' so the top link men on that turn would also not necessarily have their own engine. So No.1 link saw a lot of common users shipped in, albeit the best of the common users, and generally A3s in preference to A2s. However, since No.1 link had other diagrams which demanded a class 8P locomotive, in the summer an A1 from No.2 link could be allocated on certain turns. Thus could the allocation of engines in No.2 link also fall apart.

No.2 link was structured in the more usual way with 12 diagrammed turns, but again with 12 Drivers paired with 6 engines. Here, the allocated locos were the five A1 Pacifics, plus A3, 60096 PAPYRUS. Again, as in the top link, the engines and men rotated on a two week cycle. It always struck me as somewhat odd that in a link where class 8P engines were rostered work appropriate to that power classification, an A3 was the odd engine out. The A3s were class 7P and I could never understand why one other A1 was never allocated to 64B. It does however, say everything about the A3s in that they could generally work turn and turn about with the A1s, on equal terms.

This link had, during my time, the better turns from a socially acceptable point of view and again had three Newcastle mileage turns and also worked to Perth, Glasgow and Dundee. The structure of No.2 link in terms of locomotives, Drivers and rostered turns in 1957 (Winter Timetable) is shown at top right:

No.3 link in 1957 had 15 turns of duty, 12 turns of which were steam worked, and 3 DMU operated. On the weeks Drivers were covering the DMU turns, their Firemen were rostered as spare. This was a temporary arrangement until Leith Central, a DMU stabling, fuelling and maintenance depot, became properly operational and Drivers were allocated there. When that happened, No.3 link reverted to the

Turns	Loco.	Driver
1. 04.30 Glasgow/08.32 ex-Glasgow	60160	Bogie
2. 15.00 Glasgow/18.00 ex-Glasgow		Cuthbert
3. 10.00 Dundee/12.30 Aberdeen Fish	60161	Craik
4. 23.20 Newcastle/22.15 KX		Dunlop
5. 06.40 Dundee/08.55 Arbroath	60162	Gibson
6. 14.40 Dundee/17.17 Aberdeen		Burrows
7. 09.05 Glasgow/13.00 ex-Glasgow	60159	Beattie
8. 22.20 Newcastle/17.15 Colchester		Timmins
9. 06.25 Glasgow/10.30 ex-Glasgow	60096	Motion
10. 16.00 Perth/19.45 ex Perth		Davidson
11. 02.45 Glasgow/07.30 ex-Glasgow	60152	Currie
12. 14.00 Newcastle/14.00 KX		Kinnear

standard 12 job arrangement as indeed did No.4 link. No.3 link did not have any allocated engines, and thus it rotated in the normal weekly manner. The early 1957 workings were as below:

reduced to the normal 12 turns, rotating on a weekly basis. This link had the Carlisle turns over the Waverley route (200 miles mileage) and worked other more local passenger turns. It fared

Turn	Driver
08.30 Newcastle/07.50 ex KX	W. Robertson
12.30 Newcastle/11.20 ex KX	W. Ross
07.30 Dundee/10.12 Class 'C'	A. Thain
20.30 Glasgow/00.45 Class 'E'	W.Robb
02.25 Class 'F' Hawick/06.45 Hawick	J. Sellars
18.45 Dundee/22.05 Class 'C'	J. Duncan
05.05 Thornton/07.22 ECS	R. Dryden
13.50 Glasgow/16.00ECS	J Clark
10.15 Berwick/12.40 Class :H'	N. Taylor
05.50 Glasgow/As Required	W. Neave
12.00Glasgow/16.00 ex Glasgow DMU	D. Lamb
15.00 Glasgow/17.00 ex Glasgow DMU	J. Bannerman
08.30 Glasgow/ECS DMU	W. Palmer
06.38 Hawick/10.56 ex Hawick	P. Robertson
18.33 Berwick/22.16 Class 'C'	A. Fraser

This was another link with good turns of duty. By 1958 this link had reduced to 12 turns and gained the afternoon 'Talisman` to Newcastle, thus working both Talisman's, and one other night Newcastle turn, (the Colchester) It also had Hawick, Glasgow, Dundee and Thornton turns. No.3 Link had some hard running Drivers in my time there, but more of that later.

No.4 Link had 15 turns but again this was an interim arrangement, later

badly with the onset of diesel multiple units and lost a lot of the local workings such as Musselburgh, Peebles and North Berwick trains. The allocation of work in the early part of 1957 was as opposite, top of page 11.

Around 1957/58 a small new link was set up, which sat between Nos.4 and 5 Links. This was known as 4A Link and was created to work the new Anglo-Scottish Car Carrier service, extended to and from Perth in the summer

Turn	Driver
12.00 Carlisle/3.22 ex-Carlisle	R. McLennan
20.00 Glasgow/23.00 Class 'E'	A. Stirling
08.05 Thornton/12.47 ex-Leven	C. Rankine
16.30 Glasgow/18.30 ex-Glasgow DMU	W. Donaldson
06.20 Burntisland/LE	G. Wemyss
14.33 Carlisle/19.44 ex-Carlisle	A. Hamilton
06.08 Stirling/10.02 ex-Stirling	R. Downie
14.45 Corstorphine/17.05 Galashiels/19.15 ex-Galashiels	T. Milroy
06.30 Corstorphine/08.15 North Berwick/10.30 ex-North Berwick	R. Smith
15.10 Corstorphine/16.45 North Berwick/17.40 ex-North Berwick	W. Stewart
08.30 Glasgow/12.45 Class 'E'	F. Dewar
18.10 Thornton/20.35 Class 'H':/20.43 ex-Leven SO	J. Smith
11.00 Glasgow/13.00 ex-Glasgow DMU	H. Brown
14.00 Glasgow/15.30 ex-Glasgow DMU	R. Hiddleston
22.15 Carlisle/04.08 ex-Carlisle	T. Calder

timetable. The diagrammed work involved only four turns including two Perth round trips and the 21.40 Car Carrier to Newcastle, returning with the 20.05 Car Carrier ex-Kings Cross

No.5 Link was the only main line Goods link at Haymarket, and had 12 turns of duty. It was in this link that the worst jobs were to be found, for many of the rotating early and late turns meant booking on around either side of midnight. It was thus known as the 'midnight movement' link. It had mainly Tweedmouth turns, a Stobs Camp (a change-over working on the Waverley route) turn, one Carlisle turn and some ECS work. No.5 Link employed numerous locomotives from other sheds; Haymarket B1s were common performers but K3s and B16s were also regular engines used in this link- see beow.

No.6 Link was the Senior Spare link, providing coverage for rest days, holidays, sickness, and so on for the train running links. Again it was arranged in early, late rotation; crews were rostered at a 'datum' time, say 10.00am and could be utilised on a daily basis to cover train diagrams up to two hours either side of that base time. What this meant is that the crew could go back to 08.00 or forward to 1200 as required. Although full crews were rostered in this link, Drivers and Firemen could be utilised separately. This was a big link, involving 24 sets of

men as I remember, and the Drivers were all younger and very experienced men, and capable runners.

The next link, No.7, was the Junior Spare link. Arranged on the same basis as No.6, this provided coverage for local train working turns and the preparation link, but also 'back filled' the Senior Spare link to ensure the Running Foremen had spare train working coverage available round the clock. Jointly, Nos.6 and 7 Links in total had some 50 rostered sets of men; in the summer months they were more or less merged to ensure coverage of at least one full crew over all the datum times.

No.8 Link was a smaller 'Control Orders' link with some allocated local train working but with crews rostered at datum times to work to District Control orders as required. In many ways it was another spare link but at the beck and call of Edinburgh Control. Again, Drivers and Firemen could, and did, work separately if required. This link also had some train running jobs including the 15.43 Larbert.

No.9 was the Waverley Pilot link and was worked effectively as a sub-depot to Haymarket, the crews booking on and off at the station. Again, for Drivers, this was an 'accommodation' link; the job was no sinecure although financially it was attractive, with two Sunday shifts rostered out of three.

No.10 Link was by far the biggest. It was known as the 'Tank Link' and consisted of pilots, preparation, turntable, disposal and relieving. Although one big link, the pilots (excluding the Waverley West No.1 and No.2 pilots) rotated within the link and were worked by the same Drivers. For example, the Haymarket Yard Pilot was three-shifted, with three Drivers rotating but with Firemen going round the link. The only exceptions were Firemen who were 'light work' men, confined to such duties as the Shed Shunt Pilot on three shifts. Again, it sounds complicated, but in reality things worked very well. This is the link in which Cleaners obtained the greater number of firing turns. Also in here were the 'sick, lame and lazy'

Turn	Driver
01.28 Tweedmouth/04.45 ex-Tweedmouth	A. Sim
18.05 Tweedmouth/20.50 ex-Tweedmouth	S. Eddie
05.25 Hawick/05.42 ex-Carlisle	P. Bowie
14.18 Tweedmouth/17.50 ex-Tweedmouth	J. Auchterlonie
00.40 Tweedmouth/As required	J. Fleming
20.05 Leith Walk East/Tweedmouth/23.06 ex-Tweedmouth	J. Turner
02.13 Niddrie/Tweedmouth/07.00 ex-Tweedmouth	A. Duncan
19.55 Carlisle/01.10 ex-Carlisle	J. Rodgers
02.30 Haymarket/Stobs Camp/00.10 ex-Carlisle	W. Barbour
13.18 Galashiels via Peebles/16.05 ex-Galashiels	W. Shepherd
02.15 Tweedmouth/06.40 ex-Tweedmouth	G.B.Kay
23.25 Haymarket/Tweedmouth/02.21 ex-Tweedmouth	R. Hutton

workings, again mainly for Drivers who had opted to come off main line work because of age, or some infirmity ('light work men') or Drivers removed from main line work for disciplinary reasons. Into this category, as 'links within the link', came the 'Queensferry Goods' (double-shifted), the 'Broxburn Goods', the 'Sub Goods', the 'Prestonpans Goods' and finally the 'big Gorgie Pilot' (three-shifted) and 'wee Gorgie Pilot' (two-shifted).

That, then, was the link structure at Haymarket when I started, (and which I eventually had to roster and control some years later). In the period when I started, it was BR Scottish Region policy to dieselise all the local train services in and around the city. The new Gloucester and Metro Cammell DMUs were coming in very quickly and steam turns were disappearing. Initially these were workings such as the Musselburghs, North Berwicks and Galashiels via Peebles. The 'Swindon' DMUs were also displacing steam from several of the Glasgow turns, so allocated work to the links was in a state of flux. It has also to be said that the Drivers in Nos.3 and 4 links were trained to drive DMUs and did so as part of the link working. This was before Leith Central was established as a separate diesel (DMU) 'Promotion, Transfer & Redundancy' (PT&R) depot with

allocated Drivers. It was coded 64H from the end of 1959.

Whilst Nos.1 and 2 links lost Glasgow turns, these Drivers were not DMU trained and were only trained for the new Diesel Electric locomotives as they entered service during 1959-61.

N15 0-6-2T 69169 is the 'big' Gorgie Pilot. Kept in sparkling condition by the regular crews it is seen here at Haymarket obviously just after a visit to the coaling plant and waiting a crew to take her round to Gorgie and back to work. It was on this engine that I had the privilege of working with Driver Davie Anderson, then one of the regular Drivers at Gorgie, who taught me all about driving engines. (M. Robertson/Transport Treasury)

4. LOCOMOTIVE ALLOCATION

These notes concern the allocation when I started work in early 1957 and though there was little alteration during my time at 64B, there were one or two changes which caused howls of outrage at the time. I will tell of these later… The principal, and most famous locomotives on the complement were the Pacifics; Gresley, Thompson and Peppercorn varieties. The Gresleys were loved, the Peppercorns liked and the Thompsons, well they were tolerated. In all there were:-

A1 4-6-2: 60152, 60159, 60160, 60161, 60162.

A2/1 4-6-2: 60507, 60509, 60510.

A2/3 4-6-2: 60519.

Peppercorn A2 4-6-2 with multiple valve regulator: 60529.

Peppercorn A2 4-6-2: 60530, 60534, 60535, 60536, 60537 all with single chimneys

A3 4-6-2: 60035, 60037, 60041, 60043, 60057, 60087, 60089, 60090, 60094, 60096, 60097, 60098, 60099, 60100, 60101.

A4 4-6-2: 60004, 60009, 60011, 60012, 60024, 60027, 60031 (all with corridor tenders).

V2 2-6-2: 60816, 60819, 60824, 60827, 60920, 60927, 60951, 60957, 60959.

B1 4-6-0: 61007, 61076, 61081, 61178, 61219, 61221, 61244, 61245, 61333, 61404.

D11 4-4-0: 62685, 62690, 62691, 62692, 62693, 62694.

D49 4-4-0: 62705, 62709, 62719, 62743.

J36 0-6-0: 62535, 62543.

N15 0-6-2T: 69169, 69220.

J83 0-6-0T: 68457, 68460, 68473, 68481.

J88 0-6-0T: 68328, 68339.

V1/V3 2-6-2T: 67610, 67615, 67620.

We had a grand total of 80 locomotives.

Our five single-chimneyed A2s never had the sparkle of their sisters fitted with the Kylchap arrangement and double chimneys. So it was surprising that Peppercorn, when he took over the reins from Thompson, considered self-cleaning smokeboxes (which determined single chimneys, by virtue of available space) preferable to the proven free-steaming abilities of Kylchap locomotives. These A2s were in no sense bad engines, but could be a bit shy of steam on occasions.

In the account of my time at Haymarket which follows, much reference is made to Pacifics and 'big' engines. This is not exaggeration, but merely the way that we, as both Cleaners and Firemen, regarded such engines. Forty-six locomotives, over half of our total allocation, were big engines in every sense of the word and to these we can add the Pacifics and V2s which came in from Gateshead, Heaton, Carlisle Canal, Dundee and Aberdeen, all of which required preparation before they worked home. Such was daily life at Haymarket.

All pilots together! Here, at the top end of the shed, stand J36 65243 MAUDE, although the name has not been painted on after the last overhaul, and J88 68328. The J36 was the regular engine on the Broxburn goods trip and the J88 was the 'wee' Gorgie pilot working the sidings there that could not be accessed by the larger wheel-base N15. Both engines have been moved off the ashpits after fire cleaning and are waiting to be backed into the shed. This indicates that it is probably a Friday evening and the working week is finished, since the trips did not operate on Saturdays. (Transport Treasury)

A pre-nationalisation photograph of the D11/2 Director 4-4-0 2690 THE LADY OF THE LAKE, one of several 'Directors' allocated to Haymarket for its entire life. The engine is in wartime LNE black with the abbreviated lettering, NE on the tender and in a state of cleanliness quite foreign to Haymarket, but indicative of the labour shortages of the time. Fortunately, she was restored to some of her former glory in my time at Haymarket and was the last 'Director' to remain in service there. Indeed, in mid-1958, she worked the through coaches off the Down FLYING SCOTSMAN right through to Aberdeen. (Transport Treasury)

5. CLEANING DUTIES

This was the Haymarket I reported to, early in 1957. On that first Monday morning, I crossed the front of the Running Shed to the General Office at 09.00 and was struck by the number of engines standing at the front of the shed, with smoke pouring from chimneys, steam blowing off and the glare of flames from the wick 'pouries' of preparation crews. The steam, gloom, noise and much more put me in mind of the portrayal I had seen of Dante's Inferno, not a bad analogy as it turned out. After being processed, measured for overalls, hat and duffel jacket, the Staff Clerk, David Galbraith, took me, not to the Gaffer Cleaner, but to the fitting shop where I was put in the care of the Leading Fitter, one Jimmy Johnstone. He quickly passed me on to an Apprentice Fitter with the instruction that I was to be shown round locomotives and acquainted with all the constituent parts. So commenced a somewhat strange week! The young Fitter did as instructed but was obviously bored by the whole thing and left me very much to my own devices for a lot of the time. I was befriended by the Whitemetaller/ Turner, Tommy Shepherd, who explained his duties and how bearings were whitemetalled and turned, in order to protect the more valuable brasses, and gave me much further insight into the finer details of locomotive construction. Between times, I washed down and cleaned, with paraffin and cotton waste, side rods and other parts of disassembled motion from locomotives under attention.

On the Wednesday of that first week, I was sought out by Andrew Fairgrieve, the Firing Inspector, who took me to a 'dead' A3 in the fitting road. There, he proceeded to probe my knowledge of the locomotive by questioning me on the various parts. Now this is where my early days with the Hamilton men came to the rescue and I was able to comprehensively describe the locomotive, part by part, the generation and action of the steam, injectors, ejectors, valve lap and lead and other things, much to his growing amazement and amusement. I do know that I had impressed him and he muttered something about 'going out' before again leaving me to my own devices. He returned again on the Friday and took me into the cab of a V2 in steam, going over, in greater detail, the controls and what they did, the generation of steam, the passage of steam from the boiler to the cylinders, the action of the Walschaerts valve gear. He asked how an injector worked and the difference between a live steam injector and an exhaust steam injector. This was quite

a probing to which, I think, I responded well.

On the Saturday morning, I was rostered 06.00 cleaning and, for the first time, joined my peer group in the cleaning squad, though I remember little of the day otherwise. I did however learn the hierarchy of the squad. The senior (oldest hand) Cleaner was responsible for drawing the cleaning oil, a foul mix of white turning oil and lubricating oil which gave it a green tinge. This was known, for no obvious reason, as 'mickey'. He drew the cotton waste on an engine-by-engine basis from the stores, and was responsible for ensuring the 'Not to be Moved' boards were set in place, front and rear, before work started, and were taken down after work was completed. He cleaned up the used waste and barrowed it to the 'top end', where it was burned.

The three next senior Cleaners were allocated the boiler, one to each side and one to the smokebox and they rotated round these duties. The smokebox was the most unpleasant task since they were generally very hot and the cleaning oil sparked and sizzled as it fried on contact with the hot metal. The top of the boiler/smokebox was cleaned by the Cleaners climbing on to, and balancing on the handrails, with no other protection. What would the present Health & Safety Inspectors make of that? The next three Cleaners had the tender, one to each side and one to the tender end, again rotating round. Here, the Cleaners did have some help. A trestle, constructed of boiler tubing, allowed the Cleaners to reach the higher points of the tender sides. The drawback, however, was that the trestle weighed a ton and had to be manhandled over pits and carried around tenders. Then the next two Cleaners were allocated the 'paints' which were the cab sides, the running valance and cylinder covers and the front buffer beam.

The next four were allocated to the wheels and motions with another two on tender boxes and the remaining few went underneath and cleaned framings, centre motions, axles and springs. On the big engines, the framing and axles were painted red, so any slacking was immediately obvious. Each Cleaner on the wheels, framing and axleboxes was also issued with a scraper to ensure all dirt was removed before the parts were washed down with paraffin and then polished up. Accordingly, cleaning underneath for the junior Cleaners was a form of purgatory since they were exposed to paraffin drips and splashes from the outside wheel Cleaners, as well as having to work in a stuffy and

claustrophobic situation. The only lighting to be had were wick pouries which gave off a smoky, choking light. A wick pourie was very similar to an oil pourie but with a long tapering spout of larger diameter. It had a long wick which descended into the body of the can, which was filled with paraffin. The wick blazed away merrily when lit, affording some degree of light and lots of the aforesaid smoke.

This was cleaning, Haymarket style, and each squad was under the control of a Gaffer Cleaner, two of whom were ex-footplate men. Charlie Reid had fired regularly on the then A1 No.2567 (latterly 60068) SIR VISTO when it first came new from the North British Locomotive works to Haymarket in August 1924. Jimmy Blake, an ex-Dalry Road (and Caley) Driver, had two sons, Eddie and Jimmy, both Passed Firemen at Dalry Road and the other Gaffer, David Adams, was an ex-Permanent Way Ganger from Grantshouse. They stood no nonsense nor did they accept any slip-shod work. Haymarket engines were cleaned, and how they were cleaned. Cleaners worked rotating early, late and night turns of duty, as follows:

Early 06.00/14.00

Late 13.00/21.00

Night 00.01 to 08.00 (MO) 22.00/ 06.00 (MX)

No cleaning took place on Sundays although two Cleaners, on a rotating basis worked 22.00 (Sat) to 06.00 (Sun) to be available should a need for any additional Fireman arise.

In the winter period, there were some 35/40 Cleaners per shift so, even allowing for a greater number being employed on each engine, it will be obvious that there were more Cleaners than were actually required for each engine, but an insufficient number to run two separate squads. Sometimes two or three 'trusties' would be given a 'dead' engine to clean by themselves and this was considered a full shift's work. However, there were some other interesting tasks thought up to keep all employed and one Cleaner, again a lad who could be trusted to work on his own, would be given a pot of red paint, and made to go round painting or touching up the background to engine nameplates. Another would have a pot of black paint and do likewise, for Haymarket engines had either only red or black backgrounds on all nameplates.

Yet another would be given a pot containing a mix of sand and ground bathbrick (a calcareous earth which came in brick form) and oil which formed a paste. With this unlikely mix the brass work – nameplates and

building plates – was cleaned, while two or three more would be given several sheets of emery paper and instructed to clean the 'steels'. Now, on the A4s and A1s, this consisted of burnishing whatever was already burnished on the front of the engines, and indeed 60162 SAINT JOHNSTOUN, formerly allocated to Willie Bain and mate in No.2 link, but by now in the equally capable hands of Frank Gibson and Willie Burrows, was the finest example of an engine so finished. The steels included buffer faces, coupling, handrails, front and side, smokebox dart and hinges, front cylinder covers, all external motion and even the faces of the 'policemen' or rail guards. To clean the steels meant washing them down with paraffin to remove the old grease, burnishing them and then again lightly coating the cleaned steelwork with petroleum jelly to prevent rusting. Of course, this coating trapped all the insects of the day while the engines were out running, and quickly became a sticky mess of squashed wildlife. The sheer volume of dead insect life cleaned from the steels on a daily basis at 64B might go some way to explain why the east coast of Scotland did not suffer a midge problem!

The same engines were generally cleaned at least once every day, the top link engines sometimes twice, and cleaned to perfection. However, this meant that they were never really filthy and this eased the lot of the Cleaners. The paintwork was covered in a coating of 'mickey' which removed any grime there might be, and this was then polished off using clean cotton waste, leaving the paintwork gleaming. The motion, wheels and tender boxes were washed over with paraffin as was the

job where they could earn a living, and took little or no interest in the railway. Others were, like myself, keen to make a career and were keen to learn as much as they could. Others came and went just as quickly, whilst one or two, it has to be said, were just one jump ahead of the police. This was particularly so with many of the Cleaners who followed me, when it was becoming apparent that there was no future in this particular branch of the industry. Dieselisation had a demoralising effect on many and, strangely, it was to the Post Office that many went, attracted I suppose by the prospect of greater job security. Many of the older hands were first year Firemen, meaning that they had gained the required number of firing turns to warrant being paid as Firemen while still graded as Cleaners. 279 firing turns triggered this rise in wages. The very oldest hands in the cleaning squads never cleaned but were firing all year round, but again, they were still graded Cleaners.

Inevitably, a fair bit of bullying took place and one or two Cleaners were unfortunately singled out for a fair bit of rough treatment. The Gaffers were generally on the ball, however, and did not let things get out of hand. On one particular night we observed justified retribution, when one of the more aggressive Cleaners was giving Gaffer Jimmy Blake a real hard time. Jimmy was a short and very round elderly man, but nevertheless he only stood so much before stopping the miscreant short with a vicious short jab which came from nowhere, taking the hapless lad right in the solar plexus. There was never a further cheep from that young man.

This story would not be complete without a description of where the Cleaners lived whilst on duty at Haymarket. This was the Cleaners' bothy, situated between the Material and Oil Store and the Running Foreman's Office on the north side of the depot. It was a low, square, flat-roofed, brick building, painted outside with a peculiar terra cotta red distemper which adorned all the buildings at Haymarket. Inside, it was hard to determine if it had ever been painted and, all-in-all, it was a bleak, cheerless place. It had metal framed windows (with much of the glass missing) on three sides and was furnished with a few long tables and benches. A cast iron stove sat against one wall and on this stove is where our bottles of tea were placed to heat, ready for mealtime. When placing your lemonade bottle, or whisky bottle or whatever else sort of bottle, containing cold tea on the hot surface of the stove, it was imperative that the stopper was loosened else you came in at 'coffee-up' time (the local term for meal break) to find your bottle smashed and the bothy reeking of stewed and burnt tea and sugar. The stove also provided the only heat in the building.

In one corner, partly hidden by a short partition wall, which held coat pegs, was a single stone sink with a single cold tap. Here we washed prior to taking food or going off duty. Two electric light bulbs hung from naked wires and provided all the illumination there was. In daylight, it was not too grim, but on the nightshift, and particularly in winter, it was a cold, dull, dreary, miserable place. Here we messed but there was little enthusiasm to hang about or put off time after food had been consumed. The cleaning of the place, such as it was, was the duty of the senior Cleaner, as was the tending of the stove, in addition to his other responsibilities, described earlier.

In truth, whilst the bothy was poor, it was not all that different when compared with the Drivers and Firemen's bothy to the east side of the Running Foreman's Office, although this was better lit, weatherproof and warmer, but then again, it was seldom unoccupied, night or day. The Cleaner's bothy was only used when Cleaners were coming on duty, for about half an hour in mid-shift for meals and for the 20 minutes or so we had to clean up before booking off. This then was home to up to 35/40 Cleaners per shift in the late 1950s. However, if a Cleaner was on a firing turn, he was permitted to use the Drivers' bothy; thus, in summer, the Cleaners' bothy saw little use indeed.

framing, before again being brought to a shine with clean waste. Indeed, cleaning materials were never skimped and the 'Gaffer' would inspect each engine closely to ensure that dirt had not been polished into the paintwork, before declaring himself satisfied. It was a very odd occasion indeed when the squad were made to go over an engine again, but it was known. The squad generally cleaned between 8 and 10 engines in a shift.

My fellow Cleaners were a real mixed bunch from all walks of life. Many looked on the work as merely a

6. FIRST FIRING

The following week I was properly placed in a cleaning squad, which turned out to be the same squad I had been accommodated with on the previous Saturday, and I started my first backshift week, booking on at 13.00. Being a junior hand, I went underneath to clean. The week ground on, but there was a lot of fun as might be expected when a large group of young men were thrown together, and time passed quickly. I very quickly realised that not all my contemporaries were in fact as 'railway daft' as myself and the majority were there because it was just a job. A few were keen and had some ambition to drive, but regrettably, most just did the work and took little or no interest in the greater railway. This very quickly worked to my advantage, since I asked questions about everything and undertook every task to the best of my ability. In short, I became noticed and was classed with the relatively few others in the same mould. After several weeks, as the year passed into early springtime, on one Thursday afternoon when we took duty, there was some considerable excitement, for the daily roster was up for the Saturday, and the squad were all booked on firing turns. Even me! Only weeks in the job and here I was, booked as Fireman on the 14.00 'Coal Pilot'. I worked my remaining cleaning shifts in a dream and just could not wait for the Saturday to dawn.

On the Saturday, I booked on early and made my way across to J83 68474, on the coaling plant road. The engine sat at the head of a rake of loaded coal wagons and was otherwise unattended. Eagerly, I climbed aboard and had a good look round. The previous Fireman had left a good fire behind the door, the boiler was full and steam pressure sat some way below blowing off point. The footplate had been swept and hosed down and everything was just so. I waited impatiently for my Driver to appear, and the 'off'. The Driver was one David Drummond, who had been at the controls of A2 60530 SAYAJIRAO that fateful evening on the 17th December 1953 when, working a 00.50 parcels special from Edinburgh to Newcastle, the train struck a piece of pre-fabricated trackwork which had fallen from an Up Goods train and jammed between the platforms, just moments before, at Longniddry Station. The engine, running at around 65mph, struck this obstruction, was thrown off the track and turned right round through 180 degrees to finish facing Edinburgh, on the main road adjacent to the railway. His Fireman, Robert McKenzie, was killed instantly and David suffered serious injuries. He eventually resumed work, but could only walk with the aid of a stick and had, since his return to work, been accommodated on light duties, in the shape of the Coal Pilot.

David (Davie as he was generally known) eventually appeared, climbed aboard, greeted me, had a good look round and said that he was away for a blether and would be in the running Foreman's Office if I needed him. Off he went and I was left in glorious isolation. I fired a shovel or two of coal in the box at odd intervals to keep the fire alight, and topped up the boiler, but otherwise, I was bored until 22.00 came. We had turned nery a wheel. My first firing turn had been on a 'standing pilot' and my firing had been confined to a few shovels full of coal. What an anti-climax on my special day!

In retrospect, I realised just how circumspect Sandy Mercer, the Roster Clerk, had been in rostering me for this turn, for I was just weeks in the job, had not been passed out and thus my inexperience would certainly have not given rise to any harm on the Coal Pilot. Indeed, some time later, I was able to observe first hand how such inexperience could cause chaos of monumental proportion. This particular black comedy was played out later that summer on a Saturday. Haymarket was humming, engines coming on shed, engines being prepared and engines going off to work trains. In the midst of this hustle and bustle, which was not at all unusual, the engine booked for a relief London job was failed by the examining Fitter and a replacement was urgently required. The only spare was our own A3, 60098 SPION KOP but she was facing north and had not been coaled for a Newcastle turn. It was a case of all hands to the pumps. A Passed Firemen and his young mate were dispatched to get '98 on to the turntable and turned and then up to the coaling plant to be fully coaled.

To ensure that the engine did not then become trapped in the 'one way' system of moving the engines through the servicing procedures, a man was sent to the turntable to stop any movements up towards the coaling plant until '98 could be reversed back, and slipped though the hand points connection between the coal road and the loop. The engine eventually moved down and stopped short of the points. On the footplate, the Driver instructed his mate to drop off and set the hand points. The Fireman duly obeyed but did not re-appear. After a moment or so the Driver crossed over the cab and looked out, and there was his mate, standing outside of the cab with his hands on a points lever. 'These yin's?' he asked. 'No, the set up beyond the engine, son', was the response. Off he went, set the road as directed and waved the Driver on. What he had failed to say was that he had already pulled the points between the engine and tender. The Driver tugged open the regulator and his tender was 'off', all wheels off! After aid had been summoned, he took his Fireman aside and had a word or two in his 'shell-like'. In his official report, he (the Driver) stated that '*after the derailment, I inquired of my Fireman, as to the length of his service and breadth of his experience, and he informed me that he was, on that very day, making his debut as a Fireman at Haymarket, whereupon I assured him that he was, without any shadow of a doubt, the most outstanding debutante of the season!*'

Now I cannot recall these words actually being spoken, as the roars of the Driver were heard all over the shed that day, but it runs in my mind that what was said was somewhat more earthy in content, as the young Cleaner got his blessings. This was a classic example of the inexperienced being asked to do more than they were ready to do.

Opposite. J83 68457 at the top end of the shed on 31st May 1953. This was the Haymarket Yard pilot and I spent many happy days firing (and driving) on this engine whilst we shunted the yard. In the right background is an unidentified 'Shire' temporarily rendered a 4-2-0. (J. Robertson/Transport Treasury)

D49/1 62705 LANARKSHIRE at rest in the shed loop on 14th August, 1949. This was the engine we had on the very last day of steam working on the 3.43pm Edinburgh/Larbert. On return from Larbert, the diagram then called for empty coaches to be worked up from Craigentinny to Waverley and since the 'lift' was a big one, a rear end pilot had been provided on each of the previous days. On the Saturday, there was no pilot and 62705, working tender first, had to put in a Herculean effort to lift a big train of empty coaches up the hill to Waverley unaided. 'It was a close run thing'. In the left of the picture behind the buffer beam is the Shed Labourers Bothy. (J. Robertson/Transport Treasury)

7. PASSING OUT

On my next day shift week, on the Tuesday morning just after 07.00, I was once more sought out by Andrew Fairgrieve or 'Fairy' as he was generally known, although never to his face. After he had had a few words with the gaffer Cleaner he said 'away and get your coat and 'piece' (sandwiches etc.), you're with me today'. Off I shot, collected my bits and met him outside the Running Foreman's Office. 'Let's look for '37, he said, 'she's on the Thornton and your going to fire her'.

Well, I knew exactly where '37 was, A3 60037 HYPERION to give her full title, for hadn't I just finished cleaning her? We walked across the shed and climbed up into the cab. The Driver, Dick Hiddleston of No.4 link greeted us, and his Fireman, Bobby Lemmon, looked very happy at the prospect of a trip 'on the cushions' while I did his work. Pleasantries over and the tank having been topped up, Dick gave a warning screech on the whistle and, with cylinder cocks roaring, we slid out towards the shed exit signal. As we shuddered to a stand, Bobby took me with him to show me this part of the drill and we dropped off to telephone the Signalman in Haymarket Central Junction. He showed me how to wind the handle on the side of the 'phone and when the Signalman answered, he said '37 for the 08.05 Thornton'. 'Wait for the signal' was the curt reply. Words were never wasted at that 'phone.

I checked that the lamps were set and as we regained the footplate, the disc came off. Dick tugged open the regulator and we slipped over the North lines to access the South lines and so down to Waverley. I shut the cocks at a nod from Dick and had a quick look in the firebox. The fire had nicely been made up behind the door and into the back corners, but the rest of the firebox was almost bare. However, we also had half a glass of water and pressure was sitting nicely at 180lbs. I looked over the side as we clanked our way through Haymarket station, the Gresley 'knock' music to my ears. We plunged into the Haymarket tunnel with a screech of the whistle and the footplate was illuminated by the glare of the fire. I was extremely excited but was also becoming somewhat worried. This was a 'big' engine. 'Would I manage?' I wondered.

We slid through the Gardens and into the Station, where I had to couple up to the train under the eagle eye of 'Fairy'. This done to his satisfaction, I was instructed to set a single lamp at the chimney denoting a stopping passenger train, and returned the other

headlamp to the cab. By this time, Bobby had sloped off to the train, for a sleep no doubt. 'Now son', said Andrew, 'take the shovel and push some o' that fire around the sides of the box'. I reversed the firing shovel and levered the burning coals around the box. Dick gave a touch of the blower and the languid yellow flames turned to incandescent white. 'Put half a dozen doon each side son'. This done, Andrew said, 'noo, look at your chimney'. A grey haze was shooting straight up into the cold morning air. 'Good, jist as it should be for you must always remember it's a crime to make black smoke or blow off in the Station. Noo, fill up that hole below the firedoor'. I shovelled until the coal was level with the bottom ring and then filled in the back corners of that wide firebox. I was getting used to the half-trap door and had now mastered the knack of giving the shovel blade a twist to shoot coal right into the back corners.

'Right', said Andrew, 'five minutes to go. Get some water in the boiler'. Steam pressure was now rising quickly with 210lbs showing, and the safety valves were beginning to sizzle. 'Pit another dozen roond the box'. 'Oh, for heavens sake, I've only one pair of hands', I thought as I shut off the injector and picked up the shovel. 'Noo, I am going to stand ahint your seat and watch you,' said Andrew. 'I winna' interfere, but I will keep you richt if needs be, son. Everythin's looking good, so dinnae worry'. Dick gave me a wink.

Away back the train, whistles blew. I crossed over to the Driver's (left) side of the cab and looked back. A green flag waved at the rear. Dick gave a blast on the whistle as he tugged the regulator open. Cylinder cocks roaring, '37 gave a wee slip and then the driving wheels caught and we blasted our way out to the Mound Tunnel. I watched the train followed out the platform, as I was required to do by the Rule Book and then crossed over and closed the cocks. I sat myself up on the comfortable bucket seat so thoughtfully provided by Sir Nigel Gresley for his crews, and looked out as we pounded our way through Princes Street Gardens. Steam pressure was just below blowing off point and we had ¾ glass of water.

We entered the North Haymarket tunnel with a screech, and the footplate and tender end were illuminated as if by bright sunshine, and the glare of the fire bounced back off the tunnel roof. The noise was indescribable as we roared through the tunnel. I caught sight of a small circle of light ahead rushing towards us and then, with a loud hiss,

Dick dropped the brake handle and we slipped out the tunnel with brakes grinding and came to a smooth halt at Haymarket station. Once again I crossed the cab and looked back. Doors slammed, whistles blew and the green flag was given once more. Again, Dick pulled open the regulator and '37 gave voice at the chimney. As we roared away from the station, I bent to pick up the shovel, but 'Fairy' stopped me. 'Wait a wee bit until the blast has an effect on your fire', he said. Back up into the padded bucket seat and head out the window. We were approaching the depot and as we rushed past, I gave a wave to my fellow Cleaners. As I soon learned, nobody fired when passing the shed, but sat looking out and giving the impression that all was well with the world even although, in truth, steam pressure might be dropping and a 'cold run' looming.

Anyway, Dick had been winding '37 in by shortening the cut off and now had the regulator full out against the stop. The syncopated exhaust beat was clear above the crashing din on the footplate but the engine rode smoothly with just a slight rise and fall on the tender plate beneath my feet. Prompted by 'Fairy', I picked up the shovel and sent a dozen or so shovelsful round the box with another half dozen into the back corners. Pressure was holding up well, almost on the red line, as I put on the exhaust injector. Andrew just nodded and took notes in his wee book. Speed had increased on the long straight past Haymarket West Junction and we swung away to the right at Saughton Junction, parting company with the Glasgow line. Here, we dropped down the short 1 in 110 curving, falling gradient, on to the wee level stretch and up over the switchback 1 in 140 rising to 1 in 110 falling hump, towards Turnhouse. Then another long straight past the Airport till we crossed the River Almond Bridge. The Turnhouse intermediate block signals were clear to speed us on our way, and again, at the Inspector's prompt, I bent to the task of feeding that hungry firebox. Water and pressure were holding up well as we hit the 1 in 100 rising gradient which would take us up to the Forth Bridge. Dick let the reverser out a turn or two and '37 barked her way up this hill. I made to pick up the shovel but again 'Fairy' stopped me. 'Dalmeny stop' he said.

We started away from Dalmeny station and ahead I could see the long viaduct leading on to the Forth Bridge proper. I was filled with excitement since I had often been over the bridge in a

train, but this was the first crossing on the footplate. I sat mesmerised as we proceeded into the spiderwork of girders and cross beams, with the river glinting in the morning sunshine away below us. The sun was up and was spreading a golden carpet up the river. The noise was unmistakable, and quite peculiar to the bridge. One would have to be both deaf and blind not to know when you were on the big 'Brig'. Even down in the streets of South Queensferry, when a train was crossing, the noise was unmistakable, that unique, rumbling reverberation high above the Forth.

Slowly we proceeded across and dropped down through North Queensferry and into the tunnel on the steep 1 in 70 downgrade. This North Queensferry tunnel had marker lights installed, a reminder of the fateful Sunday evening on 7th March 1954, when Haymarket Top Link Driver Storie, with 60024 KINGFISHER, working the 18.55 Aberdeen to London sleeper with 13 coaches, a train weighing 467 tons tare and representing an overload of 17 tons, slipped to a stand on the rising gradient. The slipping had been intermittent on a new rail which had only been installed that same day and Storie was working both the regulator

and reverser to try and check it, but was unaware that the train had actually come to a stand and was slipping backwards. In the foul darkness he tried to touch the tunnel walls to ascertain if he was still moving when there was a bump from the rear as the last three vehicles derailed at the catch points just outside the northern portal of the tunnel. Fortunately the buckeye couplers held, thus preventing the three derailed coaches from being precipitated down the steep embankment. Only one passenger sustained slight injuries. Her Majesty's Inspecting Officer of Railways, Brigadier C.A. Langley, in his Investigation Report, recommended that marker lights should be provided to assist trainmen in tunnels with such steep inclines and both North Queensferry and the next tunnel north at Inverkeithing South were so fitted, as was Queen Street tunnel in Glasgow.

But to return to my journey. We ran down the hill in easy steam to stop at Inverkeithing station, bang on time. On departure, I made up the fire again. This next part of the journey could be a heartbreak for locomotive men and surely made the Edinburgh to Aberdeen road one of the very hardest to run to time anywhere in the country. From Inverkeithing, we were either rushing up hills or dropping down hills and

screeching round corners. High speed was impossible and it was here that the penny dropped with me sometime later, that the art of firing was not always to have full pressure and a full boiler, but to control the firing to give steam where required and to prevent waste when it was not required. But on that beautiful early spring morning we pounded up to the summit at Dalgety and then rushed down along the Fife coast, now parallel with the river estuary and directly across the water from Edinburgh.

We had left Edinburgh firstly heading west and now we were rushing due eastwards having described a full 180º turn as we crossed the River Forth upstream. Our stops at Aberdour, Burntisland and Kinghorn were successfully completed and we stormed up the 1 in 183 to top the rise at Invertiel Junction, before dropping down into Kirkcaldy. As we approached Kirkcaldy, my nose was assailed by a most peculiar and all-pervading odour. Not unpleasant, but strong. This was the smell of the ingredients for linoleum manufacture for which Kirkcaldy was famed, which included turpentine and linseed oil. No one could ever miss Kirkcaldy and as we drew into the busy platform I was reminded of a famous children's poem by C.S. Cocker in which

Thornton at 09.40, and standing there until 09.58 to allow the faster 07.05 Aberdeen to Edinburgh express, conveying through coaches from Aberdeen to London Kings Cross, to overtake. The engine was a Dundee V2 and was in good order. Again, the Dundee Fireman gratefully went into the train to continue to Edinburgh as a passenger, whilst I did his work. The fire was in apple pie order and there was a full boiler of water. The Driver confirmed that 'she was a guid yin' and we sat waiting for departure. The Aberdeen ran through and at 09.58, we set off in pursuit. This was another 'all stops' to Edinburgh, due at Haymarket at 11.04. The V2 was a pedigree engine and not 'off the beat' in any way. So we blasted our way back round the Fife coast and I had no trouble with steam or water.

On arrival at Haymarket, we took our farewell of the Dundee men and walked back up through the yard to the shed. Andrew spent just a bit more time with me going over the relevant Rules for footplate staff, until it was time to book off and make for home. What a day it had been! The following day, we repeated it all again, once more with 60037 HYPERION on the outward leg, but on the return journey Dundee Tay Bridge depot had provided A2 60527 SUN CHARIOT. This was my first introduction to a single chimneyed Peppercorn A2 although we had five of our own at 64B. Again, I had no cause for concern and though I did think that I had to work just a wee bit harder on the return journey, the engine steamed and rode well. The train was a fairly light train in any case and was very easily timed, so there was no panic.

The next day, Andrew again collected me from the cleaning squad and took me in to see Mr. Cherry, the Shed Master, who asked me questions on the mechanics of a steam locomotive, the theory of steam production and then we had a session on Rules and Regulations applicable to footplate staff. At the end of this session, I was advised that I was now a 'Passed Cleaner', could officially act as a Fireman as necessary, and was then directed back to the squad.

every verse finished with the lines ' an ye ken by the smell, that the next stop's Kirkcaldy'.

Whistles blowing put thoughts of poetry out of my mind for we were now faced with a long three mile climb up to Dysart on a ruling gradient of about 1 in 110. As I fired round the box, '37 barked her way up past Sinclairtown and Dysart to breast the summit and turn our head northwards. Here, Andrew motioned for me to put the shovel down and, climbing up on to the seat, I looked out ahead at this unfamiliar road. Dick had braked heavily and was checking '37's progress to the point of being funereal, but looking ahead I was fascinated to see the track alignment looking like a switchback as we slid down past Randolph Sidings Box. Colliery working and subsidence was the cause, requiring very severe temporary speed restrictions, for this area lay on the eastern reaches of the big, and very productive, Fife coalfield. We continued down, to finally come to a stand at the sinking hole that was Thornton Junction Station, on time, at 09.19 on the dot. At Thornton, Bobby rejoined the engine, having us coupled off on his way up. Dick turned to me and said, 'good trip son, when are you coming with me again?' Praise indeed and as I collected

my jacket and satchel, I overheard Dick say to Andrew 'he did very well and seems to have a real grasp of what's required in firing. I really am quite impressed.' 'Well', said Andrew, 'his theory was excellent and he has not disappointed me today either'. I went off with my ears ringing.

We sat on a seat and had our sandwiches, then Andrew took me across to a siding in which were stabled some corridor coaches. We got down into the four foot at the end of a coach and he put me through the operation of buckeye couplers and how to lift and drop them. He showed me why buffer saddles were required when the buffers were pulled into the long position when the buckeye was dropped, then made me take off saddles, shorten the buffers by pushing them in, and lifting and setting the coupler head. This was all very useful and relevant, for our seven A4s all had buckeye-fitted corridor tenders. His last words, which later came back to haunt me, were, 'remember laddie, if you're coupling on to buckeye fitted coaches using a screw coupling, always check that the buckeye is doon and the buffer saddles are in place!'

Our return working soon ran in. This was the 08.30 Dundee to Edinburgh stopping passenger train, due at

D49/2 4-4-0 62743 THE CLEVELAND and the only one of the 'Hunt' class allocated to Haymarket, at the west end of the shed on 1st September 1957. This locomotive was fitted with Lentz Rotary Cam poppet valves and this in turn afforded some no little amusement to us idle bystanders on the occasion, when, after attention had been given to the valves and pistons in the new fitting shop and the engine had been steamed, she just stood still and see-sawed when the driver pulled open the regulator. The valves had been fitted in reverse on one side! Red faces all round. (Transport Treasury)

Haymarket top link Driver Bill Stevenson leans from the cab of A2 Pacific 60534 IRISH ELEGANCE as he storms up the 1 in 66 incline out of Dundee Tay Bridge station, on his way to the Tay Bridge proper with a heavy express from Aberdeen on 20th April 1953. This was a heartbreaking start with locomotives which were not 'warmed up.' (J. Robertson/Transport Treasury)

8. MORE FIRING TURNS

The year moved into late spring and the depot holiday season, and the first 'shift up' occurred. This was the movement in the weekly rosters caused by annual leave. All such leave was rostered to ensure a fair distribution but, more importantly, to ensure that adequate coverage was maintained at all times. It was covered by the 'Spare' men, the ensuing 'holes' in the spare link covered by men stepped up from the preparation link. Then Passed Firemen were stepped up driving and Cleaners firing. This roster movement was known as the 'shift up' and occurred at the commencement of the (staff) holiday season as described, then the summer timetable when Haymarket was required to work many more booked trains, and then again at the Scottish Trade holidays and the later English holiday season, when many additional special trains were added to the depot workload.

The senior Cleaners from each squad went out firing first in strict order of seniority, and the remaining Cleaners were then divided equally into three groups and three new squads set up. This meant that you could find yourself under a different Gaffer and this happened several times each year at the 'shift ups' and 'shift backs'. Of course, on the way up, the squads got smaller and smaller until nearly all Cleaners were being utilised on firing duties. If you went firing as a 'red ink' man, this meant that you had the job for a complete week. Otherwise, the younger hands were put up firing on a daily 'as required' basis and could be cleaning one day, firing the next. It sounds a complicated system but it did work. Moreover it was fair and since Haymarket had a lot of mileage work which meant additional pay, it generally ensured that the proper men got the mileage turns and avoided a whole lot of hassle.

More of the rostering procedure later but, obviously, from a Cleaner's point of view, it was much more satisfactory when full weeks of firing came along. I was not at that time, nor for some time thereafter, a 'red ink' man but was now being lifted more and more on a daily basis for firing duties. These were, in the main, preparation duties although I did enjoy a day or two on the pilots now and again. It was also, when firing on an odd day basis only, often a case of being in the right place at the right time. Firing turns on preparation came along on a fairly regular basis, but every Cleaner's dream of getting out on the

main line was much more unlikely since there was the cushion of the Spare links to provide for that. However, sometimes the unexpected did arise and a main line turn was achieved.

Preparation duties were possibly some of the hardest turns for young Firemen at Haymarket. National Agreements stated that an hour was to be allowed for the preparation of 'big' engines. This was related to heating surface area and all the Pacifics, V2s and B1s fell into that category. The smaller engines were allowed 45 minutes for preparation and so at Haymarket, in the preparation link, in theory at least, a preparation crew could prepare seven 'big' engines in an eight hour shift, being allowed 20 minute break for food 'between the third and fifth hour'. Some of our preparation turns had indeed seven Pacifics diagrammed. In the height of the summer, and particularly at weekends when great demands were placed on Haymarket to provide engines for numerous specials in addition to the normal increased summer workload, we might prepare up to ten engines in a shift as an 'obligement' to the Running Foremen. Such 'obligements' never, ever, went unnoticed and was at some suitable time later on, repaid in full.

In preparation, the engine had come off the ash pits where the fire, ashpan and smokebox had been cleaned. Generally there was a small amount of fire in the box and the Fireman's duty, after checking the level of water in the boiler, was to ensure that the smokebox door was properly closed and tightly fitting, the drop grate or rockers were closed and secured, the brick arch was in good condition and that neither the fusible plugs nor the tubes were leaking (although generally, with a 'foreign' engine, if it came in with leaking tubes, it went out with leaking tubes!). This done and with the front framing carefully swept of ash and char, attention was turned to the fire. It was generally necessary to spread what fire there was around a bit, and then add more coal. The blower was turned on full and whilst waiting for the fire to burn through, the tender would be trimmed and a full kit collected, including a set of fire-irons and two firing shovels. This sometimes had to be achieved by searching around the shed area and even 'thieving' the necessary components from other engines awaiting preparation. It was however, an unwritten rule, which was almost always abided by, that once an engine

had been prepared, the kit, shovels and fire irons were 'off limits'.

As the fire burned through, it was spread again and then the hard work of filling up the back of the firebox started. Pacifics with their wide fireboxes could lose a ton or two of coal 'behind the door' and so the preparation Fireman shovelled and shovelled and filled the back of the box, including the back corners, right up to the flameplate, or bottom ring, of the firedoor. If the engine was due out shortly, he would work on the fire and get a good fire well burned through down each side of the box. Otherwise, the big 'back of the door' sufficed, since the engine would stand quietly for a longish time, yet with a good mass of live coals to spread around when needed. This done to satisfaction, both injectors were then tested and the boiler filled to about ¾ glass. Then, with the live steam injector still on, the floor would be swept clean, then washed down with the slaker pipe.

Lubricating oil was poured over the faceplate from the top down and then the hose turned on to wash it down too. The oil emulsified and took any dirt with it and a gleaming, shining faceplate was the result. Copper and brasswork were then rubbed up and gauge glasses, protectors and all gauges cleaned as were the side windows and front spectacle glasses. By this time, the Fireman was on the last lap, but not necessarily the easiest, for this is when the sandboxes would be checked. Woe betide you if they were empty or part empty for then, firstly, the sand-pails had to be found. It was standing instruction that these should always be returned and left adjacent to the sand kiln after use, but human nature being what it is, these were always spread to the four winds and so the great sand-pail hunt began. Sand pails were round galvanised pails, somewhat larger than a standard watering can, and with a wide spout. They held about 60lbs of dry sand. Now, time was ticking away and a lot of your hour had already been used up. When the sand-pails were found, they had to be taken to the kiln and filled, then carried back across the shed to where your engine was standing. This had the effect of lengthening arms by about six inches, or so it felt. Then, the full sand-pails had to be lifted on to the running plate generally above head height. I am 5ft 8in tall and a Pacific's running plate was always way above my head. This was muscle cracking work which had to be repeated until all the sand boxes were full. After they had been filled, well, you just threw the sand-pails away in relief. Finally, the headlamps and gauge glass lamp were filled with paraffin and rape oil respectively, and left in the cab.

So all that effort had to be crammed into 60 minutes and your mate, who until that point had been oiling round (the two of you would barely meet until work was completed) would carry out a quick check round. Then you went looking for the next engine, and the next, and the next. On a hard diagram, a preparation Firemen could, and often did, shovel around 15 tons of coal, or even more, but we were young and getting fitter by the day. All this was undertaken surrounded by hot metal, some of it so hot that it would just sear skin right off if you came in contact with it, a veritable furnace full of raging fire that could, and sometimes did, blow back, singeing eyebrows and hairline,

and boiling water and steam just waiting to scald the unwary. Burns were an everyday fact of life and cuts and bruises added to the pain. Preparation could be, and often was, conducted in a sea of pain from the minor injuries as described, to the muscles which ached in protest. Sweat poured from every pore and I consumed gallons of water during a preparation shift. And yet I, and many of my colleagues, revelled in this and I can never recall any time when I did not book off duty after such a shift with a feeling of great satisfaction. Leaving the job never entered my head although, sadly, more than a few Cleaners quickly threw in the towel. But not all preparation diagrams consisted solely of preparation and more than a few had also an element of relieving or engine changeovers as well, which added variety to the otherwise drudgery of the job.

Haymarket B1 61245 MURRAY OF ELIBANK in considerably less than sparkling condition and with a badly burned smokebox door, approaching Craigentinny with what appears to be an Up Special express passenger service, with a motley array of coaches, in the early 1950s. It was whilst driving this locomotive one night on ECS working that I ended up with my forearm gashed from wrist to elbow. The usual weekend array of out-stabled locomotives from St. Margaret's shed line the Piershill loop in the background. (M. Robertson/Transport Treasury)

9. MAIN LINE DEBUT

Some weeks after being passed out and with several preparation turns under my belt, I was backshift cleaning, and the senior hand. I had started at 13.00 but around 14.45, the Running Foreman, Ross Dougan, came up and instructed me to go over to V2 60827 and lend a hand in preparation. Away I went across to the front of the shed and No.2 road, where 60827 was standing, facing north. I climbed aboard but there was no sign of any Fireman and so I started going through the procedure with which I was now quite familiar. I was concentrating on the fire and filling up the box when the Driver came up and spoke to me. I was a bit surprised since preparation Drivers were generally younger Passed Firemen and I thought to myself that he was a bit older than the run of the mill 'prep' men. He was pleasant enough and went off to continue oiling round. With the cab looking spruce, a good fire in and half a glass of water, '827 was making steam but not too quickly, so I then turned my attention to the dreaded sands, wondering where on earth the regular Fireman was, the one I was supposed to be assisting. I was startled out this reverie by the Driver asking about the sands. 'They're nearly full,' I shouted down to his inquiry. 'Weel, make sure

they're full to the top and working properly,' he shouted back. Groaning, I set of on the pail hunt but fortunately, four or so pail loads topped them up.

I trimmed the tender, and with a final check round, went to climb off, when the Driver came back to the cab with his oil cans. 'Where was I going?' he asked. 'Well I've prepared the engine as asked and I'm now going to report back to Ross Dougan, job done,' I replied. 'What did Ross tell you, son?' he asked. 'Just to assist with the preparation of this engine,' I responded. 'Naw, you've only got half the story. You're my Fireman for the day, for that lazy b*****d, Willie L***, who was booked for the job, will nae doot be hiding somewhere, waiting until we're off the shed because he doesnae fancy the hard work,' my Driver said. 'OK, but where am I going?' I asked. 'We are working the 16.00 Perth, son, and I know you hivnae much experience but Ross says you're keen and we'll get on fine, I've nae doot,' was the response. The 16.00 Perth was a No.2 link job, and my Driver was none but J. Cuthbert. He ran A1 60160 AULD REEKIE with his opposite number, Joe Bogie but today we had one of our own, good V2s whilst his own steed was in Doncaster for a general overhaul.

Since I was to be in the hot seat, I quickly went over everything again just to ensure that I had not forgotten or omitted some essential factor. The fire was in good order, although still mostly at the back of the door at this time, the boiler nicely full but with a bit of space in reserve and the tender nicely filled and trimmed, with good, hard coal. Having collected my jacket and satchel, I'd stowed my tea bottle behind the injector steam pipe, just as real Firemen did, I thought. My Driver blew off the brakes whilst I released the tender handbrake, and with a blast on the whistle and roaring of cylinder cocks, we drew out of the shed and stopped at the water column. Tender filled, we slid out to the shed exit.

I phoned off shed and, after the exit disc cleared and we were slipping quietly down to Waverley, the butterflies started again in my stomach. 'What was this Perth road like?' I asked myself. After coupling on to a fairly heavy train and setting one lamp at the chimney, denoting that this was, strangely, only a Class 'B` stopping passenger train, I set about building up the fire, the lessons learned just weeks ago on 60037 still clear in my mind. I had already, in preparation, built up a good fire at the back of the door and back corners so,

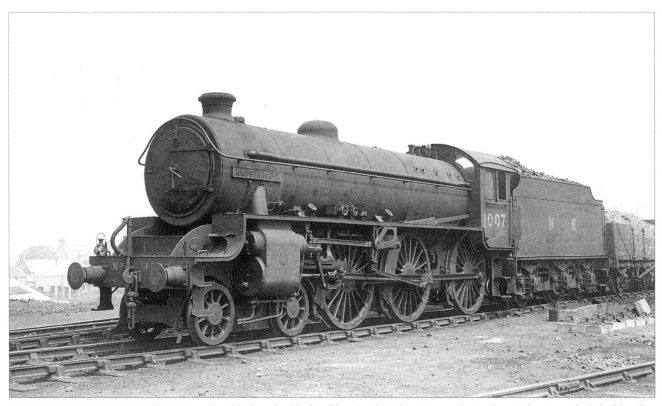

B1 4-6-0 1007 KLIPSPRINGER in LNE wartime black and with the abbreviated NE lettering on the tender, at the top end of shed heading what appears to be the ash train. The engine is in very run-down condition but is in the livery it first appeared in as 8308, in 1944. It was initially allocated to Darlington shed but only for a month, after which it was transferred to Haymarket, in the May of that year. It was renumbered 1007 between January to March 1946 so this photograph is after that date. It was with this engine, by then 61007 in BR times, that I had my first really 'cold' run, due wholly to my own stupidity. (W. Hermiston/Transport Treasury)

with words of encouragement from my Driver, spent the time feeding the sides with a small charge of coal and watching the chimney. The centre of the firebox was still more or less just the bare firebars and that helped keep the smoke down to a grey haze as we waited for the off. Pressure was rising nicely and I still had some water space left in the boiler to avoid blowing off in the station if the need arose, 'Fairy's' words of warning still very fresh in my mind. My mate had blown up the vacuum and a brake test had been carried out and, as the clock on the *North British Hotel* slowly ticked round to departure time, I fed several shovels of coal to the centre of the box, filling up the void there. The haze at the chimney darkened significantly but at that moment whistles blew and we got the 'right away' from our Guard. As my mate pulled on the regulator and we started to move, across the station, the chime whistle of A4 60012 COMMONWEALTH OF AUSTRALIA on the 16.00 Glasgow gave a long blast which reverberated around the Gardens and she also started to move out parallel to us. I had forgotten about the simultaneous departures at

16.00, and now looked forward to the 'race' which would take place after the Haymarket stop.

The 16.00 Perth at that time was a fairly heavy train of 10 coaches, 360 tons, conveying through coaches from Edinburgh to Inverness via Carrbridge, and also Edinburgh to Inverness via Forres, plus a restaurant car and, as we blasted through the Gardens, I had a good look at my fire. As we stood waiting the off at Haymarket, I fired another dozen or so shovelsfull round the box and set the exhaust injector. Hanging over the Driver's door, I had one eye on what was happening back the platform and the other on the 16.00 Glasgow in platform 4. We got the right away from our Guard and Jim had '827 on the move before he gave an acknowledging blast on the whistle. Behind us, I saw '12 begin to move, her melodious chime whistle again raising the echoes around the station.

Jim was giving '827 some stick now as we powered our way up towards the shed, where there always was an audience to watch the two 16.00s go past. Our boiler pressure stood rock steady, but '12 slowly began to reel us in and as we passed the shed, she got her streamlined nose in front. We exchanged waves with her crew as she slowly pulled away from us, and acknowledged the waves and gestures of encouragement from the Glasgow passengers as they slid past, for this was a 'race' which the regulars enjoyed as much as the train crews. We then held

our own out to Saughton Junction, running parallel with the rear coaches of the Glasgow until we swung away northwards towards the Forth Bridge. My mate gave me the nod to start firing and I took this opportunity to repair some of the damage the blast had done to the fire, whilst Jim wound the reverser up and the barks at the chimney diminished to a dull roar. This engine was perfection both in riding and steaming for the injector had kept the boiler level up despite the hammering she had taken. Although pressure had dropped to around 200lbs, my bout of firing soon had the needle moving upwards once more, much to my relief. We took up our Dalmeny stop, slipped gently across the Bridge and dropped down to Inverkeithing station, through the two tunnels.

As we stood at the station, my Driver described the road ahead. We were faced with an unbroken climb of 11 miles on a rising gradient averaging 1 in 95 or thereabouts, with a station stop at Dunfermline Lower and some severe curvature around the chord line from Touch South Junction (pronounced 'Tooch') to Townhill Junction. This was quite a prospect with a heavy train. 'Just keep firing little and often, son, said Jim, and watch your chimney and water level.' I shot another dozen shovelsfull round the box, and then concentrated in getting the back corners as full as I could. On the right away, with '827 down in about 50%, we blasted out underneath the road bridge and

Below. Aberdeen based V2 E851 on the ash pits at the west end of Haymarket shed in unlined black livery. Originally 4822 when new, she carried this number from January 1948 until January 1951. She has just come from the coaling plant and one hopes that the crew are still aboard as she is in full forward gear, a crime if the engine is left unattended. (M. Robertson/Transport Treasury)

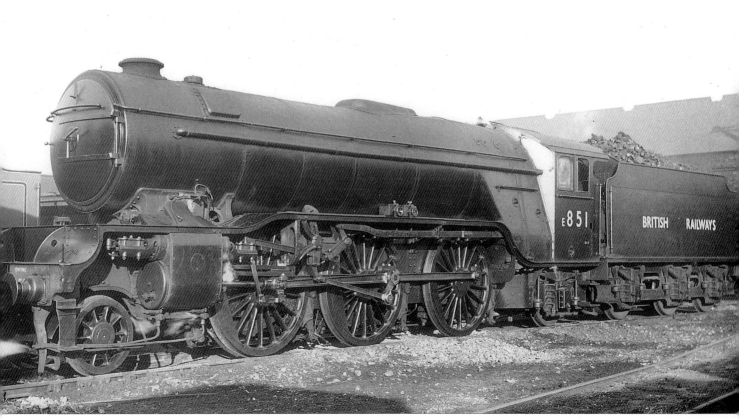

immediately swung to the left and on to the curving climb and then long straight, up through Rosyth Halt to Dunfermline. Looking out, the exhaust was shooting straight up into the air and was a healthy dark grey. The syncopated beat of the exhaust, once described as 'one, two and a handful' was music to my ears as Jim shortened the cut-off to about 30% and pulled the regulator into big valve. We pounded our way up the five miles to our next station stop at Dunfermline Lower.

After Dunfermline, we swung to the right and up round that severe, curving rise through the trees at Touch South, the left-hand lines going on to Dunfermline Upper and Stirling. I was now firing more or less constantly, pausing only to brush the spilled coal from the floor and to give it a wash down to lay the dust. The boiler level was being maintained by the one injector and the pressure gauge needle was wavering just below the red line. We stopped at Cowdenbeath just short of the top of the hill, and on receiving the right away, blasted up the last few yards to Cowdenbeath North Junction where '827 dropped her nose down the 1 in 80 falling gradient, towards Kelty. Once again, we were in the heart of the broad Fife coalfields and like the Aberdeen road, our route ahead was littered with temporary speed restrictions because of colliery subsidence. We slowly rocked our way over the switchback alignment down to Kelty with the engine blowing off fiercely, much to my chagrin. After departure from Kelty, we left the coal workings behind as we blasted our way up to Blairadam. From here to Glenfarg the line was a series of wee ups and downs, but some speed was possible and we powered our way round the Lomond Hills and over the fine farming country of the Howe of Fife, with Loch Leven glinting in the afternoon sun away to the right-hand side.

As we approached the top of the hill at Glenfarg, the rails ahead seemed just to disappear from sight. This was the fearsome Glenfarg bank, some seven miles of 1 in 70, which I had heard about. At this point in our journey we were descending the gradient, but I could not help but think that I had to provide steam to get us back up this incline later in the day. However, my mate motioned me to leave the fire be and shut off the injector. Partially closing the flap on the firedoor, I sat back and enjoyed the run down through the trees. The road ahead gently swung right and left through the forests and down the hill and '827 was riding like a carriage. Down through the two tunnels, a long swing to the left brought us out of the glen to run diagonally down the hillside into Strathearn, and to our final stop at Bridge of Earn. Here my Driver instructed me to push the remaining coals at the back of the box forward with the poker, set the injector and close the flap. This I did as we

climbed up the short gradient to Hilton Junction and swung right into the rock cutting which was the precursor to the 1,210 yard long Moncreiff Tunnel. As we cleared this long tunnel, the city of Perth lay before us in the sunshine, and we ran into Perth General Station dead on time at 17.46.

After coupling off we ran round and proceeded back to Perth South shed, where we cleaned the fire and prepared for our return journey. After tea and sandwiches, I went off to have a look round. Perth South was the former LMS shed and was home to many Black Fives and Jubilees. I was also impressed by two Princess Coronations being prepared for their nightly journey southwards, and not envying the Crewe North Drivers and Firemen this marathon journey.

Soon, it was time to return to the station ready to work our train home to Edinburgh. This was the 15.20 from Inverness, due to depart Perth at 19.19, and another heavy train. The train ran in two minutes early behind two Black Fives and as they were being uncoupled, I set about building up my fire, taking care not to create too much black smoke. We coupled on and a brake test was completed. The exhaust injector was set to keep '827 quiet in the station and Jim used this time to give me some more good advice. 'We dinnae stop at Bridge of Earn, son, but run richt through tae oor first stop at Kinross. As we clear Hilton, just dae as you did coming up and fire her light and often. You micht need the ither injector as weel, so watch your water. An' by the way, you'll sin see why I needed the sands full!'

At 19.19, we got the right away and steadily accelerated away from the station, '827 announcing her departure to the 'douce' (that is, sedate) folks in Perth. With the heavy train well on the move we pounded into the long Moncrieff tunnel, out again and swung left at Hilton Junction. Over the all but level gradient to Bridge of Earn, Jim had the engine accelerating steadily in big valve whilst I set to with the firing shovel. The needle on the red line, ¾ glass of water and the injector singing away sweetly, did little to calm the concern I was feeling. I had heard so much about Glenfarg and although all appeared well at the moment, I knew in my heart that I was really very inexperienced and might not be able to cope if everything started to go pear-shaped. We blasted through Bridge of Earn station and the junction with the Newburgh line and Jim started to let the reverser out half a turn at a time. The heat from the fire was intense as I stood before it firing, and my gloves were smoking. I had been given a tip by a Passed Fireman mate with whom I had worked on preparation, to put the first shovelfull or two just inside the front of the firedoor to reduce the temperature of the fire there, whilst

firing round the rest of the box. This I had tried, and it did work.

I was aware of '827 now giving voice at the chimney as the increased blast pulled the fire into an intense, shimmering, white mass. Pausing to wipe the sweat from my face, I glanced at the gauge glass. Water level was holding up well so far. The pressure gauge showed the needle back off the red mark, and as my mate let her out a bit more and the roars from the chimney increased in volume, I could feel the heavy train now hang back behind us and drag the speed down. The sands were now fully open and remained so until we got over the top. I fired another round, then another until I was firing continuously, glancing only at the pressure gauge and gauge glasses at frequent intervals. The exhaust from the chimney was almost black now as we crashed our way into and through the first tunnel. Steam had rallied but the water was now coming down a bit. I put on the live steam injector and took the opportunity to lay the dust on the floor, before bending to my task yet again. After each round, I dropped the flap and was mightily relieved to see the pressure hold up just short of the red line again, the boiler showing about two thirds full. However, we were on a 1 in 70 rising gradient, and I knew that the true boiler level would be somewhat less when we levelled out, if we ever did, I thought.

Back to the shovel and in went another dozen or more round the box. By this time I was really feeling pain and the sweat was pouring down my face and back. Jim gave me a prod and motioned me to stop firing. I stood upright for the first time in a while and looked out. We had just cleared Glenfarg station and were topping the climb. Jim wound the reverser back as we went over the top and gave me the thumbs up. The noise level diminished almost to a comparative silence as I hung my head over the side and gulped in the sweet evening air.

The remainder of the trip was much easier compared to Glenfarg and we ran into Waverley a few minutes to the good. However, I was still thankful to see Haymarket shed and leave the engine on the turntable. The V2 was a first class engine for both the Perth and Aberdeen roads and, as long as they were in good order, many Drivers preferred them to the Pacifics. Our particular ones were well looked after and the valve setting at Haymarket could stand comparison with the best anywhere at that time. Despite my aching back, legs and arms, I had enjoyed the experience and my mate, who had given me much help, was not slow to tell Ross Dougan that I had coped well, all things considered. Personally, I was painfully aware of the small errors such as too much black smoke and the engine blowing off too often.

A2 4-6-2 60535 HORNET'S BEAUTY at rest in the shed loop in October 1955. It was with this engine that I had a memorable day on a local Dundee working, by firstly washing down the roof in the North Queensferry Tunnel (and covering my Driver, W. Donaldson in sooty water to boot) as we caught the water on entering the tunnel and then having the turntable at Dundee derail as we were turning the engine there. (J. Robertson/Transport Treasury)

10. GRIEF, PAIN AND PLEASURE

After my sojourn to Perth, an unexpected but welcome interlude, I had a few other firing turns on shed preparation, run of the mill grinds, as described. I then started my nightshift week on cleaning, although I was now one of the more senior hands. There was, at this time of the year, a lesser prospect of firing turns on the nightshift, and so we cleaned our engines from stem to stern under the eagle eye of the Gaffer. However, on the early hours of the Friday morning around 04.30, Jimmy Austin, the deputy Running Foreman sought me out. 'Book off at 05.00 with a guaranteed day, son', he said, 'and come out for 17.00 preparation tonight'.

This 'Guaranteed Day' (GD) was allowed by National Agreement and was a vehicle by which a Cleaner could be turned around, shift-wise, in 12 hours, this being the minimum rest period between shifts for locomotive men. Whilst there was a lesser demand for Firemen on night shift, there was always a big demand on both day shift and backshift. Booking me off at 05.00 meant that I could be swung on to the backshift for firing duties at 17.00, as was happening in this instance. Whilst quite a proper arrangement, it was not always popular with people like me who lived some way out of Edinburgh and relied on public transport. On another occasion I was, whilst on nightshift, booked off 02.00 GD to start at 14.00 later that day and had to cool my heels sitting around the shed until the first train home at 06.00. Nevertheless, I was officially having 12 hours rest. The guaranteed day arrangement ensured that full payment was made even although only part of a shift had been worked.

Anyway, I did as I was bid and made my way to Princes Street station to cadge a lift home on the 06.00 empty coaches to Fauldhouse, the Driver very kindly agreeing to steady up to permit me to alight at Addiewell, which was the nearest station to my home. Later that afternoon I returned to Haymarket, booked on just before 17.00, and learned that my Driver was a Passed Fireman, Davie McNeill, a quiet man but a very good mate as it turned out. We were on a 'Fridays Only' preparation turn and, very quickly, Willie Elder sought us out and instructed us to prepare A2/1, 60510 ROBERT THE BRUCE for the 'coast' i.e. a Newcastle turn.

We found '510 standing outside the 'new' fitting shed obviously just off repair and, more obviously, not long kindled. My heart fell to my boots, for this was the very worst type of preparation job, a real nightmare for both Driver and, especially, the Fireman. As I looked at

her standing there, not even over a pit, I could see the oily blackish, yellow smoke just roll from the double chimney. In the cab, the smoke was rolling up the face plate and seeping out under the rubber fairing between cab and tender and also through the cab windows. In the murk I could also see great orange flames play up the face plate. The first thing I had to do was to find out if she had started making steam, in order to get the blower on and clear the cab, and so there was nothing else for it but to take deep breath and get up into that hell.

I climbed into the choking, smoke filled cab and immediately my eyes and nose started streaming. It was purgatory and I could see almost nothing so, by feel, I put my hand up to clean off the face of the steam pressure gauge. As I did so, my sleeve rode up and my bare forearm, between glove and sleeve, brushed across the injector steam valve wheel. You might have heard my yells a mile away as I drew my arm back. I had lost the skin on my forearm. It had just seared off and I was left with a burn some 6/7 inches long and about two inches across, a burn that was already weeping and covered in soot. The tears in my eyes were for real this time but, taking more care this time, I put my hand up again and managed to partially clear the gauge. My spirits lifted very slightly when I saw there was about 30lbs showing, and I quickly opened the blower. It took effect to a degree even at that low pressure, and immediately the smoke stopped billowing from the firedoor, the flames subsided and the cab began to clear. Now all this took place in much less time that it takes to tell and in an instant, I was back down on the ground and seeking out Davie. I told him what had happened, showed the evidence and said I was off to report the injury and seek First Aid.

I went to the Running Foreman's Office to enter the mishap in the Accident Book. Willie Elder was there with the second Foreman. He took one look at the burn and went for the First Aid kit. His mate held my arm whilst Willie proceeded to spoon on dry baking soda to the wound and completely covered it. That stung, how that stung! He then wound a dry bandage over the wound and covered the first bandage with a tubular bandage sleeve and asked if I wanted relief. This I declined and said I would just return to '510. This was the standard treatment for burns at the time and it has to be said that the pain subsided very quickly and within a couple of weeks I was left with a perfectly clean wound covered in shiny new, pink skin which eventually healed up without any noticeable scar.

Back to '510 I went, to find steam pressure on the up. I left the cab alone meantime, checked the smokebox door, swept off the front framing and then collected a full kit and filled the sands. The outside jobs done, I turned my attention to the cab, and the filth in which it was coated. I had, by this time, enough steam to get the live steam injector working, so, helping myself to oil from the engine oil can, I liberally poured this over the top of the boiler end and down the faceplate. When I was sure that I had spread the oil all over the full faceplate, I stood outside the cab window and turned the slaker pipe on the faceplate. The oil emulsified and ran off taking all the soot and dirt with it, leaving a shining faceplate and pipework. I turned the hose on the cab roof and then the tender end, until I could see the green paintwork gleaming through again on the latter. It was then a case of setting to with some waste and wiping down all the pipework, gauges and glass. In a very short space of time the cab was gleaming and all gauges were again fully visible and shining. I then turned my attention to the fire and started building up the back corners and behind the door in time-honoured fashion. Injectors tested, the boiler filled and the cab swept out and hosed down again, I reported to Davie that I was finished. He had oiled around as far as he could, so climbing aboard, he blew off the brakes and we moved '510 round to the front of the shed and over a pit, where he finished off his oiling underneath the engine. Preparation had taken well over the allotted hour but on completion, and after topping up the tender, we looked with some satisfaction at the finished job. '510 was, once more, a worthy Haymarket product.

We went of to report to the Running Foreman and enquire what he required of us next. 'Oh no, he said, now you take the engine light to Craigentinny and collect the coaches for the 22.40 Coast and work the empties round the 'Sub' (the Edinburgh Suburban circle) and back down into Waverley when they're ready for you.' The pain in my arm subsided. Here was an unexpected adventure. I had never been to Craigentinny or round the 'Sub' before. We collected jackets and bags from the bothy and re-joined '510. Blowing off the brake, Davie told me to set the lamps and, this done, I walked out ahead of the engine to 'phone us out. After a short wait, the disc came off and we slid out on to the main line. I picked up the shovel to spread the fire around a bit but Davie stopped me and said 'just put half a dozen shovels down each side and across the fore-end'. Seeing my mystified look, since there was not much fire there at all, he smiled, and said, 'don't worry, do that and drop the flap, and by Craigenntinny it will be well alight. We will not be working hard enough to pull a lot of cold air into the firebox.' I complied with this instruction and regained my seat as we whistled prior to entering Haymarket tunnel. Even after all those years, I can still recall to mind the unique smell inside that tunnel – oil, steam, smoke and dampness, a virtual melange of odours which was quite peculiar to it. We slid through the Gardens and were signalled down the North Loop through the station. This was now foreign territory as we cleared the east end and dropped our nose down the hill through Calton North tunnel. I was now in a state of high excitement, and crossed and re-crossed the cab to see as much as I could of this new piece of railway. We whistled our way under the road bridge and through St. Margaret's shed, (yes, through St. Margaret's shed since it was split between both sides of the main line) and finally were signalled into the reception roads at Craigentinny, ready to collect the coaches for the 22.40 Edinburgh/Kings Cross Sleeping Car service.

While we were waiting for a Shunter to appear, I looked at the fire; just as Davie had said, it was burning brightly

now all round the box. I tucked that wee bit of information away for a rainy day! I placed another round of coal in the box and then made up the back of the door and back corners. Pressure was rising nicely and I put on the right-hand injector to fill up the boiler. Our Shunter arrived and joined us to travel down through the depot to where the train of sleeping cars was waiting. We soon backed up and coupled on to the train. This, the Shunter did for me as I watched, and I noted that he had also coupled up the steam heating bags. Setting the headlamps for the ECS position, I re-joined the cab whilst the Shunter phoned the signal box. Craigentinny was going like a fair and it was obvious they wanted us away as quickly as possible to clear another siding.

Davie described the 'Sub' to me as we waited, and I was soon made aware that there was an awful lot of 'up' before we went down. The pressure was standing at 220lbs and the valves were beginning to hiss a bit. This caused me concern, for the boiler was sitting quite full and, inevitably, the engine started to blow off. Davie was quite unperturbed and I got the impression that Craigentinny was not Waverley, and that no one was going to make an issue of this. Our Guard had now joined us and gave us the load. '14 on, equal

to 495 tons', he shouted above the din of escaping steam. 'I'll just climb in the front van and walk through the train.' I watched him go back and he gave a wave as he joined the train. I confirmed this to Davie. There was now a bit of water space in the boiler so on went the injector and I also opened the steam heating valve, and the safety valves shut with a distinct pop.

The signal cleared and we pulled out on to the main line. Davie had the reverser well out and the regulator in first valve to get the heavy train on the move. The Pacific made herself heard as we barked out past Portobello West Signal box and through Portobello Station, the Signalman standing at his window watching our slow progress. As the rear of the train cleared the yard, Davie pulled the regulator out into big valve and '510 responded immediately. Gradually he pulled her back and then all but closed the regulator to steady our progress at Portobello East Junction where we were signalled to the right and on to the 'Carlisle' road. We lurched over the junction and immediately the regulator was fully opened and '510 roared up round the rising, right-hand climb towards Niddrie West Junction, where again we were signalled to, and duly took, the right-hand line at the Junction, and on to the 'Sub'. I started to fire and put around 15 shovels or so

around the box and set the exhaust injector, then regained my seat to take in this new road. We banged and crashed our way down to Duddingston and, swinging round again to the right, we took the wide sweeping curve to Cameron Toll road underbridge and got our nose on the 'Sub' proper. Here, Davie let her out a full turn of the reverser. How '510 gave voice as we blasted up through the quiet, leafy residential suburbs of Edinburgh's south side. Through Newington Road and the island platform with the kink in the track, then up towards Blackford Hill where we were in cutting. We were largely out of sight but our passing could not be going unnoticed, unless of course, the population of the affluent south side were deaf. We banged our way up the hill with this heavy train, maintaining, I estimated, a steady 30mph, if that. I gave her another round. The pressure was sitting up on the mark and the injector was easily maintaining ¾ glass of water. Blackford Hill station was now behind us and Davie motioned me not to put any more on. We breasted the hill at Morningside Station and pushing the regulator closed and winding her into 25%, the noise died away. In comparative silence, we coasted down the hill through Craiglockhart, under the 'Caley' and then under the Union Canal to swing through Gorgie East station

and so to a stand at Gorgie East Junction. There, under the provisions of Rule 39a, the Signalman allowed us to draw forward to the starting signal where we were destined to sit until Waverley was ready for us. I looked at my fire and was pleased to see that it was fairly uniform and level, although well burned down. As this engine was going through to Newcastle I could not let the back corners and back of the door burn down too much, so at intervals gradually filled it up, but without making much steam, or indeed, black smoke. As I worked, I mused that someone was now going to work this big train forward to Newcastle and then work back again. Some night's work.

We sat until just after 22.00 when we were called on to the South Main line and routed back down through Haymarket, before being signalled into platforms 10/11, the South Main, at Waverley. As we ran along the platform I hung over the side and looked at the great throng of passengers who were waiting to join the train and then sleep their way to London. At the east end of the platform, we slid to a stand at the platform starting signal and were joined by the No.1 link crew who were taking the train on. The Fireman had a look at the fire and appeared pleased with what was there. He and the Driver, however, were much more concerned at just how

much water we had used up, and shouted to the Platform Inspector that they needed to take water. This required the engine to be coupled off, and, under the authority of the Signalman in Waverley East signal box, to pass the platform starting signal at Danger to access the water column ahead. To help out, I coupled off accordingly. The necessary authority having been granted, the engine drew forward the few yards. After assisting with the filling of the tank, we then took our leave to walk back to the shed (40 minutes walking time allowed) to book off. Quite a night! Quite a thrill!

V2 2-6-2 E819 at Haymarket; she had originally been allocated (as 790) to Aberdeen Ferryhill, but was subsequently transferred to Edinburgh. She only carried the number E819 from March 1948 until December 1949 which dates this photograph. The clean lines of the class are seen to advantage here and of course, it goes without saying that they were extremely well liked by the Haymarket men. (M. Robertson/Transport Treasury)

The picture that says it all and demonstrates just how clean Haymarket engines really were in their heyday. Possibly one of the most photographed A1s, 60162 SAINT JOHNSTOUN was allocated to No.2 link and Driver Willie Bain during his time there. The clock on the *North British Hotel* shows 12 noon and the engine is leaving Waverley at the head of the *QUEEN OF SCOTS* Pullman service for London Kings Cross, with all but a clear chimney. Note the burnishing of the 'steels' right down to the leading edge of the rail guard irons. I did have the privilege of firing this locomotive, with Driver Bain at the controls, on the *NIGHT SCOTSMAN* one evening in 1958. (J. Robertson/Transport Treasury)

11. SOME PILOT DAYS

Weeks moved on and we had another shift up and then another, as the summer timetable came in. I was now getting firing turns on a daily basis and was doing little or no cleaning. The bulk of the turns were preparation, a couple of nights on the turntable and some pilot work. The first pilot on which I was booked to work was the 14.00 Haymarket yard pilot. After booking on, I walked the short distance to the yard which sat on the north side of the main lines, between the 'Caley' bridge and Haymarket station. The former carried the Princes Street to Leith North line over our North and South Main lines, and immediately on the north side of this bridge stood Coltbridge Junction Signal box.

At the yard office I joined J83 68457 with Driver John (Jock) Braidwood for an afternoon's shunting. Jock was one of the regular Drivers on this pilot and, as it turned out, an excellent mate and mentor. When I climbed aboard, he asked me my name and how long I had been 'out', that is, passed for firing. I told him what he wanted to know and what I had done. 'Aye, but have you fired on any pilots, son?' he queried. Well, the answer to that was simple, a straight yes and no, for I had been rostered Fireman on the coal pilot but never actually fired the blessed thing, as I have related earlier. That amused him no end and set us off on the right foot, I think, for he was a mine of information and a good help as I came to terms with a shunting pilot that virtually never stopped for the full shift, save for our short 'piece' break. I was taught to fire only one side of the firebox at a time and to allow this to burn through before firing the other side. In this way, black smoke was almost entirely avoided and pressure was controlled to avoid blowing off. Haymarket yard was bounded on one side by private houses and the noise of shunting around the clock must have been bad enough for the long-suffering residents, without the added annoyance of blowing off and black smoke.

I also very soon picked up the handsignals, including the 'home grown' ones, as given by the Shunters and quickly realised that the Fireman had to be as alert as the Driver during shunting operations. On the backshift, after 'office hours' we shunted the coal sidings belonging to the respected Edinburgh coal merchants, Bruce Lindsay Ltd. at their coal depot just immediately west of Haymarket station. This depot contained a well-known landmark which survived into the early 1990s, the most decrepit, ramshackle, black wooden 'garage' where the coal

lorries were serviced and kept; it stood almost on the site of the original Edinburgh & Glasgow Railway original Haymarket engine shed. On this shift, we also shunted the flour mill which sat on Haymarket Terrace (now long gone) and was accessed by a curving line from the yard that hugged the perimeter wall. It was only a couple of hundred yards or so away from the yard area, but was an adventure never the less. The Haymarket pilot seldom stopped on any shift and we shunted and made up trains with only the agreed 20 minutes break. As a result, my first shift with John passed quickly and I was pleased to have the opportunity of firing to him on many more occasions.

My next time on this pilot was a dayshift turn and that had its own particular periods of interest. At around 10.00 each morning, when a convenient gap appeared in the main line train services, the pilot crossed the main lines to shunt the Haymarket Distillery. This was served by a line which paralleled the Down South line and entered the Distillery just a few yards west of Haymarket Station. Frequently as we shunted, or sat waiting to shunt, we would see the Customs & Excise men at work. They were testing, we assumed, the proof strength of the whisky, assisted by labourers who handled the casks. These were tapped, a sample withdrawn by syringe and decanted into a measuring jar which was taken into an office for testing. What was left was brought back out and should have been poured, as far as I was led to believe, down the drain by the said labourers.

Whisky, on which the duty has not been paid, is literally worth very little indeed – even more so back then. The point of this story is, however, that this whisky, expensive or cheap, never saw the drains but was certainly drained, down the necks of the aforesaid labourers. I have never been a whisky drinker and indeed have little knowledge of whether this was raw or seasoned spirit, but alcoholic spirit it was and the Distillery had a number of inebriated staff wandering round most mornings by about 10.00. It was hard to believe that the powers that be were unaware of what was going on but, I assume they merely chose to turn a Nelson's eye to the matter, perhaps in the knowledge there would be lesser chance of illegal pilferage.

By this time, Jock was letting me take the controls at the easier spells in the day and I was quickly learning the secrets of shunting and how couplings had to be stretched out gently when pulling away and when propelling back and braking. After many snatches and

tugs, with dust and rust billowing from way back in the 'lift', I finally got the knack of good shunting. This was without, it must be said, suffering the indignity of any broken couplings, though I think it was a close-run thing during my first days at the regulator.

I had, some time later in the year, another full week on days on this pilot, but with a young Driver, Alec Fisher, who, when he found out that I had put in some time on the pilot, used to leave me in charge whilst he went for his 'morning rolls'. I never knew where he went for these but it might well have been that he went to Glasgow and baked them himself, for he always returned around mid-day each day, just to catch up on what had been going on in his absence. This was not, as things turned out, the only time I was to fire to Alec, although the next time was definitely 'big time'. So I was left on my own as we shunted away, firing and driving and having the time of my life on my lovely little J83. They were lovely engines to work on and totally suited to shunting work since the arrangement of brake, regulator and reversing lever meant that the Driver could keep the Shunter in sight and be in control at all times. They had few vices, steamed well, were strong, had a good brake and were, all in all, a pleasure to drive and fire.

My other experience on pilots was on the 'big' Gorgie Pilot. This was a three-shifted pilot located at Gorgie East and worked by N15 69169, one of two we had at Haymarket. Here we shunted the cattle market, the large Gorgie East goods and coal yard and the cattle banks at the Slateford Abbatoir or 'slaughter hoose' to give it the popular name. This pilot also provided rear end banking assistance 'as required' for freights going round the 'Sub', up the hill as far as Morningside Road. I fired many times on this pilot, but always with the same one Driver, again a regular on this pilot, and something of a legend at 64B. This was David Anderson (Davie) who had been the Driver involved in the tragic Castlecary accident on the 10th December 1937. Davie, as a young spare man, had been at the controls of A3 2744 GRAND PARADE, working the 16.03 express to Glasgow. Whilst running at around 70mph in atrocious weather conditions and falling snow, his train collided with the rear of the standing 14.00 Dundee to Glasgow train at Castlecary Station. The casualty list was grievously long with 35 dead and 179 injured. Davie himself, and his Fireman Willie Kinnear, by now recently elevated to a No.2 link Driver at Haymarket, were almost unhurt, largely due to the strength and height of the steel front of the tender.

The blame lay fairly and squarely with the Signalman on duty at Castlecary and to a lesser degree the Station Master. A distant signal was allegedly showing a false clear and had been seen, and accepted as being clear, by both the Driver of the preceding train, and Driver Anderson. Nevertheless Driver Anderson was arrested and taken into custody, albeit for a short time only. He was exonerated at the subsequent Inquiry. He was, at the time, and without any shadow of a doubt, unfairly treated, by both his employer, the LNER, and the upholders of law and order and was made the scapegoat for other peoples shortcomings and downright carelessness, but common sense prevailed in the end. In other publications, it has been recorded that Anderson never drove on the main line again but this is untrue. Davie Anderson went on to take his place in the top link at Haymarket and worked the Non-Stop when it ran as the 'Capitals Limited'. He came off the main line voluntarily when he was 60 years of age and I, even yet, consider myself having

been privileged to have fired to this extremely keen and competent engineman.

My first turn with him was on the 14.00 shift. Having booked on at the shed, I walked up the line to Gorgie and joined the engine. As was the form, I was beginning to realise, Drivers had to know everything about their Fireman, and what experience they had had. His famous piece of advice was 'always dae whit yer Driver says, son.' On that backshift, the first duty of the Fireman was to clean the fire, ashpan and smokebox in the wee pit on which the engine stood at Gorgie. This was one of the few occasions when a Fireman did have to be involved in fire cleaning. On an N15, this entailed shovelling the fire out through the firedoor and over the side, and this had to be done just so for Davie, with no spillage on the footplate. After the fire had been cleaned, I crawled underneath to clean the ashpan, a most unpleasant task. You had to judge just in which direction the wind was blowing else you ended up with a faceful of hot ash. This was one

of the most unpleasant tasks with steam locomotives, closely followed by cleaning the smokebox. When all this had been done, Davie came and inspected the handiwork, after which the fire had to be made up properly, without black smoke and the cab swept and washed out. Davie, it was, who first demonstrated how to drain off the water from the Detroit Sight Feed Displacement Lubricator and fill it with steam oil; this became a daily task which fell to me thereafter. When steam pressure came up, so the work began. Shunting on the big pilot was not quite as frantic as, say, the Haymarket yard pilot, and the pace of life was somewhat more sedate although, when required for banking, it was all hands to the pumps. This pilot was known as the 'big' pilot to distinguish it, strangely enough from the 'wee' Gorgie pilot which was a J88, No.68339.

The smaller engine shunted the locations where the larger wheel-based N15 could not access, such as the North British Distillery, and also the infamous Cox's Glue Works which stood in Gorgie

all Drivers and some Passed Firemen at the depot. We shunted Gorgie on days and through nights, and in doing so, my awareness of what exactly firing a steam locomotive entailed increased, as did my self confidence.

On the Big Gorgie pilot, there was a booked Saturday night/ Sunday morning turn and I fell heir to this Sunday turn when rostered for a full week of nights on the pilot during the following year. Now, as I was to find out, there was in fact little or no movement required of the engine on this turn and shortly after reporting to the Yard Bothy, the Yard Inspector, Shunters and my Driver began to settle down for a good night's sleep. Each had a chosen place whilst I, as the lower order, had to find my own. Fortunately I have always been able to sleep almost anywhere, and so I put my satchel down on the concrete floor as a pillow, lay down and drew my reefer jacket over me. I was quickly asleep and awoke at daybreak to observe the others regarding me, somewhat sourly, I thought. I was right. They just could not believe that I could sleep on the hard floor and because of this they had had a sleepless night watching me sleeping.

The only other pilot on which I ever fired was the Waverley No.1 Pilot, J83 No.68481. This J83 was unusually finished in lined out BR black and was kept in a highly polished state by her regular Drivers and their mates. The three Drivers were all ex-main line men who had opted to relinquish main line duties and included in their number was Stuart Storie, the ex-Top Link Driver who had been involved in the run back in North Queensferry tunnel referred to earlier.

My first experience of this pilot came with the 00.01 Monday turn with a young Passed Fireman, Willie Brand. 68481 came on shed on a Sunday afternoon to have the fire cleaned and any mechanical attention that might be necessary. She was then coaled, watered, and prepared. We prepared her and then took her back down to Waverley to commence work, work which thereafter seldom stopped. This began with the arrivals of the first night trains from the south, carrying through sleeping cars for various destinations which had to removed and re-marshalled at Waverley. Both 'West End' pilots were required and it goes without saying that these movements were made with the greatest of care since, generally, most passengers preferred not to be tipped out of bed in the wee small hours. By the time the last of the early morning connecting trains were on the way out, empty coaches then had to be set in the platforms for the morning service trains and then the later Down services were arriving and had to be dealt with.

A shift, any shift, on the Waverley pilots passed very quickly and whilst the firing was no more onerous on these pilots, the Fireman was required to maintain a higher level of attention and relay Shunters' handsignals to the Driver. Many of the shunts were long shunts requiring the engine to pull away through the Mound Tunnel with a lift of coaches, and reading and interpreting the handsignals correctly left no room for inattention. On top of all that, the Fireman, assisted by the Driver, cleaned every inch of the engine, bit by bit, as the opportunity arose between shifts

The regular Drivers were all very skilled men and the brake setting and ejectors on the engine were maintained to the highest level to ensure that brakes could be 'blown off' in the shortest possible time. The speed at which some of the long shunts were carried out and completed was remarkable and a tribute to the skills of the Drivers, and the Shunters, concerned, especially since many of the shunting moves, particularly in the mid-morning and early afternoon, were required to be made with passengers in the coaches being shunted, as portions were taken off and re-marshalled. The Waverley pilots were popular with young Firemen since they were three shifted and the crews worked two Sundays out of three. The earning potential was therefore, higher than many of the shed jobs and preparation turns.

The other pilots worked at Haymarket were the 'shed shunt', a three-shifted pilot worked by the other J88, 68328, and involved the movement and placing of dead engines on an as required basis, and the Coal Pilot, a two-shifted pilot, previously mentioned. I never fired on the former job, which was seen as mind-numbingly boring by most of the Cleaners. Nevertheless, it suited those who were partial to slipping down to the Roseburn Bar or Murrayfield Indoor Sports club (at the back of the shed) for a quick pint. Again these pilots had regular Drivers who were all light work men and indeed there were two 'accommodated' Firemen also rostered on a regular basis. The most notorious Driver on this job was Andrew Airns, another Driver who had come off (or had been removed from) main line work and who was fond of a pint. He was also famed for some of the long shunts he would undertake. At night, the Running Foreman must have often wondered just where Andrew and 68328 were bound for, when they slipped away into the darkness towards the shed exit, hauling half a dozen or so 'dead' engines.

Road, the latter, happily, now long gone. These glue works were a satanic huddle of factory buildings surrounded with racks and vats of suppurating, foul smelling, steaming liquids and piles of hides, hoofs and bones. It was a foul, malodorous place and yet the spot where the day shift men on the wee pilot often took their break. The seagulls which frequented this site were like rapacious eagles and of course squabbled and swooped whenever a variation of their staple diet of offal appeared. You had to fight to hold on to your sandwiches, but if the truth be known, few men ever had any great appetite in this charnel house of a place anyway.

Davie was another Driver who encouraged young Firemen, if they played the game and were keen. When he was satisfied that I could meet all demands made on me by the job in hand, I was then encouraged to take the regulator and brake, but never in an unsupervised way. He was always there, correcting, advising, instructing and encouraging, which was not something which could be said about

A1 60152 HOLYROOD passing Haymarket shed on the South Main line on a stopping train to Glasgow Queen Street on 29th June 1952. At this time the engine is still fitted with the plain stovepipe chimney as built, though fitting of the new lipped chimneys had commenced in 1950. (John Robertson/ Transport Treasury)

A1 60160 AULD REEKIE heads an express passenger to Aberdeen away from the Haymarket stop. The train is likely to be the 4.15pm service from Waverley, judging by the shadows. In the left background behind the coal dump is the triangular roof-end of the original train shed which was the terminus of the Edinburgh & Glasgow Railway before the tunnels were driven through to Waverley. The building to the right is the Haymarket Distillery, now converted into flats. (W. Hermiston/Transport Treasury)

12. SHED WORK AND SPARE WORK

As the summer passed on, I enjoyed almost continuous firing, on a variety of different jobs. I spent several nights one week on the 'turntable' job, firing to Tommy Glass, another Passed Fireman. This job did not entail any actual firing. Incoming engines were left in front of the kit store, previously referred to, or on the turntable if it was otherwise unoccupied. The store was our abode whilst we waited for incoming engines. The environment, described earlier, was no better, and indeed might be regarded as somewhat worse, than that generally found at 64B. The entrance was on the level from the shed yard side, but there were steps up on to the platform on the incoming side where engines were relieved. The best that could be said for this dark, malodorous place was that there were always Firemen coming and going to fill lamps and the 'crack' was good.

When an incoming engine was relieved, it was then set on the turntable if this had not already been done by the incoming crew. Engines made their appearance on the turntable in no uncertain fashion, each wheel banging on to the table in turn. The engine had to be balanced to ensure trouble-free turning and this was not always easy since it had to be judged by the movement of the turntable as the weight reached dead centre. Balancing was essential before turning started, since there was little room for manoeuvre with a Pacific and an overall wheelbase of just short of the 70 feet of the table, especially when it was halfway round. The Haymarket turntable was a Ransomes & Rapier product and was fitted with a vacuum tractor. All that was required, after the engine had been balanced, was that the vacuum bag on the engine was coupled to the long hose on the tractor, and the vacuum then blown up by the Driver. By holding the control lever forward or back meant that the turntable went clockwise or anti-clockwise, but it mattered not. The only other thing that you had to be aware of whilst operating the turntable, were the securing catches. If you threw the lever over before the catch had lined up, it would kick back quickly and, if your head was in the way, well an egg sized bruise was the likely result if you were lucky, a more serious injury if you were not!

When the engine was placed to satisfaction on the table, we both then watched the window of the Running Foreman's Office across the front of the shed. From there would come a signal given by one of the shift Foremen, either a 'turn' signal (circular movements with one hand) or a 'straight-on' wave. Based on this we either turned the engine or

moved straight off, again accompanied by the individual bangs as the wheels crossed the gap, and up to the coaling plant. Here, whilst the Driver positioned the tender correctly under the chute, the Fireman would enter the little concrete control hut and await the shout from the Driver. The chute could be swung to lie to the right or left (front end or rear end of the tender coal space) but care had to be taken when pressing the 'start' button to ensure that there was not a large lump of coal already resting in the chute. This, by sheer size and weight, could alter the lie as the coal started to flow, resulting in either the cab roof (and cab) covered with coal, or the tender end filled with coal. Experience soon taught everyone to start and stop the flow to ensure the coal was going to fall just where it was required. After coaling, the engine was placed on one of the ash-pits, secured and left to the tender mercies of the fire-droppers, whilst we enjoyed a stroll down along the outside of the shed and back to our 'howf'.

My first few attempts on that first night meant that I was calling for a wee bit forward or a wee bit back as I tried to determine when the table was balanced. This, in turn, met with much displeasure on the part of my mate, for juggling a Gresley Pacific on the table with the vertical reverser and vacuum brake only, was not physically easy. As a result, my first impressions of my mate on the first night, were that he was a grumpy bugger, and no doubt he was thinking that I was a right no-use bugger. However, we did not fall out, although he was more than cool to begin with.

After we had finally succeeded in getting several engines safely pointing the right way for their next turn of duty, and during a lull in the proceedings, we shared a can of tea and this broke the ice, so to speak, and we started chatting. He asked about my length of service and when he found out that this was my début on the turntable, he became distinctly more amenable and offered some advice on just how to watch the movement of the turntable. It also turned out that he was, like myself, a keen railway modeller and the discussion then turned to the pro's and cons of what currently was available 'off the shelf' for the hobby. Tommy turned out to be, after that first difficulty, one of the nicest and most genuine of men, a good mate who both encouraged and tutored, and eventually a friend. By the end of my few nights with him, he had allowed me, under his supervision, to drive locomotives on to the turntable and taught me how to balance them from the Driver's viewpoint. What I had thought a boring job turned out be an

enjoyable learning experience with a really good mate.

In my first year at Haymarket I was only once involved in disposal, but that adventure must wait for a later chapter. I use the word 'adventure' carefully for was it not the case that everything I was being required to do was an adventure. Preparation was becoming 'old hat' and I, like many of my cleaning colleagues, had preparation off to a fine art and muscles were no longer creaking in protest. What I did not immediately realise was that I'd become physically much stronger and mentally much more confident and self-assured. However, much as I took preparation, and there were a great many preparation turns over that summer, in my stride, and indeed revelled in the sheer hard work, there were preparation diagrams which came as a surprise and offered yet more adventure.

One such turn was preparation diagram CD.2. This entailed booking on at 06.30 and this I duly did when I found myself rostered for it one Monday morning. My mate for the day was a Passed Fireman, John Stavert. After signing on and reading the notices, he collected his oil pourie and we set off to look for A3, 60087 BLENHEIM which we had to prepare. This was duly found and we set to work. The locomotive finally prepared, Jack, as he was known at the shed, explained the diagram to me, for this was a preparation turn with a difference. Basically, the turn involved preparing an engine for the 10.05 Carlisle, the 'Waverley' express passenger from Edinburgh Waverley to London St. Pancras, via the 'Waverley' route and the Midland main line. The preparation crew then took the engine light to Corstorphine and coupled to 10 coaches forming the 08.34 passenger train from Corstorphine to Edinburgh Waverley, calling at Pinkhill, Balgreen Halt and Haymarket. The train was worked to Edinburgh, all of a 14 minute journey, where the nine corridor coaches were pulled off and re-platformed to form the 10.05 Perth. With the non-corridor coach disposed of elsewhere, the engine would be taken round through the station and coupled to the 10.05 Carlisle in platform 9. An adventure indeed!

We filled the tank and, after ensuring everyone was well clear of the engine, pulled forward to the shed exit. Just to step back for a moment, it was essential, before any locomotive was moved, for the crew to ensure that anyone who might be working on or underneath or in the vicinity of said movement were properly warned of what was to take place, and thus in a normal day the shed echoed to calls of 'all clear, engine xxx, out below engine xxx, all clear' as the crew walked round the locomotive concerned.

At the shed exit, I set the lamps and 'phoned out. On the clearing of the disc, we slipped out to come to a stand behind the disc on the Up North Main line just under the Caley bridge. Here we reversed and crossing to the Down North, ran westwards to Haymarket West Junction and on to the Corstorphine branch which initially ran parallel to the North lines before sweeping away, firstly to the right and then left to Corstorphine terminus. After coupling to the train, we settled down to a fairly lengthy wait until departure time. As we waited, I took stock of Corstorphine station. It was larger than I had envisaged, with two very long platforms and a very busy goods yard. It was situated very much in the heart of what had been Corstorphine village but what was now a suburb, and a very affluent suburb, of Edinburgh. The station was 4¾ miles west of Waverley.

At around 08.15, passengers started arriving and I was surprised at the sheer number of people joining the train. The Guard had given us the train details and the Station Master himself came up and passed the time of day with the Driver, an indication of just how important this train was, and also of just how many Railway Officers from the Edinburgh Divisional Office at 23, Waterloo Place, used the service. I set to making up my fire and by 08.30 had a full boiler, a nicely burned through fire and steam pressure sitting just below blowing off. I hung over the Driver's side as we both

waited for the right away. Back the train, whistles blew, hurrying a few latecomers into the train and then we got the green flag and with a tug on the regulator, '87 gave a slight slip, regained her feet and we were off. We blasted down behind the houses towards our first stop, a mere 1½ miles away, at Pinkhill. As we ran in, again I was surprised at the large number of passengers waiting our arrival. Away we set again to our next stop at Balgreen Halt, another ¾ miles on and again, with a goodly number of passengers. As we stood, I fired round the box just to keep up pressure for the final sprint to Haymarket, 1¼ miles on, and then into Waverley. We ran into platform 16 at Waverley on time at 08.48, where, after uncoupling, I enjoyed watching the hordes of pretty girls making their way to the ticket barriers.

After the coaches were lifted, we reversed out and ran round to Platform 8, where we coupled to two coaches which were, in fact, the leading two coaches of the 'Waverley'. The complete train at the height of summer was too long to be accommodated inside the signal at platform 9. This arrangement meant that at about 09.50, and after the departure of the 'Elizabethan' from No.10 platform, these coaches were then shunted on to the head of the train with the locomotive then standing out ahead of the platform starting signal for the few minutes before departure time. No sooner had I coupled on than we were relieved by the Carlisle Canal crew who had worked in earlier in the morning. Now, the next part of this preparation

diagram required that we cool our heels until the arrival of the 09.18 Aberdeen/Edinburgh at 13.09. This express contained through carriages for London Kings Cross which ran forward on the 'Heart of Midlothian', the 13.30 Edinburgh/London Kings Cross, commonly known to all at 64B as the 'Diners'. On arrival of this train in 19 platform, we relieved the incoming Haymarket No.2 link crew and, when the through coaches had been detached from the rear of the train, we worked the remaining empty coaches forward to Craigentinny. This generally involved running round through Abbeyhill to Piershill Junction to avoid the main line, where we then ran on the duplicated slow lines to Craigentinny. We then sat until the 'Diners' passed when we were then permitted to cross and enter the carriage sidings. It was then a matter of waiting for a suitable path for the light engine movement back through Waverley and on to the shed.

This diagram became a firm favourite of mine and I was fortunate enough to work it many times in the future. On one memorable occasion in the following year, I was rostered on this turn for the week, firing to a senior Passed Fireman, George McGeachie. Now he was first class mate with a fiendishly wicked sense of humour. As I have described, the passenger train at Corstorphine was made up of nine corridor coaches and a single non-corridor, the latter immediately behind the tender. On the Wednesday morning, we had the Carlisle Canal A3 60093 CORONACH. At Corstorphine, a young couple came

A1 60159 BONNIE DUNDEE on the Haymarket turntable with the vacuum pipe connected ready for turning. Because of the situation of the shed, lying as it did on an east/west axis, the light conditions made this a favourite spot with photographers. (W. Hermiston/Transport Treasury)

down the platform around 08.15 and the young man spoke to George. After a brief conversation, they joined the front compartment immediately behind the tender. George said nothing at the time but later, as we started off from Corstorphine, he shouted me across the cab and suggested I keep a good look out as we pulled into Pinkhill.

We ran into the crowded platform at a speed which was somewhat higher than normal, and at the last moment he made a very full brake application stopping with the front of the leading coach immediately on the platform end. The passengers moved to join the train and a group of young ladies near the end of the platform made to walk back a bit when there was a shout and they immediately streamed into the leading compartment. George just laughed and off we went again. At Waverley, the young man alighted and said something very, very uncomplimentary and calling George's birthright into question, as he walked past the engine. One or two of the young ladies worked in the Edinburgh Divisional office and George spoke to one he knew. There was a fair degree of hysterics amongst the girls but gradually the story emerged. The young couple were regulars on the train and knew it was almost too long to fit in the platforms en route. The young man, when he spoke to George, had asked if the front compartment of the leading coach would be off the platforms going in to town and George confirmed that he would ensure that this would be the case. Bent on amorous pursuits (at 08.30 in the morning) the couple repaired to the privacy of the leading compartment. Of course, on (purposely) stopping the train with the coach still on the platform at Pinkhill, the couple were caught 'in flagrante' and, as the typist then told George, the young man's face was a picture as he struggled to get his trousers back on, in front of his unexpected audience. Life does have its ups and downs for some people, and their trousers, especially when a Passed Fireman with a warped sense of humour is involved.

On one occasion in early in 1958 I'd prepared A3 60100 SPEARMINT for diagram CD.2, working the Corstorphine-Edinburgh leg with a Passed Fireman, Bobby Millar, a man who died all too young a few years later. After coupling to the 10.05 'Waverley', we were asked if we would work the train forward to Hawick, where we would be relieved. Something, I don't remember now exactly what, had caused delay and the incoming Carlisle men were not available to take up their back working. Bobby, who had signed for the road, at once agreed and I had my first venture over part of what was commonly known as the Waverley route.

I built up a good body of fire behind the door and got the boiler almost full before the off since I had heard about this most difficult of roads. Bobby, whilst we waited for the 'right away', described the road to me and what I might expect. At 10.05 on the dot, we received the green flag from the rear of the train and Bobby got SPEARMINT on the move. As with all southbound departures, we had a 1 in 78 falling gradient from the platform-end and there was no drama in getting the big train, 10 coaches, 370 tons gross on the move. We slipped down through St. Margaret's and shimmied round the reverse curves at Portobello. At Portobello East signal box we had the road to the right for Niddrie West and the south. Immediately we were on a 1 in 80 up grade and Bobby let the reverser out a bit as he pulled the regulator into big valve. We blasted up to Niddrie South Junction. At this point, I had begun to fire round the box and had the exhaust injector set in preparation for what was to come.

At Niddrie South there was respite on a length of level track before we were climbing again, up through what was to become Millerhill Marshalling Yard in the not too distant future. At old Millerhill station, the gradient eased to 1 in 230 and by here, I was firing in earnest. At Hardengreen Junction, with a full boiler and pressure sitting just on the red mark short of blowing off, we hit the 1 in 70 which we had to climb for the next 10 miles. The reverser was wound out further to somewhere between 30 and 35% and a column of near black smoke was being pushed straight up into the morning air as we blasted up the hill. The noise from the chimney was incredible as we pounded up through Newtongrange station and on past the huge colliery complex which was Lady Victoria Pit, one of the deepest and most productive collieries in the Lothian coalfields. At Gorebridge we entered the climb up through the Moorfoot Hills proper. By Fushiebridge, '100 was flagging, the level of water in the boiler was coming down and the pressure was off the red mark. These single chimney Gresleys did not particularly like this sort of treatment and tended towards shortage of breath over long drags such as this. They, with their 6ft 8in driving wheels, had not been built for long hard slogs and I was firing almost continuously now, desperately trying to keep fire in the box. Speed was well down and the reverser was let out another half turn as we cleared Tynehead. The summit at Falahill was only two miles away now but pressure was back under 200lbs. despite my best efforts. My shirt was a wet rag sticking to my back whilst the sweat did not as much drip, as trickle from my nose as I bent to my task of firing this insatiable firebox. Bobby gave a shout and nodded that I should have a seat. I looked out and realised that we had topped the climb and were passing Falahill signal box on the summit of the bleak Middleton Moor. Quickly, I set both

injectors to bring back the water to a more acceptable level in the boiler, and gave the cab floor a quick sweep round. Pressure quickly rallied and with a full boiler once more, I settled back in my seat to enjoy the run downhill.

As we swept through the lonely outposts of Heriot, and then Fountainhall, where the Lauder Light railway swept away to the left, it was now all downhill, running alongside Gala Water to Galashiels some 15 miles to the south. I could now take time and admire the beautiful rolling border hills as we wound our way down the long valley. We ran into Galashiels station on time at 10.58 where I had some three minutes to repair my fire. Actually, the fire was in good shape despite the terrible pounding it had taken on the ascent of the Moorfoots. At 11.01 we received the 'off' and proceeded over the wee switchback between Galashiels and Melrose under the shadow of the Eildon hills. We galloped through the beautifully kept station of Melrose with spectacular views of the magnificent ruined Abbey to the left, and then along the Tweed valley past Ravenswood Junction where the single line branch from Earlston and Duns converged soon after passing over the elegant and beautiful Leaderfoot viaduct. Here we passed close to the site of Newstead which had been a large Roman settlement in the early days of Scotland's history.

On through St. Boswells, and firing was just a matter of a little and often as we traversed what had been, in the old days, the debatable lands, where the actual boundary between England and Scotland moved regularly. It was a land where the Border Reivers had rampaged over the old Middle March of the Scottish Borders. On, over a series a ups and downs which caused little problem to SPEARMINT and our progress, and all to soon we were dropping down into Hawick, coming to a stand in the long curving platform, high above the street level on the viaduct over the River Teviot, at 11.34, bang on time. Here, Carlisle Canal men were waiting to relieve us and work the train forward. I was sorry for I had also been told of the wild, bleak and difficult terrain over the Cheviot Hills lying to the south of Hawick, and longed to experience this but, for the moment, Hawick became my southern boundary.

After a brief break we joined the 12.17 passenger train from Hawick, back to Edinburgh and, with someone else doing all the hard work, we arrived just in nice time to book off at the shed at 14.30. Yet another adventure. When the A3s were fitted with double chimneys, the revised draughting arrangements made a significant improvement and the engines so fitted steamed effortlessly whilst being absolutely flogged, as I was to find out some time later.

In true Haymarket condition, A2 60534 IRISH ELEGANCE has backed down to the shed exit but appears to be making a shunt into another shed road as it is in forward gear. On the left of the engine is an old air raid shelter, long out of use but proving a convenient store for purloined pianos on one occasion. (J. Robertson/Transport Treasury)

13. TRAGEDY

Back to 1957; I was backshift spare and turned out to work the late turn Haymarket Pilot. When booking on, another Cleaner named Brian McGovern, somewhat senior to myself, was booking on at the same time to work a relieving and ECS diagram. We chatted for a few minutes before I made my way down to Haymarket yard. During the course of the afternoon I saw he and his mate go past the yard in a V1, 67610, towards the shed, running bunker first. At around 16.45 or thereabouts we could see flashing blue lights up at the shed and much activity in the shed loop where the V1 was sitting at the head of the empty coaches for the 17.15. Glasgow. These coaches had been brought up to the loop from Craigentinny earlier in the day, as they were every day, to make space there. They were then worked down to Waverley later in the afternoon to be set for the 17.15 departure, a heavy and very busy commuter train. On that particular day, time went on before the coaches went past down to Waverley, with a B1 at the head and another crew on board, running very late.

It was much later in the afternoon, as we stopped for our break, that the tragic news filtered down. The Fireman had been trapped when coupling up and killed immediately. It was a tragedy, one which could have happened to any of us, and caused largely by the earlier carelessness of a Shunter somewhere.

What had transpired was simple. Brian went down to couple on as the V1 moved on to the train. He went in between, in contravention of the Rule Book as, I must say, did we all, to throw the shackle over whilst the engine was still setting back. Unfortunately, the last coupling movement with this coach had involved a buckeye and although this had been properly dropped and the buffers pulled into the long position, the Shunter had omitted to place the buffer saddles on the buffer shanks. As 67610 came in and made contact, the buffers slid into the short position and the Fireman's head was trapped between the bottom of the gangway and the buffer beam of 67610. His neck was broken and he was dead before he was released. A sense of great shock was felt throughout the depot at the tragic loss of a young life, but the rail management quickly acted to distance themselves and the Board from blame, citing the requirements of the Rule Book and the fact that employees were forbidden to go in to couple on before the movement had come to a stand. This had not been complied with, and thus the Fireman was responsible for his own actions, which cost him his life.

Now this stance was, whatever the circumstances, entirely proper and had he complied with the Rule Book, he would not have been killed. Nevertheless, it was the general opinion at the time that this was an unfeeling attitude. The upshot was that every Fireman and Cleaner were later taken, in groups, down to Leith Central station where coaches were stabled and were required to lift and drop buckeyes, set buffers, and were then given a lecture on what to watch for, and of course the absolute necessity to comply with the Rule Book at all times, by the Locomotive Inspectors. I went, remembering how Andrew Fairgrieve had taken me through exactly this process all those months ago, at Thornton.

The following day when I turned out at 14.00, I found I was required to cover this same diagram and make exactly the same moves as McGovern, only 24 hours before, but this time there was the Running Foreman, Ross Dougan and a Locomotive Inspector, Jimmy Fyfe, on hand to observe that I complied fully with the Rules when I coupled on to the coaches in the loop.

A3 60100 SPEARMINT, once the steed of Driver Norman McKillop, and in original condition, makes a smoky departure out of Leith Central with empty coaches for Edinburgh. Most likely it will form the 10.47am passenger from Waverley to Dundee. It was with this engine that we were required to work the Up *WAVERLEY* express passenger train as far as Hawick one morning when the incoming Carlisle Canal crew were delayed on the down leg of their diagram. (J. Robertson/Transport Treasury)

A3 60099 CALL BOY, now fitted with a double chimney and Kylchap blast pipe (July 1958) has come off the turntable and is waiting its turn to go under the coaling plant. It is standing in the area of the points referred to in the text, when another A3 was inadvertently derailed by points being pulled between the engine and tender. (W. Hermiston/Transport Treasury)

A3 60097 HUMORIST, for many years the only A3 with double chimney (and smoke deflectors) stands on the Haymarket turntable. She was always a star performer and I enjoyed one trip out to Glasgow with her on the 10.00am passenger from Waverley. The photograph is undated but the engine appears to be finished in blue livery which she carried from November 1949 until November 1952. The low, flat-roofed building in the right background is the new Cleaners' Bothy. (W. Hermiston/Transport Treasury)

14. ANOTHER NEW ROAD

A week or so passed, with most of my time spent in the relentless grind of preparation. Now I enjoyed the physical work involved in preparation and time just flew by when so employed, but I did find being constrained to the shed a bit of a bind sometimes.

One morning, in the middle of an early turn of duty on preparation, my mate and I were preparing the engine for the 10.00 Glasgow, A3 60097 HUMORIST, at that time the only double chimney engine in the class. This working was a No.3 link turn. Just before we had completely finished, the Driver, Norman Taylor, a very tall, thin, genial man, climbed aboard and put his bits and pieces in the locker.

While he chatted to my mate, I put the finishing touches to my work and climbed up to trim the tender. This done to my satisfaction, I returned to the cab with the firing shovel and cleared up the spillage on the footplate by tucking it into the back corners of the firebox. At that point, I became aware of Charlie Scott, the Running Foreman holding a conversation with my mate and Norman on the ground beside the cab. Spotting me, he shouted 'away and get your things and go with Norman, here.' Away I went like a rocket before he changed his mind and was almost immediately back on board with my jacket, tea bottle and piece. As I stowed it away, Norman explained. 'The regular Fireman's called off and there's nae spare man. The only Cleaner his jist been in the job for twa meenutes and he's gau'n wi' your mate. He micht jist cope wi' preparation. Your comin' wi me. Hae ye ever been tae Glasgow?' he asked. 'No, not to Glasgow but I have been out' I replied. 'Oh, weel, I'll keep ye richt, and we hiv a guid engine,' he responded.

We slipped out to the shed points and came to a stand behind 60160 AULD REEKIE, whose Fireman was already 'phoning out in preparation to work the 10.00 Aberdeen. AULD REEKIE was already coupled, tender to tender, with Gateshead A1 60151 MIDLOTHIAN, which was working the 10.00 'Flying Scotsman' south. I followed him to the 'phone and advised the Signalman, '97 for the 10.00 Glasgow'. I was somewhat staggered when the Signalman started a conversation to the effect that we should couple to 60160 and 60151 and he would then put us down to Waverley together, and that I was to let him know when this had been done. This was a favourite ploy to maximise line capacity,

and on any given day in summer, but especially on a Saturday, it was not uncommon to see up to five (the maximum permitted) engines coupled, making their way into Waverley.

I shouted up to the crew on '160 what was required and went back to Norman and told him. We inched our way forward until we had buffered up with AULD REEKIE and then I went in to couple up. The Fireman from '160 watched me do so and we both retrieved our lamps and he went to 'phone out again.

We got the road and were soon gliding down to Waverley. In the Gardens we raised quite a stir with the inevitable spectators on the two latticed overbridges, since three Pacifics, two shining from stem to stern Pacifics and one Pacific which was a disgrace, were nevertheless quite a sight to behold. Through the Mound tunnel, we stopped and firstly '151 was uncoupled and signalled down the North Loop and then '160 was coupled off and set back to her train. The road came off a third time and we slid with HUMORIST back to Platform 14 where we coupled on to the heavy Glasgow train.

Coupling on completed and lamps set, I had a look at my fire. I had prepared the engine and, as per usual, had put on a big back of the door fire to help the regular Fireman. Now I was reaping the benefit. Norman had a look at the fire. 'What you do, laddie, is bang in coal all roond the box, but dinnae spread what you've got at the back o' the box. Jist leave it and on the way tae Haymarket, it'll catch nicely and we will hae plenty of steam when we need it.' Shades of Davie McNeill and 60510 all those weeks ago, I thought. 10.00 approached and we had just 200lbs showing and half a glass of water. I was somewhat concerned. Norman just nodded as he blew off the brakes and that filled me with some confidence. At least someone thinks he knows what he's doing, I thought.

Back the platform, whistles blew and the green flag waved. Norman pulled open the regulator before answering with a blast on the whistle and with a momentary slip, HUMORIST's drivers bit into the rails and we slid smoothly into the Mound tunnel.

I had seen the 'Aberdeen' just move forward before we did and as we blasted into the Gardens I was looking across, directly into the windows of the middle part of the Aberdeen. People waved and made gestures urging us on. We were really barking now, or as much as a

double-chimney engine ever barked. I looked at the pressure gauge and my heart nearly stopped. Pressure had fallen back to about 180lbs. I jumped for the shovel but Norman stopped me. 'Hiv a look at yer fire,' he shouted above the din. I looked into the box and saw an incandescent white fire covering the grate. Norman just nodded, and so I climbed back into my seat and enjoyed running alongside the Aberdeen. Soon we plunged into Haymarket tunnel and Norman eased off. As I watched, the pressure gauge began to rise, and rise quickly and, as we slid to a stand at Haymarket station, we were near blowing of point. 'Git that injector on noo, son and put anither round on,' shouted Norman, before his head disappeared out the cab window. On went the exhaust injector and round the box went about twenty shovels of coal. Whistles blowing again, I leaned over the cab to watch the receding platform as we moved off to blast our way out of Haymarket with our train accelerating nicely. I went back across to my side of the cab to see where the Aberdeen was and was pleased to see that it was only an engine length ahead. The heavy exhaust from both engines was darkening the skies around. The race was on!

The pressure gauge was on the red mark as I fired another round and went back to observing the race. The Aberdeen was the heavier train and slowly but surely we drew alongside '160. Norman came across and hurled some friendly abuse at Joe Bogie, the Driver, who responded with a blast on the whistle. Both engines were roaring at the chimney and the Fireman on '160 had his back bent to some effect. Reluctantly, I too returned to the shovel and as I finished, it was in time to see '160 lean to the curve away to the right and speed away towards Turnhouse and the Forth Bridge. With a final wave to the passengers, I returned to the matter in hand.

This was another new road for me although I had travelled it by train. 60097 was purring along well notched up and the pressure was sitting easily on the red mark. The exhaust injector sang away and I had the water gauge showing ¾ full. As we rushed over the flatlands around Gogar I fired steadily, repairing some of the damage caused to the fire in the first few miles. The A3 responded by blowing off. Norman waved me into my seat and winked. Bathgate Junction came and went then Broxburn Junction followed by

Winchburgh Junction. Through the historic town of Linlithgow we roared and I looked across the town with its stone church tower, later to be topped by a futuristic spire, and of course the Palace, birth place of Mary, Queen of Scots and in ruins. Little did I think that this town would become my home some years in the future.

Norman was soon applying the brakes and we slid smoothly to a stand at Polmont, our first stop, on time, at 10.33. I fired another round, paying particular attention to the back corners before looking out and back for the right away. There was the green flag. A blast on the whistle and Norman had '97 on the move again. I stopped on his side of the cab since I wanted to see Polmont engine sheds on the left-hand side of the line. Polmont was home to freight engines in the main, and ex-NB engines to boot. There was also an allocation of Ivatt 2-6-0 'doodlebugs', something that I was to become acquainted with in due course.

Falkirk tunnel loomed and, whistle shrieking, we plunged into the darkness and then out again, rushing through the Falkirk High station. From here, the line, although to all intents and purposes level, ran along the edge of high ground, parallel to both the Union Canal, which was soon to drop through a series of locks to join the Forth and Clyde canal, and also to the line of the Antonine Wall. From this lofty vantage looking away over the carse to Stirling and the Highland hills, one could understand why the Romans had created such a defensive position along this high ground. Tearing myself away from the splendid views and historical musings, I returned to the task in hand. Although '97 with its double chimney steamed very freely, too freely as I had found out, the task of firing her was not at all over-strenuous. This I was enjoying and I had a mate who was helpful and appeared relaxed. Certainly we had plenty of steam and water.

Through the incredible rock cutting at Croy we rushed and, on leaving it, ran into the northern edge of the Lanarkshire coalfields to be greeted by collieries on both sides of the track. Again, we steadied and then brakes went on for our Lenzie stop. This was now the Dark Interior so far as I was concerned. We slowly ran along the platform and gently stopped. Norman turned to me and said, 'spread the back o' the door roond the box but dinnae pit any mair coal oan and see we hae a bit o room in the biler. Hae ye ever been intae Queen Street?' I shook my head. 'Weel, the ane thing ye cannae dae there is blaw aff. They hing ye fur that, so jist let her come doon a bit an' we'll be a'richt.'

Whistles blew, and we were off on the last lap. I did as I was told and pushed the fire forward and shut the flap. Passing through Bishopbriggs, I shut off the injector. Pressure was still holding on

the red line. We steadied again and ran past Eastfield Motive Power Depot with an interesting array of engines on parade, before swinging round the right-hand curve through Cowlairs station. I could hardly believe my eyes. Ahead the line seemed to just disappear. As we cleared the platform, the cutting and steepness of Cowlairs bank came into view. The track dropped steeply away into a smoky cutting and the sunshine of the morning disappeared. I peered into this Stygian gloom and the ever-deepening cutting as the brake shoes ground on the driving wheels, steadying our descent. This was incredible. I could now see the black portal of the tunnel loom ahead and at that, an engine, working hard and wreathed in smoke and steam, burst out of the darkness and blasted its way up past us. The coaches slid slowly past with curious passengers peering out. At the rear of the train, there was another veritable explosion of sound and smoke as the N15 banker followed out of the tunnel, putting its all into getting the train up this 1 in 45 bank.

We plunged into this smoking darkness. The air was foul and I could see nothing, not even the tunnel walls reflected in the firelight. This was my idea of Hell. We appeared to rumble down the tunnel for ever. There was a flash of dim light then followed by another, and I realised that we had just passed under one of the two ventilation shafts. The darkness lightened and we slid, brakes squealing, into Queen Street station with its glorious single arched roof spanning the platforms. I looked at the pressure gauge mindful of Norman's dire warning, for I had no desire to be 'hinged', and was relieved to see that it had come back to just under 200lbs. Half a glass of water bobbed in the gauge glasses as we ground to a final halt under a huge low beam at the platform end.

There we sat as our passengers moved along the platform, some smiling to us, one or two nodding but others walking past as if we were not there. I understood that I did not couple off here for did we not bank our own coaches up the hill? Eventually, we felt the bump as the pilot, another N15 without a doubt, coupled at the now front of the train. 'I would try an pit a wee bit roon' the box', said Norman, 'since we hiv tae get back up the hill, but watch your chimney an' dinnae make black smoke. They hing ye fur that here'. I decided Queen Street was not the place to be if you had no desire to have your neck stretched, nevertheless, I obeyed and kept the centre of the grate free from coal. Norman cracked the blower and a pale grey haze hit the beam above. This action had a marked effect on the pressure gauge and the fall steadied and then began a very slow climb.

A cock crow was heard from the pilot and we saw the repeating signal come off. There was a tug and Norman

opened the regulator and set '97 against the buffers of the coach. Slowly, but with increasing speed, we slid along the platform. Tender first, we plunged back into the tunnel. The atmosphere was now 100 times worse as we followed the pilot engine up the bank. We were giving voice at the rear but in turn were suffering from the smoke of the pilot's efforts. I had a look at the fire and saw that the bars were bare in places. I banged in another round of coal and put on the injector just as we slid out into marginally better air. What an engine this '97 was. Pressure was back above 200lbs and we were blasting away to no little effect as we pushed the train up the hill. The coaches turned the brow of the hill and we came to a stand in Cowlairs platform. I quickly coupled off and set my lamps, and we followed our train to the platform starting signal, stopped, and waited for the road into Eastfield shed. At the shed we dropped off and I learned that we did not have '97 on the way back, but that we picked up a fresh engine at Eastfield and worked a parcels train back from Sighthill. After a much needed cup of tea and a bite to eat, we went looking for our new steed. Here was yet another adventure for we were booked to have 73107, one of Eastfield's new(ish) BR Standard Fives.

On joining the engine, I had a quick look around and decided that this was very much like the Black Fives I had worked on at Shotts. Norman confirmed that he also thought highly of these engines and expressed the view that it would be 'nae trouble'. I waited to learn which heinous crime on a Standard Five carried the death penalty, but it was never mentioned.

The return working was a sinecure. We had a light train, the engine rode well and steamed well, too well indeed, and I overdid the firing a wee bit. Running past Haymarket West Junction we got shut distants and were stopped immediately outside the shed. There, waiting, were a spare set of men ready to relieve us, since after platforming the train, the engine was then required for something else. Gratefully, and not looking the proverbial in the mouth, we made our way across the shed to book off. 'Happy?' queried Norman. I replied in the affirmative. 'Weel, ye can come with me again sometime laddie fur ye did a'richt'. More praise indeed. I began to have just a wee bit, as it was soon to turn out, overconfidence and was impatiently waiting to get 'on the coast', as the Newcastles were known.

15. CONSORTING WITH THE ENEMY

It was just a few weeks or so later, as senior nightshift Cleaner, that I was called into the Running Foreman's Office around midnight and asked if I knew how to get to Dalry Road shed. I replied in the affirmative and was then instructed to get over there just as fast as I could. There was nery a mention of transport. I collected my jacket and satchel and walked round Murieston Crescent to Dalry Road proper, then up the narrow lane known as Coffin Lane between Dalry Cemetery and Dalry Road shed, entering by the stairway from Dundee Street. I reported to the Running Foreman's office there. Now this was not an entirely unusual situation and in summer a Haymarket Cleaner would sometimes be loaned for a shift, and usually for a night turn. One Cleaner, somewhat senior to me, went across one night and found himself firing a Black Five on the 23.50 Birmingham 'Sleepers' as far as Carlisle.

The Running Foreman was one John Buchanan who was later to become a Locomotive Inspector, and he instructed me on what to do. They were short of a Fireman for the 1.40am Crewe Junction to Clyde Iron Works (Glasgow) freight and I was told to seek out and prepare a Black Five, No.45360, in readiness for working the train. My mate was a Passed Fireman, Bob Ellis, I think his name was. I found the engine which was standing out alongside the south wall of the shed and introduced myself to my Driver for the night. He asked if I had any idea of the 'Caley' Glasgow road and when I told him I lived at West Calder and had indeed used these very trains as transport home in the wee sma' hours when on the backshift, he laughed. I was of course, thanks to my Hamilton mentors, wholly familiar with the cab layout and firebox of a Black Five and had no difficulty with the preparation. My mate re-appeared, stowed his oil cans, had a good look around and declared himself, satisfied.

I had no great concerns at this strange working since I was on familiar territory and had seen at first hand, just what a Fireman had to do to keep those big heavy freights on the move, for the load behind the tender would be Norwegian iron ore which was imported through Leith Docks and carried by rail to the great iron works complexes in the Motherwell/Glasgow area. I 'phoned off shed, and soon we had the road out at Dalry Junction. We then had to reverse to run tender first northwards down past Dalry Middle signal box and over our own North and South Main lines at Coltbridge Junction.

Soon we arrived at the Scottish Crewe, a series of sidings lying to the south of Granton, to where the wagons of iron ore had been tripped after loading in Leith docks. We were called back on to our train by our Guard who then coupled on, whilst I set one headlamp below the chimney and the other on the centre of the buffer beam, as instructed, to indicate that we were running as a class J unfitted freight. As the Guard gave the Driver the load, I set about filling up the rear half of the long, narrow firebox, not neglecting the front sides and fore-end as I had seen Dalry Road Firemen do when I travelled home on the footplate. I was always deeply suspicious of the injectors provided on Black Fives since these did not always pick up as quickly and cleanly as our own Pacifics, but both the live

A3 60098 SPION KOP was another Haymarket locomotive and in July 1959 (fitted with a double chimney) is being shunted to the shed after fire cleaning at the west end. It was just after she returned from Doncaster with the new chimney that I fired her on the afternoon *TALISMAN* to Newcastle, with Driver Peter Robertson. In the right background can be seen the steps leading into the Scottish Rugby stadium grounds at Murrayfield. (W. Hermiston/Transport Treasury)

steam and exhaust steam injectors on '5360 appeared to be in good order, and well set up.

As we waited for the right away, Bob quizzed me about what took me to Haymarket and how I managed to travel to and from West Calder. He was highly amused when I said that I often worked my passage home on this very train, amongst others, when on a late turn of duty. Both the Signalman at Coltbridge Junction and the Driver of the train on the night were generally amenable to slowing up to allow me to join the footplate. There never was any trouble in alighting at Addiewell, which was the nearest station to my home, since it sat on a 1 in 100 gradient and these heavy freights were only proceeding at walking speed at that point in any case.

The 4-6-0 began to blow off and I was somewhat concerned since Crewe Junction was surrounded by houses but, before I could get the injector on, the yard exit signal cleared; away back the train, the Guard gave a green lamp from his van. With the reverser well out, Bob

swung the regulator handle up into first valve and, with cylinder cocks roaring, '5360 moved the heavy, unfitted train out on to the main line. I closed the cocks on the nod from Bob and with the very distinctive bark at the chimney, '5360 accelerated the heavy load up towards Craigleith and on to Murrayfield. At Coltbridge Junction, the road was cleared for the right-hand fork which would take us up to Slateford Junction and the main line. Having watched the regular Firemen firing these engines many times as I travelled home on the footplate, I followed their example and began to spear coal down each side of the firebox, filling the rear of the box right up to the lip of the flameplate. I lifted the flap but kept the firedoors open, and set the exhaust injector.

For some reason, the ex-LMS (and Caley) men ran with the water level very high in the gauge glass, indeed almost out of sight and so I followed suit. We barked our way up to Slateford and saw the distants lying off. We were right away. Up went the regulator into big

valve and the reverser was back around 40/45%. The roar from the chimney was incredible, a noise that I was wholly familiar with since, as a boy and for as long as I could remember, I would lie in my bed of an evening and listen to the same Black Fives. They hit the start of the gradient up to Benhar Junction, at West Calder, and I'd hear the staccato bark at the chimney as they struggled with their heavy trains up the long haul. They would approach, oh so slowly, then pass close by our home, crawling up the long, weary climb over the moors, gradually becoming fainter and fainter.

At the end of Slateford platform we hit the 1 in 102 rising gradient which marked the long, unremitting uphill haul to Mid Calder Junction, some 9½ miles away. Up past Balerno Junction we slogged, speed dropping down to a little faster than walking pace. '5360 was throwing fire out just as fast as I was feeding it in to the blindingly-white furnace, the chimney a veritable volcano in the darkness. The trailing boxes were knocking badly and every revolution of

the driving wheels was accompanied by a bone-shaking, crashing thump. The tender fall plate rose and fell and shimmied from side to side as the engine rolled and lurched which made firing all the more difficult. The reflected heat was incredible and reminded me as to why the LNER half trap firedoor was much more preferable.

Up the 1 in 142 past Curriehill, and then inchingly slowly, the lights of the lonely Ravelrig Junction signal box came into view. I was firing continuously now and conscious of the fact that I was shovelling a lot more coal than ever I would on a home-grown steed. It also must be said that the pressure gauge remained rock steady on the red line but I had to use the live steam injector to supplement the exhaust injector which had been on continuously, to put back what was being taken out of the boiler. I took time to quickly stick my head over the side and breathe in some of the cold, fresh night air. With Ravelrig now behind us, we crawled on to the long straight but uphill stretch with the lights of the Camps Junction signals

showing clear and the street lights of Kirknewton village shining in the distance to the left.

Bob came across and, after checking the tender water gauge, shouted, 'we'll stop for water at Mid Calder Station!' He immediately whistled to let the Camps Signalman know we wanted water at Mid Calder, the low deep blast of the Caley hooter echoing around the district. I pondered this event. Here we were, only some 20 miles, in round terms, from our starting point, and it was now considered prudent to take on water though in fairness, Holytown, 23 miles further on, would be the next available point and, given the climbing which was still before us, it might just have been tight to reach there. I still had plenty of coal falling on to the shovel plate but I had made some inroads into what had been a very full tender.

We clanked to a stand at the water tower at Mid Calder Station, the level crossing gates closed across the line ahead of us. We spent seven or eight minutes topping up before the Driver gave a blast on the whistle to let the Signalman know we were again ready for the off. We faced just over one mile of 1 in 120 uphill running before we slipped over the top at Mid Calder Junction to take the deviation line to the right to Uddingston. As we passed the lonely and isolated tiny signal box which was Mid Calder Junction, Bob pushed the regulator closed and wound back the reverser. The silence was sheer bliss as we dropped our nose down the 1 in 130 falling gradient and the weight of the train did the rest. '5360 started to blow off as the weight of the train accelerated us down hill. The short level stretch approaching Newpark station steadied our speed before it then began to fall away as we hit the short upgrade before the next level stretch at Limefield Junction approaching West Calder. On this stretch, I began to build up the fire once more and set the injector. Bob just looked over and nodded.

As we cleared the platform of my home village, a platform on which I used to spend much of my waking time when I was a lad, the regulator went up into the roof and the reverser was wound out a turn or two. We were now back on a 1 in 105 rising gradient which would remain almost constant for the next seven miles except for a short portion of level track at Breich. Here we were climbing up on to the bleak moorland country of the Midlothian, West Lothian, North Lanarkshire County Marches and over the basin of the Lothian/ Lanarkshire coalfields. At this stage of our journey we were still traversing the centre of the Scottish shale oil industry. Just beyond West Calder we ran parallel to the huge, red 'bing' or heap, of spent oil shale, one of many defacing both Mid and West Lothian. This was Addiewell bing, created by the dumping of the spent oil shale mined from underneath this area and burned in the

retorts of Addiewell Oil Works, the largest in the oilfields. This extracted oil in the form of a heavy, thick 'smoke' which was then condensed to leave a heavy crude oil. It was little wonder that the stretch of line from just before West Calder right through to Shotts was littered with temporary speed restrictions, a consequence of mining subsidence. Over the moors we crawled, past lonely Woodmuir Junction signal box and on and up to the summit at Benhar Junction, another lonely, isolated signal box, sitting in a cutting. I was still in familiar territory for Benhar Junction was one of the signal boxes I had worked under the eagle eye of a relief Signalman, Wallace Dougall, from Shotts, when I worked there. Indeed, one of the regular Signalmen here, Neil Gemmell, was brother to our own top link Driver Gemmell at Haymarket.

Here the hard work was over. We ran down through Shotts and it was merely a question of checking the progress of this heavy train on the down grades through North Lanarkshire. Ahead, the glow in the sky told of the many blast furnaces and steel works in the Clyde Valley and around Glasgow. That was our destination. We slipped down through Holytown and over the main lines from Carlisle to Perth just south of Mossend yard before dropping down the Bellshill bank. We received clear signals and were able to join the west coast main line at Uddingston Junction, unchecked, for the remainder of our journey to Clyde Iron Works, close by Polmadie Motive Power Depot. After disposing of our train we were coaled, the fire was cleaned and we turned and watered before enjoying a very welcome break. Our return working to Edinburgh consisted of a full train of empty 16 ton mineral wagons but it was with relief that we arrived at Slateford Yard to detach our train before running light to the shed. I was permitted to telephone myself off duty before seeking transport back to West Calder and a very welcome bed.

That one night put into perspective the difference between the so called 'glamorous' high speed passenger work at Haymarket with the finest of engines, and the many, many enginemen who went about their decidedly unglamorous daily (and nightly) business of serving Scottish industry. I reckon I know who the real unsung heroes were.

Another star performer. A3 60096 PAPYRUS in very clean condition, stands in No.11 Platform line at Waverley West End in preparation for taking forward an incoming service from the south, possibly the NORTH BRITON, on 10th May, 1952. (John Robertson/ Transport Treasury)

A Haymarket A3 in action. 60094 COLORADO heads the southbound *HEART OF MIDLOTHIAN* at Penmanshiel whilst climbing to the summit at Grantshouse deep in the Lammermuir Hills, on 31st May 1952. Despite the 1 in 96 rising gradient, the exhaust is clean and the safety valves are showing a feather of steam, so all's well with the world. (J. Robertson/Transport Treasury)

16. DISPOSAL

Summer was slowly passing when, towards the end of July, I was booked for a full week's firing on 14.00 Disposal. My mate was Davie Booth, one of the older Passed Firemen, who had done sterling work firing to Jimmy Swan on the 'Non-Stop' in the early 1950s. He had received a special mention in Norman McKillop's book *Enginemen Elite*, written under the pseudonym 'Toram Beg'.

I booked on in good time on the Monday afternoon and was soon joined by Davie. 'Have you been on disposal, son?' he asked. 'Yes, but just for the day,' I replied. 'OK, lets get to the top end and see what's what.' The 'top' end of the shed was actually the west end where we would do our work in the coming week, for disposal meant moving the engines off the ash pits after fires, ashpans and smokeboxes had been cleaned, filling the tenders, and then setting them in the shed roads under the instruction of the 'third man' as the third Running Foreman's Assistant (generally a Driver) was known.

The work was constant but not hard, at least that is how it should have been, but I was in for a lesson in Work Study. We had disposed of a couple of engines when the 14.30 set of disposal men came on duty and joined us at the top end. The Driver, another Passed Fireman, was known to me although I had never

fired to him. His Fireman was a cleaning colleague with whom I got on well. Round the clock, there were two sets of men on disposal, booking on at 06.00 and 06.30, then 14.00 and 14.30 and finally at 22.00 and 22.30. This meant that there was always an overlap and a crew on duty. On the late shift as we were, it could become quite onerous as the early shift engines were coming back on shed to be prepared for late turn duties and foreign engines were coming in to be turned around to work home. Time certainly did not hang heavily at the top end.

The two Drivers were in conference as we waited, then Davie came to me and said 'that's it agreed then, you and me will work on today and we can have the short day tomorrow. Then we'll do the same for the rest of the week, so we work full shifts again on Wednesday and Friday.' I was flabbergasted. What was this, and how did I get so much time off? All was explained, and the 'normal' way of working on disposal was spelt out. One crew would cover one full shift instead of two crews, but this required that the Driver and Fireman worked independently of each other. In short, one person acted as two when it came to disposing, and the booked crews alternated so that each had a short shift every second day. I was still amazed, but came to realise that this

way of working was only entered into if the Firemen were reliable and up to driving on their own. Otherwise no chances were taken and the roster was adhered to. This highly unofficial arrangement must have been known to the Running Foremen, but a blind eye was turned as long as everything went as planned. If it did not, the sky just fell in on the crew involved as I was to discover in the following year. Of course, the turning of a blind eye also put the perpetrators in the Running Foreman's debt as I was again to find out, and how.

The means of covering disposal with one crew was as follows. The Driver would take one engine, fill the tender with water, reverse it up to the long headshunt adjacent to the Scottish Rugby Football stadium at Murrayfield and then set the points for the appropriate shed road, before rejoining the engine and driving it to its required location. The Fireman did exactly the same, working engine about with his Driver. This made the job somewhat more difficult with more climbing up and down tenders and more running about in the yard, setting points. There was, however, a further refinement just to make life a wee bit easier and in the hour or so that the other crew were on duty before slipping off, Davie took me in hand and showed me what to do.

The replacement A3 60090 GRAND PARADE (the original being scrapped after the catastrophic Castlecary collision in December 1937) stands opposite the coaling plant on the shed loop on 16th March 1958. The large tank holding the main water supply for the shed is immediately behind the locomotive; it was kept topped up with water drawn from the Union Canal. (J. Robertson/Transport Treasury)

In essence, it meant moving the engine into the headshunt and stopping. It was then reversed (or set in forward gear depending on which way it was facing) and, before the brakes were blown off, the regulator was opened and quickly closed. With the brakes then being blown off, the Driver or Fireman quickly dropped off and ran forward setting the points while the engine, with brakes now off and steam in the steam chest, moved slowly along behind him. When the route was set, all one had to do was wait as the engine come up alongside, re-join the footplate and drive it to the required resting place.

This then is how disposal was conducted 'normally', and how we set about work on that week but, to be fair, time passed very quickly and the early finish around 17.00 every second day, was most welcome. The week passed without event.

However, as intimated, I had a ringside seat when things did go wrong – but I must jump forward a full year to recount the sequel to this tale. I was booked for an 18.00 ECS working and on the Friday of a splendid early June late afternoon, had walked down the 'Sub' from the bus stop in Gorgie Road and had started to walk across the front of the shed to the Shed Office to book on, when I was brought up by a magnificent sight. There, standing at the foot of No.6 road, facing west, was our own A4, 60031 GOLDEN PLOVER shining from stem to stern. She had been taken out of service a few days earlier to be prepared for the 'Non-Stop', 'The Elizabethan' express, due to commence service on the following

Monday. The few Cleaners, augmented by Shed Labourers on overtime, had obviously spent the day polishing and burnishing '31 to perfection and there she stood, gleaming in the June sunshine, a sight to behold.

As I stood lost in admiration I became aware of a roar, just like an engine running quickly. Suddenly, from the gloom of the shed, our own J36, 65235 GOUGH shot out like a cork from a bottle and, still under steam, collided heavily with the front of GOLDEN PLOVER. This had the result of stopping GOUGH in her tracks while '31 wore a very pained expression for all to see. I ran across and shut the regulator on 65235 just as the posse arrived from the Running Foreman's office, closely followed by the crew from the top end. For a minute I had difficulty in convincing the Running Foreman that I was not the demon train wrecker and had merely been 'in the audience' as it were.

65235 was quickly set in reverse and moved back. There was remarkably little obvious damage other than a fractured buffer casing, but '31 was in a far worse state with considerable damage to the front of her streamlined casing, a buffer sheared off and, as it was later ascertained, her main frames buckled. She did not work the Non-stop that year, being removed a few days later to Doncaster for repair. After examination, 65235 was soon back in harness. The only other casualty of the day was the Gaffer Cleaner Davie Adams, who had hysterics when he saw what had happened to his pride and joy. And the cause? Well, I have

described the 'short cut' to disposal and, on the day in question, this is how the disposal crew had been working. Unfortunately, the Fireman was a Cleaner of no great experience. He had collected 65235 from the ash pits, filled her tender and run her up the headshunt. So far, so good. He had put the lever into the full forward position, opened the regulator, released the steam brake and jumped off to set the road ahead, expecting old 65235 to creep down behind him. On the J36s and other ex-NB locomotives, the steam brake released slowly so all should have been well, except that *he had not closed the regulator*. Having set the road, he turned to watch 65235 come down behind him but to his amazement and, no doubt, great consternation, 65235 passed him like an express train and disappeared into the bowels of the shed.

It was a matter of the utmost luck that No.6 road was otherwise unoccupied, and that no staff were in the vicinity. On the other hand, it was also a matter of luck (though not entirely so for GOLDEN PLOVER) that she was where she was since otherwise, 65235 would most likely have run unchecked, out at the shed exit and could have caused mayhem with main line trains.

The disposal procedure at the top end returned to a proper and safe footing thereafter. The culprit, before the disciplinary procedure was completed, took himself off to the Post Office to pursue a less exciting career as a Postman. The Driver accepted his punishment and lived to fight another day.

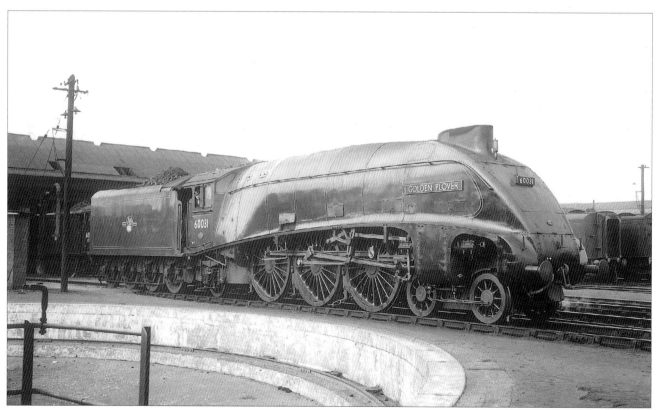

A4 60031 GOLDEN PLOVER, fitted with double chimney in March 1958, appears to be undergoing preparation since the coal on the tender has not been trimmed, but it is in full back gear. The condition of the paintwork would suggest that the date is around the time it came back from Doncaster in 1958 since it is still very fresh. The Fireman peeking from the cab cannot be identified. (W. Hermiston/Transport Treasury)

17. ANOTHER MAIN LINE TURN

On the Saturday of my week on disposal, I booked on for 14.00, but early as usual (around 13.30) mainly due to the vagaries of public transport. As I booked on, one of the most senior Cleaners, Andrew Outterston was at my back. Now, he was so senior that he was never seen in the cleaning squad, but fired permanently, although an un-appointed Fireman. Promotion was, as I previously indicated, extremely slow at 64B because men were unwilling to transfer away, lured by the high earnings of the mileage work at the depot.

Anyway, on hearing me call to the Timekeeper, '14.00 disposal' he immediately asked me if I would swap jobs with him. 'What was he on?' I asked. '2.40pm Dundee,' was the answer. The swap was made there and then. I then went to the rosters to see who my Driver would be on the Dundee and found that it was Willie Donaldson in No.4 Link. I then had a look at the diagram to ascertain just what the job entailed. The 2.40pm. Edinburgh to Dundee was a Saturday Only turn and involved an all-stops (except, strangely enough, Haymarket) passenger service, due into Dundee at 5.34pm. Hardly an express, I thought. The return working was somewhat more interesting in that we worked back the 5.17pm Aberdeen to Edinburgh express due out of Dundee at 7.18pm and due in Waverley at 9.12pm. No hanging about with this train I thought.

I then went seeking my engine and found out we had been booked Peppercorn A2 60535 HORNETS BEAUTY. She was standing across in No.1 road and so I made my way across to have a look around. I was strangely concerned, for I had only once fired a single chimney A2 before, when being passed out, and had heard stories of them being a bit shy for steam. Indeed, there has always been some question as to why Peppercorn did not give all his Pacifics double chimneys but instead, fitted some of the A2s with self-cleaning smokeboxes which precluded the fitting of the Kylchap arrangement due to space constraints. The A2s so fitted never had the sparkle of his other engines. Nevertheless, '535 looked to be in good condition and nicely cleaned. She had been prepared and everything was just so. I had just finished checking the tank when my Driver arrived. He had been told of the swap, but was non-committal about the whole thing. Indeed, he had little to say apart from seeking confirmation that the tender was full and that I was otherwise ready to go. We reversed out to the Shed exit just as my regular mate, Davie Booth walked up through the yard to book

on. He was a bit taken aback to see me look down from '535 and, as I advised him of what had taken place, he was not a little upset, especially when he heard who he had for a mate. Willie Donaldson dryly commented that he was not surprised by the reaction since my replacement would have to be 'found' several times during the course of the shift, hence the reason for the swap to a shed job.

We slid down to the Waverley where, after coupling on, I set about preparing my fire and filling the boiler. I had a big 'back of the door' fire on and soon had the box covered in a searing white fire. Boiler nearly full, I awaited the 'off', but with some trepidation. Greens given and acknowledged, we pulled out of Waverley and accelerated through the Gardens. With no Haymarket stop, speed was allowed to rise through the tunnel and we roared through Haymarket station, causing waiting passengers to step back. I watched the pressure gauge and was concerned to see pressure come back off the mark. The exhaust injector had been set fine and was maintaining nearly a full boiler of water, as I bent to the task of firing. Another round, black smoke at the chimney, soon clearing to a grey haze but still boiler pressure sat just short of the mark. We swung to the right at Saughton Junction and blazed away down the falling gradient to Turnhouse and one of the fastest bits of the Dundee road. As we passed Edinburgh Airport, '535 hit the change in gradient and now her nose was up as we blasted up the hill to Dalmeny and the Forth Bridge. The brakes went on for the Dalmeny stop and we slid to a stand. On departure, as we ran on to the Forth Bridge, I banged another round of coal into the box and suddenly, pressure was right up to the mark. On again went the injector to keep '535' quiet, and I took the opportunity to look out and enjoy, as always, the thrill of crossing the Forth. A perfect day, the sun was shining, the water was calm and blue and all was well in the world, or so I thought.

A glance at the gauge glass showed that the boiler was very full, too full indeed, for comfort, so off went the injector, but pressure was still almost on the red line. We ran into and stopped at North Queensferry. Here, in the platform, the line drops into the North Queensferry tunnel on a falling gradient of 1 in 75. Even with the nose of the engine on the down grade, there was no sight of the water level in the glass. Platform work completed, whistles blew and Willie tugged the regulator open. Disaster! '535 caught the water, the safety valves opened sending steam and

water roaring skywards whilst gouts of water shot from the chimney. I struggled to open the cylinder cocks as we slid, in a veritable cloud of steam and water, into the darkness of the tunnel. The steam and water was now hosing the tunnel roof and walls as Willie struggled to close the regulator, and we were immersed in clouds of wet steam roaring from the front end. At last the safety valves closed and I shut the cylinder cocks. The deafening roar now settled to a dull roar as we slid out into the sunshine. The engine was a mess, the footplate was a mess, and Willie was just sitting there looking, well, glaring, at me as black sooty water ran off his hat and down his face. 'This is a slow train, so there's nae need tae fire it as if ye were gauin' tae Newcastle', he hissed at me. 'Jist calm doon an' leave that shovel alane until I tell ye.' Much chastened, I set to cleaning up, so far as I could, the mess on the footplate and myself, as my mate did the same, whilst we ran, quietly this time, through the Inverkeithing tunnel and came to a stand in the station.

The water was now showing in the glass and boiler pressure was back to about 220lbs as we set off and swung round towards Aberdour and the Fife Coast. After Burntisland, we ran along parallel to the beach which, because of the fine day, was very busy, and I envied the bathers as I took to the shovel once more. The rest of the run was, to my mind, a miserable affair but with enough steam for the job. Another lesson learned. Only produce steam when steam is needed and a realisation that the Fireman must be able to keep pressure *down* to meet the engine's needs, rather than having it always at the red mark.

I was, it has to be said, already concerned at the prospect of our return trip with a big train and far tighter timings, and not a little perturbed as to how this unpredictable locomotive might perform under my inexperienced ministrations. However, that was in the future and I settled down to enjoy the run across the great Tay Bridge, curving across the gleaming waters, and down into Dundee. We stopped on time, and after coupling off, we ran forward into Dock Street Tunnel before reversing to run past our train and into Tay Bridge locomotive depot. We set the engine on the turntable and, after making sure she was balanced, I attached the vacuum bags to the turntable tractor and started to turn her. We had the engine about half way round when the turntable gave a lurch and stopped. I tried to reverse the motor, then put forward again, but it just whined and did not move. Willie dropped down with some irritation, I could see, and no doubt thinking it was my fault again, and came and took the control handle. 'That's funny' he muttered, as the table refused to budge. Leaving the handle, he told me to go round the turntable one way and meet him as he went round the other. We both reached the tender end of the engine about the same time and it looked to be sitting at a funny angle. 'Stay here son and dinnae let anyyin touch anything,' he shouted, as he made off at speed to the shed office. Looking into the table pit, I could hardly believe my eyes. The turntable had derailed from the circular guide rail in the pit and the tractor wheel was sitting on the base of the pit. We were truly in a predicament.

The Shed Foreman plus the Fitters appeared with Willie. They also were astonished. This was a new situation for all, and quite obviously a crane job. Eventually we were instructed to go to the messroom and have our break, although it was equally clear that '535 would not be coming back to Edinburgh with us. This was confirmed some while later by the Running Foreman when he came into the bothy looking for us. 'We hae a real problem noo for we jist dinnae hae ony suitable injins fur ye. The only big injin we hae in steam is a Black Five. Whit dae ye think?' Willie, in a few terse words told the Foreman exactly what he thought and it did not involve taking a Black Five back to Edinburgh. 'Weel, all I can suggest Driver, is that you jist take oan the incoming Aiberdeen injin on the 5.17pm. It's a V2 60898 and if ye're willin', I'll send doon a couple of men tae shovel coal furrit fur ye.' Now, that was music to my ears since I knew that V2s were universally liked, and indeed welcomed, on the Aberdeen road and, personally, I would feel much more competent with such a steed, since I had already fired them on the main line.

We made our way down to the Station and waited for the Aberdeen to run in, as it did, on time at 7.09pm. 60898, obviously on her first turn since coming out of the shops was in sparkling condition. The Aberdeen Ferryhill crew, who were expecting to take her off here, were a bit surprised when they learned that the engine would be running forward and were apologetic about the fact that the fire had been run down in anticipation of this. However, they filled the tank for us whilst the Dundee Firemen pushed the coal forward and I worked on the fire, building it up in readiness. The Aberdeen Driver came back up and spoke to Willie commenting that, as the engine was just back from Doncaster where her tender had been completely cleared, she had only been coaled for Dundee and that coal might be tight. Indeed, on examination, the coal level was well down in the tender. This was not in fact, unusual, since Ferryhill had a manual coaling stage and Dundee had a

60031 GOLDEN PLOVER in BR blue livery which it carried between July 1949 and July 1952, working the southbound *QUEEN OF SCOTS* Pullman service and gathering speed as it approaches Craigentinny signal box. (John Robertson/ Transport Treasury)

mechanical coaling plant and thus it was easier to obtain a full tender of coal at Dundee.

I knew then, without anything being said, the dilemma Willie found himself in, with a coal supply that was severely depleted, no other suitable engine, a heavy, important and tightly timed express train and a Fireman who was definitely short in experience. Nevertheless all he said was 'I think we'll manage.' At that point I was determined not to let this man down.

Now the departure from Dundee Tay Bridge is heartbreaking for every enginemen, especially with a cold engine. From the platform end the gradient steepens from 1 in 260, to 1 in 66, to 1 in 74 on the entry to the Bridge proper, and then on the bridge, a climb of 1 in 114 continues to the high girders where, after a short level stretch, another climb of 1 in 762 continues to the south end of the bridge. Climbing then continues to the 55 mile post at the summit just before St. Fort. In all, we were faced with a climb for four miles with an engine which was now 'cold'. I was aware of this and had, in the time

available at the station, been working on the fire. As we got the 'right away' I had a full boiler of water, pressure was sitting on the red line and I began to pack coal into the box as we pulled out of the station and up the hill. To add to the problem of the gradient, the line was also on a left-hand curve all the way from the Esplanade platforms to the high girders. Willie had 60898 down in about 45% and as we hit the former Esplanade station pulled the regulator full out to the stop. 60898 was making herself heard all over the west end of the city as we blasted on to the bridge, causing the good people of Dundee, out taking the fine June evening air along the river, to stop and stare at this mobile volcano disturbing the peace. I fired another round, packing them in to the back corners, and then another, and was gratified to see my efforts rewarded by the rock steady needle on the pressure gauge. At least what coal there was, was of good quality and not too small. The exhaust injector was set and I swept round the floor of the cab before seeking fresh air over the cabside. Willie pulled '898 up a bit and the roars subsided as

we swept past Tay Bridge South Junction signal box. The worst was behind us for the moment and we topped the summit and began the downhill high speed run through St. Fort.

Through Dairsie, another round of coal took us on to Leuchars Junction. As we waited on passengers from the connecting St. Andrews branch to entrain, Willie offered some advice. 'Its jist wee ups and doons to Ladybank an' we hae a stop at Cupar, so jist keep firing her little and often. We're gaun tae need all oor coal efter that, but she's a good yin and yer da'en fine son.' I fired almost continuously, but very slowly and deliberately after passing Ladybank and up the hill until we passed Lochmuir Box at the summit of the climb over the shoulder of Falkland Hill, with the pressure still on the red line and three quarters of a boiler of water, and we were on time. Down through Markinch and then we were steadying for the subsidence problems through Thornton station. From Thornton, I was more acquainted with the road and so we reached Kirkcaldy and our last stop. I put a heavy fire on as we left Kirkcaldy

and climbed to Invertiel summit, which took us nicely round the Fife coast in the deepening shadows of evening.

From the glare from the fire, I could see that the remaining coal was well down with just several hundredweights or so and, as we leant to the curve through Inverkeithing, I packed in another good fire. Willie was gradually letting out the cut-off as the gradient took effect. Up through Inverkeithing tunnel and I fired another round as we swept over Jamestown Viaduct and into the last, but severe, gradient in tunnel. As we blasted into the 1 in 75 gradient up through the rock cutting and into North Queensferry tunnel, I put on all but the remaining few shovelsful of coal and as we cleared the Forth Bridge, so the last of the coal went into the firebox. I dropped the flap as Willie wound her back and we started to really run downhill towards Turnhouse. I put on the live steam injector and washed down the floor and washed out the now empty tender for good measure. Passing Saughton Junction I had a look at the fire and pushed what was left behind the door down the sides.

We slid to a stand in Platform 19 at Waverley on time. The diagram called on us to work our own empty stock to Craigentinny before returning to the shed, but a hurried conversation with the Platform Inspector quickly had us the road right away to Haymarket. On arrival at the kit store, the turntable crew stepped aboard. The Driver, a young Passed Firemen, looked at the tender, now gleaming in the firelight and remarked 'rough trip, son?' I nodded. His Fireman, a very young Cleaner, had a look, then looked at me, then at the firing shovel and I could see him thinking, 'if that's what main line work is all about, I'm off!' I made for the bothy, and a good wash, whilst Willie handed his 'ticket' in. He joined me at the sink. 'Well, whit a day you've had but ye managed when it wis needed laddie.' I appreciated his generous words but knew in my heart of hearts that I still had an awful lot to learn about this engineman game.

One of the four detested 'Clans' transferred to Haymarket in October 1958, 72005 CLAN MACGREGOR stands in the shed loop on 28th March 1959, very much unloved and apparently unwanted. Within a month, she and her sister engines will be but a bad memory at 64B, although two did come back to briefly haunt us at the end of 1959. This surely was the poorest of the 'Standard' classes and even the Polmadie and Kingmoor men, who had most exposure to the class, did not have their troubles to seek when working these engines. (J. Robertson/Transport Treasury)

18. A BLACK NIGHT AT HAYMARKET

After some further firing turns on preparation, the year slipped into September and the finish of the summer timetable. Cleaners went back cleaning, including myself, and firing turns were few and far between, although we were still in the holiday period. I became resigned to the drudgery of cleaning as the days grew shorter.

I was nightshift cleaning. Winter was setting in and I found myself going to work in the dark and going home again in the dark. I never saw daylight because I slept through the day. The truth was I detested nightshift, and it was made worse on those cold, freezing and often very foggy, nights by the strange smells which pervaded the Haymarket area. Now, these were not railway smells, the wholesome smell of smoke, hot oil and steam. No, these were, I suppose, individually, not unpleasant smells, but together, well, I can recollect it yet and I still feel sick. To understand, Haymarket was surrounded by industry. Jeffrey's Brewery sat at the foot of the entrance road in Russell Road. Behind the shed in Roseburn Street was the factory where Fergusson's made their famous Edinburgh Rock and other sugar confectionery. Across the main lines lay the North British Distillery and the Duncan Flockhart Industrial Chemists establishment where, amongst other things, ether was produced in vast quantities. Further to the south were several more breweries including McEwans large Fountainbridge complex; also at Fountainbridge was the North British Rubber Company. Each produced its own distinctive odour. The yeast and fermenting barley from the breweries, the malting barley from the distillery, the ether from Duncan Flockharts, a strong smell of rubber from the NB factory and the sickly sweet sugary smell of whatever ingredients Fergussons' put into their product when mixed all together and held down by cold, frosty air, created a resultant smell which was all-pervading and appalling. I never really enjoyed eating on the nightshift and, all in all, I was miserable a lot of the time.

However, occasionally there were lighter moments to lift the gloom and on this particular nightshift in late October, around 02.00, into the shed slipped a Standard Pacific 72000 CLAN BUCHANAN, one of Mr. Riddles 'Clan' class 6MT engines. Now I had quite an exposure to these engines since they worked over the Glasgow to Edinburgh Princes Street Line whereon sat my home station but this engine immediately became the object of much interest, and various explanations were offered as to why it came to be at 64B. The real reason came just minutes later

when Davie Adams, the Gaffer Cleaner shouted 'right lads, get yersel's onto that injin and get it cleaned. Its gaun oot on the 05.05 Thornton papers.' Shock and horror for we never, or almost never, cleaned foreign engines. 'Its no a foreign injin at a', said Davie, it's been transferred here an there's three mair tae come.'

So we set to clean this very strange locomotive. That's when the problems started. The men on the 'paints', that is the cabsides and the running valances, could clean those from ground level and the cab running plate on our own engines. The cab sides and valances were out of reach on the Clan and there were no cab running plates. The tender was a funny shape and the Cleaners on the tender moaned about that. At the end of half an hour when an A3 or A4 would have been shining from stem to stern, we were still trying to come to terms with this ungainly beast. Talk about the 'resistance to change' factor. It was never more apparent than in that first hour or so and that was just the beginning.

On duty came the No.3 Link crew to work the 'Thornton Papers' and on this turn they had to prepare their own engine. The Driver took one look at it and shot off to the Running Foreman's Office. The Fireman climbed aboard and took one look at the large oval firedoor with sliding doors. Off he shot, hard on his Driver's heels. We Cleaners waited around expectantly for here was some fun. Back came Charlie Scott, the Running Foreman with the Driver and Fireman. The argument raged on, the crew refusing to put a hand near this piece of 'junk' and the Fireman declaring it a risk to safety. Other crews attracted by the furore even left the warmth of the bothy to come along and add their twopence-worth. Charlie Scott stood firm; it was a serviceable engine and go to Thornton it would. The clamour subsided and the Driver and Fireman were left looking sheepish. To ease the burden, a few of us Cleaners volunteered to help the Passed Fireman prepare the engine and set to. The Driver, somewhat mollified when he realised that there were no 'underneaths' to oil, was also lent a helping hand. The fire was made up and I certainly, for one, did not really fancy firing to the wide corners of this firebox through such a large firedoor. We looked round for the deflector plate to insert in the firebox. No deflector plate to be seen. One Cleaner was dispatched to the ashpits to ascertain if it was there, whilst the Fireman set off again to break the good news to Charlie. No deflector plate, the engine does not go off shed, was his war-cry and we all knew that if the deflector plate was missing, no ex-LNE deflector plate was going to fit.

Charlie conceded defeat, a B1 was commandeered and the Clan was failed. Common sense had prevailed.

That was not the end of the story however, for, in gaining the four Clans, 72000, 72002, 72005 and 72006, we had lost four good V2s to St. Margaret's, 60816, 60927, 60951 and 60959 to cover the additional winter sugar beet traffic from East Lothian to Fife. The moans could be heard miles away. The Clans came, but were never popular and were failed on the slightest pretext. Their availability figures at 64B must have been abysmal and they lasted only the winter. By early April they had been consigned back to Polmadie (or anywhere, in so far as the Haymarket men were concerned), our V2s were returned, slightly worse of the wear, but were soon put right, and life returned to a degree of normality.

The Clans had been intended primarily for our Carlisle turns over the Waverley route but in reality were sluggish, inordinately heavy on water, terrible to fire and were not merely disliked, but universally loathed and detested at Haymarket. Class 6 they may have been but they could not, and would never have held a candle to the V2s. They were the great mystery engines of all of the Standard Class locomotives. BR was not at all short of good Class 6 locomotives. Although originally conceived as a light Pacific for secondary Scottish routes including the West Highland line, the Clans were really not needed anywhere and certainly were, by far, the poorest of Riddles Standards. Why they were ever built remains somewhat of a mystery and of course, the original order for twenty was curtailed after only ten had been constructed They just might have been improved by front-end attention but the reality was that the power classification was just not required. They were transferred around and got as far afield as East Anglia, but lasted a short time only in each place. Polmadie and Carlisle Kingmoor men, it must be said, did some sterling work with them, but the Haymarket view was that any depot that did not like the Peppercorn A1s deserved to be lumbered with real scrap. (Polmadie men never really took to the 64B A1s, when they were briefly transferred there in the early 1950s).

The transfer experiment was repeated again, however, and in October 1959 72001 and 72002 were re-allocated to 64B, with 72003 and 72004 going to St. Margarets, so at least they had to suffer these engines as well as us. However, in that locomotive re-allocation, we also lost five V2s, 60816, 60818, 60824, 60827 and 60920 to St Margaret's, again for the winter. By June 1960 the Clans had gone from Haymarket, for good.

A4 60024 KINGFISHER standing at the west end of the shed on 5th April 1952 in the company of B1 61007 KLIPSPRINGER and A2/1 60507 HIGHLAND CHIEFTAIN. She still has a single chimney at this time and has yet to be fitted with the diamond shaped plaques displaying the badge of HMS Kingfisher, presented at the shed on 21st October 1954. (J. Robertson/ Transport Treasury)

19. AN UNEXPECTED BONUS

About the middle of November, on early shift cleaning I, and most of my colleagues, were astounded to find that on the Thursday we were booked firing for the day. The reason was that many regular Firemen were attending training days to learn the intricacies of the new steam heating boilers fitted to the diesel locomotives which were beginning to make an appearance.

I was booked 06.00 Suburban goods and my engine for the day was N15 69220. My mate was one of the regular Drivers, Matthew ('Matha') Brand who had come off main line duties on attaining the age of 60 years. He had made a name for himself as a Fireman way back on the 'Coronation' and was, I believe, one of the first Haymarket Firemen to work the train, firing to Driver John Binnie. The honour of the very first run, made on Monday 5th July 1937, went to Driver McGuire and Fireman Wilson of Haymarket. The latter, I understand, was the same Wilson now driving in No.2 link. I knew my Driver by sight but had never worked with him. I was well through the preparation by the time he appeared and little was said until he too, had completed his preparation and rejoined the cab. Now, on a tank engine, the fire irons were normally carried on one of the tank tops and though I had seen some there during preparation had not checked them individually.

We moved off shed and down to Haymarket yard where we picked up our first part of the working, a short freight for Corstorphine. My mate was cheery enough but had not a lot to say. He seemed happy enough with the way I was doing things and our trip to Corstorphine went without incident. The N15 was an easy engine to fire and although a saturated locomotive, 69220 appeared to steam freely. The firedoor on an N15 was inward opening, swinging up and into the firebox. It was operated by a ratchet lever on the right-hand side of the firebox (the Fireman's side) and when depressed, opened the door. The door was slightly concave so that, when raised, it formed the equivalent of a deflector plate in the firebox, thus controlling the amount of secondary air entering the box and ensuring the cold air could not directly strike the tubeplate. The ratchet on the lever enabled it to be set at several positions of open, as well as fully closing it.

On our return to Haymarket Yard, we again picked up just a few wagons and set off round the 'Sub' to Niddrie West. I fired the engine as I normally would and we arrived in Niddrie in due course, with plenty of steam and a full

boiler. There we shunted for a bit, then stopped for our break.

On rejoining the engine, the Guard came up to give us our load details for the journey back to Haymarket. This was a bit of a shock since it was full load for the N15. I then realised that these morning trip workings collected traffic which had been worked into Niddrie Yard overnight 'frae a' the airts' and sorted out, and was now ready for transfer, in our case, to Haymarket Yard for onward working.

Driver Brand started to give me instructions. 'Noo son' he said, 'it's a hard road roond the 'Sub' with this load so you'll hae to fire one-handed. Hae you ever done that?' 'No, never' was my glum response. 'Weel, this is hoo ye dae it,' he said and promptly demonstrated. He showed me how, after filling the shovel, he balanced the shovel of coal on the flame plate with his left hand and with his right, raised the firedoor. He then thrust the coal to the desired position in the grate and closed the door. He gave me the shovel and said 'now you hae a go.' I copied his actions, pushing the coal into the desired spot in the firebox with my left hand, and, on withdrawing the shovel, I closed the firedoor with my right. This was extremely awkward and a real strain on the left arm, but orders were orders.

Then he dropped the bombshell. 'Noo son, get the poker in and keep it handy fur ye'll hae tae gie the fire a guid rum'le aboot tae keep pressure up when we're oan the hill.' I leaned out to swing the poker in from the top of the tank and, horrors, I did not have a poker. I had two clinker shovels and a bent dart, but no poker. You could hear his moans all over the yard. I was dispatched to search the yard for a spare poker. As was to be expected, pokers just did not lie around spare in marshalling yards. Indeed, pokers did not exactly lie around spare at Haymarket Loco and were generally 'thieved' from other engines during preparation. Without any shadow of a doubt, 69220's poker had been 'thieved'.

Here was a crisis, at least in his eyes, since I had never been taught that use of a poker in the fire was a pre-requisite to generating steam but rather that the use of a poker in running should be kept to the absolute minimum, if at all, since it could cause the fire to set to the bars. 'Ye'll jist hiv tae make dae wi a shunting pole, he cried, awa and get yin.' So off I went and cadged a fairly new shunting pole from the Yard Inspector's Office, omitting to mention just exactly what we had in mind for it, and returned to the engine. As we waited for the 'right away' I made up a good fire behind the

door, using both hands, and ensured I had a bright, well burned through fire around the rest of the box. The boiler was full, the needle sat on the 175lbs mark and she was sizzling at the safety valves.

The Guard gave us the green flag and, throwing the lever full forward, Matha tugged open the regulator into wee valve. Gathering up the train, 69220 puffed (the only word to describe it) its way out of the yard and on to the main line. Duddingston distant showed clear and Matha pulled the lever back a couple of notches and swung the regulator across into big valve. 69220 responded immediately, really barking at the chimney as she accelerated the big loose coupled train behind us. I had the fire door closed so, filling the shovel with coal, I started to fire one-handed as shown. Steam pressure did not move from the red line as I set the right-hand injector and prepared to commence firing in one-handed mode. I filled the shovel, balanced it on the flameplate and swung open the door. The coal was swept off the shovel by the blast before I could push the shovel into the box. 'Aha, I thought, it's just a matter of directing the shovel to the side I wanted the coal to go and the blast will do the rest.' Firing little and often, we hit the foot of the climb at Cameron Toll still with full pressure. Despite the assistance given by the blast on the fire, firing one handed was a real bind and tiring, and sweat rolled down my face and back as I stuck at it. Despite my best efforts, the steam pressure came back off the mark as Matha dropped the lever into full forward. With the lever now full out and 69220 in big valve, the good folks of the south side of Edinburgh could not have failed to notice our passing, both by the sheer ferocity of the noise and the blanket of dark grey smoke emanating from our chimney and hanging in the frosty air. 'Stick the pole in and gie the fire a guid stir up,' shouted Matha. I complied and, opening the firedoor, I shoved the shunting pole into the fire and 'gi'ed it a guid stir up' as instructed. Black smoke poured from the chimney and the needle stopped falling and began to ease up. I withdrew the shunting pole and closed the door.

Now, the difference between a locomotive poker and a shunting pole is that the poker is made of iron. On the other hand, the shaft of a shunting pole is made of the finest American hickory wood. One can withstand immersion into a firebox, the other, well, it was a sorry looking object as I withdrew it, and one which was now unlikely to survive another foray into the firebox of old 69220.

Another round of one-handed firing,

then another and again, the order, 'stir it up!' Back went the remnants of the shunting pole back into the firebox, and then the pole disappeared for ever as once more, clouds of black smoke darkened the skies around the south side of Edinburgh. But we were winning and cleared the summit at Morningside Road with steam to spare. I am quite sure that this was not due, in any way, to the calorific value of American hickory.

The run down to Gorgie was an anti-climax. The regulator was closed and peace reigned, with only the grind of brake blocks on wheels as the steam brake was used to steady our descent. On the way back to shed with 69220, I opened the firedoor and looked in. The box was fairly well filled with a pudding of a dull red fire with some swirling, dead-looking blue flames. The firedroppers were going to be most unhappy gentlemen when we got this little lot back to the shed, I thought, as the whole lot had to manhandled out through the firedoor, shovelful by weary shovelful. Matha, however, appeared satisfied with the day's work although he did dryly suggest that if I ever fired to him again, to remember and bring at least one poker or two shunting poles.

I was young and still relatively inexperienced, certainly in the ways of our ex-NB locomotives but, at the bottom of my heart, I questioned the need, and the benefit, of one-handed firing since I honestly did believe that I had over-fired the engine, and the fire in the box at the end of the trip supported that belief. I certainly could not understand the performance with the shunting pole in lieu of poker, an exercise which only succeeded in the destruction, by cremation, of BRB property and a Haymarket Firedropper having hysterics. I know that Norman McKillop ('Toram Beg') in his book, *Enginemen Elite* made reference to one-handed firing as being practised universally on every class of NB locomotive with the exception of the Atlantics simply because the engines were just not *free enough steamers* (my italics) to stand the firedoor being opened sufficiently long to fire a round. In this general condemnation he included the superheated 'Scotts'. However, he then went on to contradict himself by remarking, later in the same book, on the free steaming characteristics of the '730' class and, later, the 'Scotts'. Indeed, he wrote: 'who said it was hard to get a Scott to steam?' Well he did actually!

I never fired on the 'Sub' goods again in the years that followed, although I did have the opportunity to fire 69220 for a whole week on the afternoon Prestonpans Goods. On the one day in that week when my Driver, A.B. Inglis, another devotee of one-handed firing, was rest day, I had a young Passed Fireman as a Driver and on that afternoon, from Prestonpans, and with 26 mineral wagons loaded with stone behind us, on the way back to Haymarket Yard I experimented and fired 69220 with both hands, door wide open and just a few inches of white hot fire dancing on the firebars. Steam, we could have sold steam and still had steam to spare, but that's another story.

60012 COMMONWEALTH OF AUSTRALIA outside the new fitting shed on 11th July 1953. She is obviously just off repair and has been kindled but is making steam as the blower is just lifting the smoke. Preparation of engines in this state was a difficult task. It was exactly in this location that, some years later, I had a nightmare preparation turn involving 60510 **ROBERT THE BRUCE**, tears and a bad burn. Just like 60012 in this photograph, '510 had just been kindled after repair. To the left front of the engine is the sand kiln and to the right, the 'shed shunt', J88 68339, simmers quietly. (J. Robertson/Transport Treasury)

20. REVENGE OF THE CLANS

Some weeks after the Clans had appeared, I was again on dayshift cleaning. The cleaning squad had been depleted again as a result of the more senior Cleaners having been rostered firing midweek for the reasons previously stated. On this particular Friday morning in late November I was senior Cleaner when, about 07.00, Running Foreman Ross Dougan sent for me and told me to prepare 72000 CLAN BUCHANAN for a 'job'. That was all. A Senior Spare Driver, Joe Sneddon, joined me. Now he was a really good mate and I was pleased to see him. We prepared the Clan as directed and then were instructed to work it light engine round the 'Sub' to Niddrie West and there uplift a full train of sugar beet tripped in from East Lothian farms and work it forward to the British Sugar Corporation's factory at Cupar. The working was more properly a St. Margaret's job, but one which that shed was unable to cover due to sheer pressure of other work, with both the lucrative seed potato traffic and the sugar beet traffic giving rise to numerous additional seasonal trains.

Before leaving the shed, I filled the back of the firebox up to the flameplate and packed the corners with coal. We had a deflector plate and this was duly set in place. The tender filled, we moved off to the shed exit where I 'phoned out. The signal dropped off and we slipped out to the 'Caley' bridge where we reversed direction and set off tender first round the 'Sub'. Despite the all-in-one cab floor and convenient layout of all the cab controls, this was one draughty engine, and coal dust from underneath the footplate swirled up around us. I was glad to leave the firedoors open just to keep warm. Boiler pressure remained just below blowing off point round to Niddrie where, on arrival, we were set back on top of a train of 12 ton open wagons (5 plankers) full of sugar beet. The Guard walked forward and gave us the load, 35 equal 50, a full load. I set to making up the fire around the back corners and down the sides for I knew that from the 'off' that 72000 would be working against the collar as we got this heavy train up and over Morningside Road.

With a full boiler and safety valves sizzling, we watched the rear of the train for the Guard's signal; on receiving it and checking the yard exit signals were clear, Joe tugged the regulator open and 72000 gave a mighty slip as the 6ft 2in drivers fought for adhesion. I watched in apprehension as my fire was drawn skyward and black exhaust was shot straight up into the winter sky. Regulator shut and immediately snapped open again as Joe caught her just as the slipping died away. She shouted her way out off the yard, the reverser sitting down around 65%. As we gained the main line, Joe wound her in a bit before pulling the regulator wide open. I was surprised that 72000 did not seem immediately to respond. The exhaust beat at the chimney was more strident, but she was not accelerating the train the way a good V2 would, for example. Joe gave me look over the cab, shrugged and just shook his head. Duddingston distant lying off, I bent to my task and, opening the sliding firedoors, set about repairing the damage caused by the slip. The back corners were re-filled and I shot a round down the sides and across the fore-end. Lifting the flap, I looked up at the pressure gauge and was perturbed to see it sitting below the 225lbs mark. I closed the doors and the exhaust darkened. Still the needle did not rise. By this time we were through Duddingston and making for the real start of the climb. The exhaust cleared and, opening the doors, I flashed another round of coal into the firebox. The radiated heat was intense and the fire was an incandescent white. Bang went the firedoors as I closed them. The pressure gauge was not rallying one bit and the injector had to go on. I could see Joe shooting glances across at the

A4 60004 WILLIAM WHITELAW (so renamed in July 1941) with the double chimney it received in December 1957, standing at the front of the shed on 21st June 1959 with the end of the Cleaners' bothy just visible above the left-hand buffer. Given the time of year, there would be few users of this abode since most would be out firing. This was the regular engine of Drivers' W. Nairn and J. Proudfoot and it was the latter gentleman to whom I fired, on 60004 on the 'early Aberdeen,' much to his initial dismay. (W. Hermiston/Transport Treasury)

gauge. We crossed Cameron Toll bridge and Joe let the reverser out half a turn or so. 72000 was giving voice now but was still very sluggish. Another round of coal and still pressure was slipping. Joe shouted to shut off the injector. This I did and pressure rallied a bit but was still just under 200lbs. This could account for the lack of spirit I thought, as I watched the gauge with concern. Pressure was still coming up but the water level was falling and we were on the up gradient so that there was a false level showing. Doors open, I fired only about a dozen shovelsfull over the flap. Doors closed, watch the exhaust. This had darkened showing that combustion was correct but the pressure gauge seemed frozen. The injector just had to go on again and as it caught, so the pressure started slipping back. I was in desperation. Joe motioned to me to sit in the Driver's seat whilst he picked up the shovel and, inserting the blade upside down into the fire, he had a look at the firebed. He then fired another round and closed the doors. Crossing over, he shouted in my ear over the crashing din that the fire was in good order and that he could not understand it. We were through Blackford Hill by this time and still on the climb. Sitting down, he let the reverser right out. Again, the crashing exhaust rose in volume but neither the pull on the train, nor speed, perceptibly increased. This, however, had the effect of starting a slow climb on the pressure gauge so, firedoors open, another round, then another and another were speared into the box at close intervals. Boiler water level was still only on half a boiler but at least we had 215lbs on the clock. This was brutal treatment of the engine but we cleared the top of the hill and the regulator was half closed and the reverser wound back. As we slid down to Gorgie East Junction and swung leftwards to Haymarket West Junction, I watched the pressure gauge and it did not rise significantly although we were almost coasting by this time. We were brought to a stand at Haymarket West Junction waiting a path and I opened the firedoors and had a look at the fire. It was in good shape and nicely saucer shaped. A classic firebed, I thought. The front dampers were properly open and I opened the rear ones just to increase the airflow. I filled up behind the doors and raised the flap. The injector was shut off but boiler pressure was slow to rally.

The remainder of the trip to Cupar was more of the same. It was, constantly, a case of mortgaging water for steam and steam for water, taking every opportunity of down grades to try and rally the boiler. We were never totally 'cold' but never had full boiler pressure available to us. It was a miserable trip with a heavy train and a locomotive which was less than impressive. When we coupled off at Cupar, we returned light engine to Haymarket, where Joe filled a repair card with some very ungracious comments about our steed. The Clan had lived up to reputation and had, at the same time exerted a degree of revenge on us unbelievers. It transpired, after examination, that the wire screen in the smokebox had become dislodged and fouled the blastpipe, this causing at least some of our difficulties. But I never was, and would never be, a fan of the Clans.

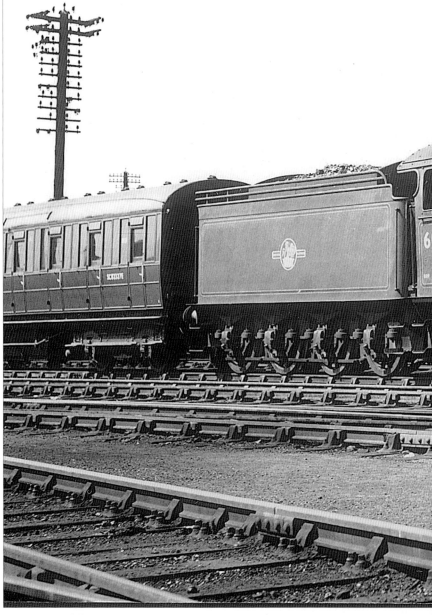

An A3 very close to my heart. 60037 HYPERION was the engine working the 8.05am Edinburgh/Thornton on the two mornings I was taken by the Firing Inspector to be passed out. On consecutive mornings, I fired this engine through to Thornton. Here it is in the condition as I first knew it, at Craigentinny on 8th June 1957, just a few weeks after my firing experience with her. (W. Hermiston/Transport Treasury)

60037 HYPERION in new guise and just back from a general repair at Doncaster where the double chimney had been fitted, standing outside the front of the shed on No.6 road, 19th October 1958. (W. Hermiston/ Transport Treasury)

21. NEW YEAR

Christmas approached but this meant little or nothing, for in those days Christmas was not a Public Holiday in Scotland and I spent Christmas Eve cleaning on the nightshift. New Year approached and since this was the traditional Scottish Public Holiday (two days) we scanned the rosters to find out which days, if any, we were being booked off. At Haymarket, the New Year holidays were rostered to ensure fairness. One year, you were booked off on New Year's day, the next year, the 2nd January and the next year you were booked off both days.

The rosters went up and, just my luck, I was down to work on New Year's day. I was booked with a Passed Fireman, Eric Dempsey at 09.00 to work the 10.47 passenger train to Dundee and return 'on the cushions'. Eric at that time was firing in No.2 link to Jimmy Dunlop on 60161 NORTH BRITISH.

I booked on at 09.00 and was soon joined by my mate. He was not in the best of moods having to work on a holiday and before we even found out which locomotive we had, he was moaning. Not about anything in particular, just moaning. We had a Dundee V2, 60822 which had been prepared for us. The engine was, however, fairly run down and looked to be a candidate for shopping, but the fire was well made up and bright, and she had been well prepared. I set the lamps and we moved off shed. This turn of duty required us to run light engine to Leith Central to pick up our coaches and work them to Waverley. The morning was extremely cold and frosty, with a thick covering of snow on the ground and, as we ran down to Leith, the engine was enveloped in a cloud of leaking steam, pouring from every quarter. I could hear the moans although I could barely see the source. Sighting signals was difficult however and my mate, both then and during the course of the journey, had some real cause for complaint.

We coupled on at Leith to our train of nine coaches, white with frost and looking appallingly cold. Coupling on, I secured the heater bags and returned to the warmth of the cab to open the train heating valve. Wisps of steam appeared gradually from the leading coach back, showing something was having an effect. My mate was having difficulty in blowing up the brake since the brake cylinders on the coaches were frozen. However, with 21 inches eventually showing and the brake test complete, we whistled for the road. Off dropped the signals and we pulled out of Leith Central in a cloud of steam. I fired gently round the box on the way up to the Waverley and, in good time, we ran up platform 10 to stop in platform 11 (the South Main) at 10.30. There was a surprisingly large number of intending passengers waiting and I did not envy them getting into a frozen train, although, without a doubt, more than a few would already have their own inbuilt central heating at work, given the nature of the holiday it was.

With a full boiler and steam just below blowing off, we waited for the green. 10.47, whistles blew and away back, wreathed in steam, a green flag shimmered. Eric pulled the regulator open and we disappeared in a cloud of steam as it rushed from the cylinder cocks. After a couple of revolutions I slammed the cocks shut and visibility improved marginally. It was soon very clear that this V2 was 'off the beat' and

A4 60011 EMPIRE OF INDIA runs off the turntable at Haymarket and proceeds up towards the coaling plant and ash pits on 24th March 1951. The lamps, unusually, have not been removed at the kit store and are thus at risk of being purloined by another preparation crew; such was engine shed life. (J. Robertson/Transport Treasury)

how, as the syncopated beats from the chimney echoed around Princes Street Gardens. Of the six beats normally, two were completely missing. I could hear the moans again!

We blasted our way around Fife in a steamy haze. The engine steamed well enough but was very rough underfoot and rolled a fair bit, caused in no little part by the badly out-of-set valves. We were just out of Kirkcaldy, climbing up to Dysart when I happened to look back the train. Well, I tried to look back the train but, behind the tender, I could see nothing: the heating bags had burst between tender and train. I shut off the heating valve and the view behind cleared, but the passengers were in for a cold journey.

We eventually slipped down into Dundee Tay Bridge station and I coupled off quickly before any of the passengers came along to wish us a good New Year (or something). The engine was deposited at its home depot with all defects duly booked (and moaned about to the shift Foreman) and we returned to the station to await our train home.

Fortunately, when it ran in, the steam heating had been more effective on the journey south from Aberdeen and we were soon ensconced in a warm compartment to sleep our way home to Edinburgh whilst someone else did all the hard work 'up front'.

Around the end of January in 1958 I started my first night of nightshift, at 00.01 am on Monday morning (no Sunday time paid to Cleaners!) and just before we set-to on the first engine of the night, I was sent for by Jimmy Austin, the Running Foreman. The Running Foreman's Office Assistant, officially designated Telephone Attendant, had telephoned himself in sick and so the office was short of a man. I was to be that man until further notice. Here was a pleasant change from cleaning. I could keep clean, I was in a warm office and my duties only involved answering the telephone when it rang, making tea at regular intervals and recording locomotive numbers against turns on the daily working sheets. I also had to record the numbers of all incoming engines as they arrived on the turntable (which was possible without leaving my seat) and had to advise, at regular intervals, engine numbers on outgoing turns to the District Control Office in Edinburgh Waverley.

The job was not in anyway strenuous and time passed quickly and pleasantly, for here I was seeing the other side of the Running Foremen and hearing the banter that passed. In the same office, to the rear, sat the Timekeeper and on the day turns, beyond him, the Roster Clerk. Little did I think at that time that I would be occupying the office of the Roster Clerk and rostering colleagues in the not too distant future.

It was also an illuminating experience to hear what the Supervisors thought of individual Drivers and Firemen, and

an eye-opener to learn that even one or two of the Top Link men were not particularly highly regarded. It was then I realised that Cleaners were not always wrong when things did not go as planned and that the Running Foremen were fully aware of this fact. They knew the good men, the obliging men and the keen men and it was then I knew that a Running Foreman's opinion of a Cleaner as a Fireman, as described to a Driver, for instance, was based very much on personal knowledge and not merely a platitude.

The reason for this (unpaid) promotion was that, when I transferred from Shotts to Haymarket, I had already enrolled in a Basic Railway Induction Course. This was a self-study course, and one of many that British Railways offered to staff who were willing to learn more about the industry. It was a commendable scheme which ran for the life of BR until 1994 and, by means of correspondence papers, students could learn at distance about various facets of the industry. Each student had a mentor, normally a volunteer Inspector or senior Clerk, who corrected and marked each paper submitted, and gave guidance where this was found to be necessary. At the end of the session, normally twenty papers/ twenty weeks over the winter, there was an examination in the subject studied. Passes were rated First class, Second class, Third class and an Ordinary pass and there was a small monetary reward, £5 for a First class pass, £3 for Second and £2 for a Third. Now this has to be viewed in the context that £5 was somewhat more than the basic weekly wage of an Engine Cleaner in 1957.

I had, in the previous April, sat the examination in the Railway Induction Course and had attained a First Class pass. Now, this did get me noticed at Haymarket, for it was apparently unknown for a Cleaner ever to avail themselves of this scheme, let alone obtain a First Class pass, and the presentation of my Certificate (the money was paid direct into wages) saw me being invited into the Shed Master's Office. Since it had thus been proved that I could read and write, I was a natural to take over from the semi-literate Labourer who normally covered the telephones. To follow on my initial success I had, for the current winter, applied to do both First and Second Year Rules & Regulations, two separate courses on the same subject, all at once. This really raised eyebrows – a loco man who was prepared to study Rules and Train Signalling Regulations.

I had a pleasant three week sojourn indoors before once more joining my peer group up on the boilers in the shed once again.

The *North British Hotel* clock shows five minutes after noon and A3 60089 FELSTEAD in sparkling condition starts the 12.05pm Edinburgh to Carlisle via the Waverley route, out of platform No.9 on 24th March 1951. Passed Fireman Mungo Scott (later to star in the BTF film *ELIZABETHAN EXPRESS* with Driver Tony McLeod and A4 60017 SILVER FOX) leans out the cab. (J. Robertson/Transport Treasury)

A3 60043 BROWN JACK just a few days back after general repair at Doncaster and sporting a new double chimney, backs down to the shed exit signal and over the sleeper crossing giving access to the General Office. The pile of ash at the side of the line is not the result of someone cleaning a fire at the front of the shed but is more likely to be some material that the Permanent Way Ganger is about to use for a purpose best known to himself. (W. Hermiston/Transport Treasury)

22. SPRING AT LAST

I sat my examinations for the two Rules courses I had been studying over the winter and was pleasantly surprised, in time, to find I had achieved Second Class passes in both. I had hoped for better but was quickly told by Mr. Cherry, the Shed Master, that this was a fine performance and that I had put Haymarket in the limelight, since it was unknown for any footplateman to have voluntarily chosen to study this subject from other than a footplate perspective. Thereafter, I became a bit of a 'font of all knowledge' to some of the staff at the depot, especially the running Fitters. They often got embroiled with each other in almost child-like arguments and would come seeking an answer to some problem or other which had, in most cases, been blown up out of all proportions by petty bickering.

The first occasion I became involved was one afternoon in the canteen, where an argument was raging and Bertie Mills, the shift Leading Fitter, came across and asked me to settle the argument. The question under debate was the weight of a gallon of water. '10lbs' I stated, recalling my days at physics in school. No, that could not be right since it accorded with none of the views held by the protagonists. I shrugged and let the war continue. Later in the day, Bertie sought me out to apologise. Someone had gone to the lengths of sloping off to the local library and had looked the answer up, and I had been right all along. From that point on I was tormented.

The beneficial side of the matter was that I was then occasionally, very occasionally it has to be said, involved in the interpretation of rules in the Drivers' bothy, a subject that no Cleaner would normally have been asked to comment upon in any way, since the view of many Drivers was that this knowledge only came with experience and 'what did Cleaners know?' It pleased me no end to be given a hearing by my betters and to be involved on an equal footing in these erudite discussions. Indeed, the whole vexed question of 'Wrong Line Order Forms' cropped up on not a few occasions. Surprisingly, these were not fully understood by many. I have to say that the discussions were never as petty as those indulged upon by the Fitters, which said a lot about the Fitters to my mind.

The year moved into springtime and the holiday roster was again upon us. Slowly, the number of Cleaners in the squad dwindled as the senior men went up firing. Odd firing turns came to me during this period, mainly on preparation and relief. Around this time, I was also fortunate enough to work some of the allocated empty coach (ECS) diagrams on which I encountered a variety of engines such as Directors, Shires and our own V1s/V3s as well as the odd B1. ECS working was mainly confined to Craigentinny-Waverley, Waverley-Corstorphine and Waverley-Saughton Junction and such turns could be quite onerous.

Saughton Junction was used to stable an overflow of coaching stock and as the year progressed and trains became more frequent, Haymarket gained a considerable number of additional ECS workings, returning coaches to south of the Border. These were known as 'Venlo' workings, after the code word in the BR Telegraph Booklet for ECS movements. These generally took place twice or, at the height of the summer, three times each week and involved fairly big trains of empty coaches being worked south to Heaton Yard around midnight, usually from the sidings to the west of Saughton Junction.

Firing turns were becoming more frequent for me since, before the onset of the summer traffic, the turntable at Haymarket was taken out of service for a complete overhaul. As a consequence of this essential maintenance, there was a demand for many additional sets of engine crews to take incoming engines round the Gorgie triangle for turning, just as had been done with the Atlantics all those years ago. The engines could not be allowed to gather up into groups for turning since the main lines had to be kept clear and so the turning of single engines did put a strain on resources, and almost all Cleaners were up firing somewhat earlier than usual. This working went on for several weeks and, given that we were firing to younger Passed Firemen, it was the norm for the crews to take turns and drive engines about. All this was good experience.

After the second shift up, I found myself firing on a more or less regular basis and 'red-inked', most weeks, mainly on preparation or pilots to begin with. I soon took to scrutinising the rosters to see who was working where, with a view to swapping turns. Since I preferred late shift turns to early turns because it made travel from home much easier, exchanging turns, especially when I was giving up early turns for the more anti-social late turns, was much simpler than I had anticipated. Neither the Roster Clerk, nor the Running Foremen generally objected, although some of the older Drivers looked askance at the very young Firemen who appeared on the footplate from time to time. There were, however, some exchanges which would not be sanctioned and generally that came down to a balance of the personalities and experience involved.

I had my first experience of a Driver who took exception to me around that time. I had swapped a dayshift Haymarket pilot week with a junior Passed Fireman who was firing in the Top Link to Bob Proudfoot, 'The Undertaker' as he was known to all and sundry, on the 'early Aberdeen', the 03.57 'sleepers' to Aberdeen which 64B worked as far as Dundee, and with a most unsocial booking-on time of 02.00. Now, at that time, Bob Proudfoot worked A4 60004 WILLIAM WHITELAW turn and turn with Bill Nairn and the 'early Aberdeen' was an onerous turn since the sleeping car train was always loaded up to maximum and was tightly timed to Dundee.

On the evening or, more properly, the early Monday morning in question, when I sought out 60004 to commence preparation, Driver Proudfoot demanded to know what I thought I was doing. He lived up to his nickname in the darkness of the early morning. He was a tall, thin man with deep-set eyes, a lugubrious look about him, and in his black railway mackintosh looked very much the epitome of an undertaker. 'I'm your Fireman for the week,' I replied. 'We'll see aboot that, laddie,' he said, and off to the Running Foreman's office he strode. I remained on No.4 and set about preparation, but not without some concerns. I knew that some of the top link Drivers were very unhappy at having to take Cleaners, whilst others proved helpful and supportive, making the best, sometimes, of a bad job.

I was not party straight away to what was said in the 'inner sanctum' but I learned later that Bob had really gone to town and refused to have me with him. There had also been some plain speaking on the part of the Running Foreman and Bob returned to No.4 with a bit of a flea in his ear and in distinctly bad humour. He said nothing, but grabbing his pourie and oil cans, disappeared under the innards of 'William'. I continued preparation and took particular pains to ensure that everything was 'just so' and the engine was prepared to perfection in order to avoid any further recriminations.

Preparation complete, he regained the now sparkling clean footplate and, after stowing cans, pourie, coat and satchel, he climbed into the driving seat and blew off the brakes. The silence was palpable and I was somewhat uncomfortable, but assumed I was, after all, going to Dundee. I took off the handbrake and, calling a warning, Bob gave a blast on the wonderful chime whistle and we slid out, cylinder cocks roaring, to the shed entrance. Here I set my lamps and telephoned for the road. Off came the disc and, pulling on the regulator, we reversed smoothly and almost silently across to the South Lines and set off tender leading, for Waverley. I had really filled up the back of the firebox and on the way down to the station fed several shovelfuls down each side of the box, but again leaving the fore-end uncovered. There was half a glass of water and pressure sat nicely at 210lbs as we slipped back into the South Loop behind the subsidiary signal and came to a stand to await the arrival of our train from the south.

Waverley was surprisingly busy at this ungodly hour and there was a fair bustle as staff prepared for the first of the early morning arrivals. At that time of the morning they had just finished with the early 'Papers' departures. Whilst we sat in the loop, I had another look around my fire, and became aware of a clattering of the cab doors and someone entering the cab. It was Andrew Fairgrieve, the Locomotive Inspector. 'Weel Bob, whit's all this aboot?' said Andrew. Bob gave vent, 'look here, he said, they've pit a wee laddie on this job an' I wanted anither Fireman but I've been telt that I've got to take him, so if he comes, you come tae, tae make sure that I get tae Dundee.' All became clear. Bob had demanded that an Inspector ride on the engine if I was to be Fireman and now 'Fairy's' sleep had been disturbed. 'Oh no', I thought, now I had two men in a bad mood.

Andrew was all sweetness and light, however, and assuring Bob that he had

passed me out, was confident in my ability to do the job properly. He gave me a nod to carry on, and stood behind my seat. I remembered, without prompting, that this would be a buckeye coupling so, grabbing the coal hammer, I slipped to the ground and, going back behind the tender, slipped the coal hammer shaft into the jaws of the buckeye coupler head and heaved it up to balance the shaft on my shoulder. With my free hand I felt for and inserted the bearing pin, and withdrew the coal hammer. I then pulled the release chain to set the jaws open in preparation for the coupling up movement. I re-joined the cab and any further concerns were cut short as our train, the 19.15 from Kings Cross, rushed in and drew to a stand alongside us in Platform 11. Off came the incoming engine and away it went to the shed. The West End Pilot moved in to take off the Fort William sleeping cars as I put another round of coal on, not neglecting the fore-end of the box this time. Pressure was rising quickly and I set the exhaust injector to fill up the boiler. The subsidiary signal cleared and we moved out towards the Mound Tunnel. The subsidiary signal for the platform line then cleared and I called out to Bob. Quickly he wound her into reverse and set gently back on top of the train. Accompanied by the Inspector, I dropped on to the platform as No.4 buffered up to the train and we heard the buckeyes engage. I waited until Bob had made a pull away test to ensure the coupler heads were engaged, then slipped underneath to couple both vacuum and heater bags. I also felt

under the coupler heads to ensure both tongues had dropped as further proof that the couplers were secure. Grabbing the lamp, I ran forward and set one over each buffer before climbing back into the cab.

Andrew, who had by this time commandeered my seat, gave me a wink and a nod. Injector off, boiler nicely filled and steam sitting just below the red line, I looked over the Fireman's door waiting the 'Off'. At 03.57 on the dot, whistles blew and a green light winked at the rear of the train. 'Right away', I called, and Bob tugged on the regulator. Smoothly and slowly, No.4 eased the big train out through the station throat and into the Mound Tunnel in the cold, grey dawn of a Scottish summer. Cylinder cocks shut, there was now an urgency at the blast from the chimney. Out through the Gardens we swung and snaked across the crossovers to the Down North Line. I glanced at the pressure gauge. It was holding up. No.4 shouted her way into the Haymarket tunnel and the firelight illuminated the cab, tender end and tunnel walls. Out into the darkness of Haymarket station and No.4 really had hold of the train. On past the shed, I exchanged waves with the top end men who inevitably watched the 'early Aberdeen' pass. At Haymarket West Junction, with signal lights showing green ahead, I picked up the firing shovel. The blast was now having a real effect on the fire and I looked into a brilliant white inferno. I began to fire round the box, slipping just a few more shovelfuls down the sides and along the

fore-end. Pressure was holding up just off the red line. On went the injector. As we swung away to the right at Saughton Junction, I was aware of Bob glancing at me every now and again. I stuck to my task as we roared up to Dalmeny and on to the bridge. As 'Fairy' was occupying my seat, I stood behind the Driver and put my head over the side. The lights of Queensferry were reflecting on the leaden water below whilst away to the west, in the sky was the glow of industrial Grangemouth. It was at such times that the real romance of railway work was apparent. Not for the first time, I thought just how privileged I was, doing something I really enjoyed doing, and where one could appreciate (sometimes) so much beauty. The words of C.E. Montague, famed novelist, man of letters and journalist with the *Manchester Guardian*, came into my mind as I looked out over the River Forth. As he mounted his bicycle in Manchester at midnight to ride to London, he said to his friends 'base is the slave who is tied to his pyjamas'. At that point, I realised exactly what Montague meant. Not everyone would, I think, appreciate the opportunity to shovel coal in the wee small hours of the night, but I certainly did.

Reflections over, No.4 dropped her nose down the hill and we slid, very sedately, through Inverkeithing and on to the difficult stretch round the Fife coast. As she swung eastwards, I could see, away down the firth, the sky lightening as the sun struggled over the horizon out over the North Sea. I bent to my task and fired little and often,

which pleased Andrew and apparently satisfied Bob. I was experiencing no problems in keeping up steam pressure and the boiler full, but was aware of just shovelling a wee bit more coal than I had previously done on the Dundee road. Bob kept No.4 against the collar as we climbed up through Sinclairtown to the first summit at Dysart. After the compulsory speed restrictions down through Thornton we again set to the climb through Markinch and up over Falkland Hill. With our nose now on the downgrade, we gathered speed down and along the Howe of Fife, there being little spare capacity, timewise, since we were due in Dundee at 05.28 and the whole road was not exactly in our favour. Steadying, we swung to the right at Ladybank Junction and then on through Cupar and St. Fort. With the sun now up over the Tay estuary, we finally swung on to the Tay Bridge and made our way across the great bridge, at the designated limit. As we crossed and dropped down at the High Girders to swing right towards Dundee, I was delighted to see seals, basking in the early morning sunlight, on the sand banks uncovered at low tide, just below the bridge. My first 'early Aberdeen' had been a magical experience, awakening such ethereal thoughts in my head.

On arrival at Tay Bridge station, I slipped down and pulled the release chain on the buckeyes after I had uncoupled the bags, and No.4 pulled forward from the train. Quickly I dropped the coupler head on the tender and rejoined the engine; we reversed in

the tunnel and made our way up to Tay Bridge MPD. There we turned the engine, took coal and went to eat. As we sat in the mess room, Bob began to direct the odd question and comment to me and was distinctly more amenable. Andrew asked him if he was satisfied with my performance but Bob was not ready to concede defeat quite so easily. 'We're no hame yit,' was all he said in response. Andrew just laughed and shook his head.

We worked the 05.47 Aberdeen to Edinburgh back. This was another big train, conveying a restaurant car in the formation. Due out of Dundee at 07.44, it was worked south to there by Ferryhill men. It ran in, on time behind 60531 BAHRAM, which was an Aberdeen engine. We changed engines and got away on time and, without any problems whatsoever, arrived in Waverley on time. As we booked off at Haymarket, Bob turned to me and said, 'weel, I suppose I'll see ye the nicht then!' Praise indeed. It must be recorded that he was the most pleasant of mates for the remainder of the week but was not a man who ever wasted words. Conversations were, as a result, of short duration.

The pleasing lines of the Gresley A3, shown to advantage in a fine side view of A3 60098 SPION KOP parked on the shed loop below the main water tank, on 11th February 1951. (J. Robertson/Transport Treasury)

Another long-time denizen of 64B, A3 60057 ORMONDE, poses outside the front of the shed; the date given is 15th March 1959. However, 60057 received a double chimney in September 1958 at Doncaster and since the tender emblem is still the old lion and wheel, I think this photograph actually dates from an earlier period. This was the engine I had on the 12.00pm Carlisle with Driver Faber Dewar in 1958. (W. Hermiston/Transport Treasury)

23. THE BIG TIME

After the usual grind of more preparation turns I found myself booked, three days in succession, on the back shift 'Ferry Goods' firing to one of the regular Drivers, Jimmy Walker. We had the usual J36, No.65235 GOUGH. This job was a pleasant turn taking us to South Queensferry by way of Queensferry Junction and Kirkliston and returning by the main line from Dalmeny Junction. On the way, we shunted at Kirkliston station and the Royal Elizabeth Naval Ordnance Stores before crossing the main Aberdeen line at Dalmeny Junction. Dropping down underneath the viaduct leading on to the Forth Bridge, we ran into South Queensferry goods and the VAT 69 Whisky Distillery. Port Edgar Naval Base was also shunted, on an 'as required' basis. We then returned to Dalmeny Junction and worked back the main line to Haymarket Yard.

This was a nice wee job and the J36 was easy to fire, and steamed well. The J36s were strong little engines, capable of some very hard work with quite prodigious loads, although our two at Haymarket led a much more pampered life than those based at Bathgate, St. Margaret's etc. There was much of interest and the shifts passed very quickly indeed.

Towards the end of the week, I was swung on to nightshift (by means of the aforementioned Guaranteed Day ploy) and on the Friday night to cover 21.30 Senior Spare. This excited me a bit, for there was always the chance of a main line turn on the senior spare link. Anyway, Friday came and I signed on around 21.15, a bit early. I had just settled into the chit chat of the bothy when Willie Elder, the Running Foreman, stuck his head round the door and shouted for the 9.30 spare Fireman. I went round to the office. 'Get your coat and away across to '162. The regular Fireman's called off sick. Willie Bain will be your mate an' he kens your coming' said Willie E. Willie B was another top link Driver who, as coincidence would have it, was on this night paired up with the engine he had been allocated to, and with which he gained a great deal of publicity, when he was in No.2 link. This was no less than A1 60162 SAINT JOHNSTOUN which had been, and still probably was, the engine which set the benchmark for clean engines anywhere in the country. Countless photographs have been published, and continue to be published, of '162 shining from stem to stern and with all steelwork and brasswork positively gleaming. Willie's regular engine now, in the top link, was 60012 COMMONWEALTH OF AUSTRALIA which he shared with George Spilsbury, and which they both had positively shimmering. However, at this time '12 was in Doncaster for general repairs and, as the diagram called for a class 8 engine, '162 had been purloined from No.2 link, a not unusual occurrence at Haymarket by this time. The booked working of the night was the 22.50 Sleeper, the 'Night Scotsman'. At last, I had got a 'coast' turn and was on my way to Newcastle.

Full of excitement, I returned to the bothy to collect my jacket and satchel. 'What job had I got?' was the flurry of questions from other Firemen in the bothy. 'Oh, just the 10.50 coast,' I replied most nonchalantly although, inside, I was a'tremble. I crossed the shed and found '162. In the dimming light of the early summer evening, she stood ever gleaming, at the head of the train in Haymarket Loop. To ease congestion at Craigentinny, it was the practice in the summer months to bring the empty sleeping cars which formed this train up earlier in the evening, and stable them in Haymarket loop. The preparation crew had taken '162 out and had coupled up for us. I joined Willie Bain on the footplate. 'Willie Elder tells me you've been oot oan the main line', he said. 'Jist where hae ye been? Hae he ever fired on the coast?' I had to reply in the negative to the last question, but he appeared to relax a wee bit when I described my week with 'the Undertaker' on the early Aberdeen. He laughed at my description of the first night and said, 'weel, Newcastle's just a wee bit further away and ye'l hae yer work cut oot the nicht.' With these words of wisdom ringing in my ears I stowed away my satchel and jacket. Putting on my gloves, I had a quick look around the fire, using the firing shovel to deflect the gases as I looked at the firebed. The engine had been well prepared with a good fire in behind the door. Boiler pressure was sitting at around 225lbs and there was three quarters of a glass of water in the boiler. The cab shone like a jeweller's shop. I swung up on to my seat to await developments. The next moment there was rattle at the door as the guard appeared at Willie's side and I heard him shout up fourteen on, 505 tons tare!' Now I was really in for it. Willie looked across. 'Full load the nicht, he shouted. Lets get the show on the road.'

I walked forward to the telephone. 'The 22.50 coast ready for the road in the loop,' I advised the Signalman. 'Wait for the road,' was the terse reply. After an up train had passed on the North line, the signal cleared for us. Willie pulled on the regulator and then gave a blast on the whistle. '162 gave an almighty slip, cylinder cocks roaring in unison. I banged the cocks shut as Willie closed, then almost immediately again opened the regulator. The time lag in the passage of steam meant that the slipping subsided as the regulator was closed, but then the pistons, with steam being re-admitted, caught the wheels when they were still just turning and got the engine over the dead point in the setting of the motion, and this time the driving wheels bit into the rails. As we swung out of the loop to the Up North Main, and with the colour light signals glowing a beckoning green in the gloaming, Willie pulled the regulator right out and into big valve and wound back the reverser. '162, with a distinct bark at the chimney, accelerated the heavy train down towards the Waverley. I fired into the back corners of the box and down each side as we entered the Haymarket tunnel since we would not be standing long before commencing our southwards journey, in Waverley. I did not however, at this point, put an injector on since blowing off, especially at night, was frowned upon in the station, and I would need all the water space I had to keep her quiet whilst waiting for the 'off'. In the Gardens we crossed over to the South lines before passing through the Mound Tunnel and running down Platforms 11 and 10. It was apparent that the holiday season was once more with us, since the length of the platform, one of the longest in the UK, was black with intending passengers. The always splendid '162 drew many admiring glances from a lot of the passengers as, almost silently now, we glided down to draw gently to a stand at the platform starting signal at the east end of the station.

Willie came across the cab and shouted in my ear, 'dinnae pit too much coal on until we clear Monktonhall for it's there that the speed restrictions end and only then will yer fire be stirred up. Ye'll only make a lot o' black smoke otherwise, and folks dinnae like it.' I nodded my thanks and set the injector to take up space in the boiler whilst keeping the needle off the red line, as we waited for the 'right away'. The station staff had done a good job of shepherding passengers into their allocated berths and the platform was now oddly empty. Five minutes to go and I packed another round of coal in behind the door and back corners. I also fired down the sides but left the fore-end alone, heeding Willie's words of wisdom. Pressure was rising quickly now and I was in somewhat of a panic in case we should blow off. At that point, whistles blew and the Guard's lamp glowed away at the back of the train. Willie wound the reverser out and pulled gently on the regulator. Steam hissed from the open cocks and perceptibly, but ever so slowly, '162 set her head down the falling gradient and eased the big train out into the half light of a glorious Scottish evening, 'Well, no one has been thrown out of bed with that start,' I thought '162 got her nose into Calton Tunnel South and with the merest breath of steam on the 1 in 70 falling gradient, accelerated the train up to the permitted 35 mph as, with a blast on the whistle, we plunged under the overbridge and swung through the centre of St. Margaret's MPD. Men paused amongst the many shadowy engines to watch us pass. Piershill Junction came and went, then Craigentinny, the yard busy with coaches being made up for early morning trains. Past Portobello station and then round the sweeping 'S' bends alongside Portobello yard. We had accelerated slightly but the engine was still running on first valve as we rattled across the junction with the Waverley route at Portobello East junction. Swinging now to the right we sped through Joppa station and passed Newhailes Junction. Willie let the reverser out a bit for the slight lift to Monktonhall and there was a perceptible spurt to our progress. Even at these lower speeds, it was quite apparent that the A1 was not in the same league as a Gresley when it came to riding and there was a distinct roll now developing as speed picked up.

Swinging again to the left we swept round the left-hand curve and over the Esk Viaduct at Monktonhall Junction. As '162' lifted her nose to the 1 in 300 gradient at Inveresk, out came the regulator to big valve, and all hell was let loose. '162 was really giving voice at the chimney and the effect on the fire was instantaneous, as was the effect on the ride. She really was developing a side to side pitch from nose to cab. I set the exhaust injector and began to fire. It was then I realised just how big the 50 square feet grate area on an A1 was. I packed the corners and fired around the sides and down the fore-end. Pausing to glance at the gauge, I was happy to see the needle just on the red line. I cleared the spillage from the floor and began to fire again. The fire wuffled back at me through the fire door as we plunged into the short, but very low, Morrison's Haven tunnel. Over the switchback of small, but telling gradients, Willie wound '162 in a bit, but she was still giving voice at the chimney. Through Prestonpans, we were soon running alongside the short dual carriageway that runs from Seton to Longniddry, and late night motorists took up the race. I paused in my firing to watch the headlights approach and draw level with us, but soon, the motorists had to brake and slow for Longniddry whilst we, in our lofty perch, continued our headlong rush, unchecked. Through Longniddry station and I returned to the shovel. A rattle

and a flash of lights as we cleared Drem and it was back once more to the shovel. I fired a round of coal, cleared and swept the floor and returned to firing, and so it went on. '162 was steaming like dream, but burning the coal at the same time. Dunbar soon passed in another flash of lights and Willie lengthened the cut off in preparation for the 1 in 200 up to Oxwellmains. We sped across the level plain through Innerwick where again, cut off was lengthened as we hit the 1 in 210 which was the precursor, gradient wise, to the climb to Grantshouse. I was firing almost constantly now, feeding the voracious appetite for coal. The injector was maintaining the boiler level nicely just above half a boiler. Willie wound her out some more as we hit the 1 in 96 and the weight of the train was really felt now as speed dropped. Out with the reverser again, and '162 was barking in the gloaming as we wound our way up through the Lammermuir hills. At around 30 mph we entered Penmanshiel tunnel, the sparks cascading down from the tunnel roof as we blasted our way through. Another round and then Willie was beckoning me to put the shovel down. We breasted the summit at Grantshouse and Willie wound the reverser back and patted the regulator half shut. The noise died away to a dull roar. I gratefully stuck my head out of my window and gulped in the cool, fresh air. The next seven miles were like a Sunday as we wound our way downhill, but with a fair bit of banging and clashing and a distinct roll, following the Eye water, a stream which had caused havoc as it swept all away before it, including seven railway bridges, after a cloudburst high up in the Lammermuirs some years before. The A1s just did not match the A3s and A4s, the latter particularly, when it came to smoothness of the ride and comfort on the footplate.

Through Reston, as we hit the dip before the Ayton curve, I returned to my fire. Pressure had dropped only slightly on our downhill rush but I was surprised to see the bars shining through as I recommenced firing. Pressure rose quickly again, a testament to the free steaming capabilities of these magnificent engines but the rate of firing was now much reduced as we swept down over the cliffs towards Berwick-upon-Tweed. We flashed past Marshall Meadows signal box which marked the end of the Scottish Region and crossed into Northumberland and England. Now I really was in foreign territory. Speed reduced, we slipped through Berwick station and across the splendid Royal Border Bridge. I took time to look down on the glittering lights of the town, reflecting in the still waters of the Tweed, whilst across to the North Sea, the evening sky was a deep purple and down the Northumberland coast could be seen the flash of lights from the many lighthouses. A slight lift up past Tweedmouth MPD, to Spittal, and then

another headlong rush downhill through Scremerston and on to the level between Goswick and Beal. We passed a freight train, looped to allow us passage, at Goswick, and speed increased again. As we passed Goswick signal box, Willie motioned me across and shouted in my ear. 'In a few minutes we'll be reaching Lucker troughs. Hae ye ever lifted water?' I shook my head. 'Weel, a'll gie ye the nod and you wind doon that handle as quick as ye can. Then I'll gie ye a shout and wind it back in as quick as ye can. OK?' I nodded again. Here was another first. We ran through Belford. Willie lifted up three fingers, then two, as I crossed to the tender end behind him and lifted the catch on the scoop handle. I also opened the 'walking stick' water indicator and noticed we still had water at the 2000 gallon hole. Willie gave a shout as the narrow strip of silver rushed towards us and I wound down the handle as quickly as possible. The effect was instantaneous as I felt the pull of water act against our forward motion. Another shout and, with much more difficulty, I wound the scoop back up, noting that water was now trickling out of the top hole, indicating a full tender. Willie gave me a nod and a smile as I returned to my shovel.

I was now feeling distinctly weary and longed for a wee break since the very act of firing on this footplate which rolled and crashed underfoot was tiring in the extreme. Across the bleak expanse of Embleton Moss we sped, the great bulk of Cheviot still visible as a dark silhouette against the summer night skyline. Up the 1 in 150 gradient which was Christon bank we roared, and up through Littlemill. Here the gradient changed once more dropping down a 1 in 170 gradient to Alnmouth as we passed the big radar station at Acklington. Another flash of lights as we rushed through Alnmouth and I thought, 'well only 30 miles or so now', remembering my geography. It was now really too dark to see clearly the most attractive seaside town of Alnmouth, clustered on a small hillside to our left above a beautiful beach, but the lights of the town sparkled and winked in the darkness. Over the myriad of small ups and downs we rushed and it felt like no time at all that we were sweeping over the viaduct that took the railway across the River Wansbeck and then the brakes were going hard on at Pegswood to steady our progress round the approaching Morpeth curve. I laid down my firing shovel and sat up on my seat as we approached Morpeth station for I had heard about this most severe curve and the fact that no one in right mind would attempt to fire while going round it. As we cleared the platform, the line swung immediately away to the left and the train slid round the curve at a sedate 40 mph with a squealing of the drivers on the check rails. We cleared the curve having changed direction to now head due south and SAINT JOHNSTOUN was being opened up again as I bent my back once more. This was now feeling like an awfully long 30 miles.

Over the wee switchback we sped and the fields gradually gave way to houses. At Forest Hall, Willie motioned that I should put down the shovel and push forward the coal at the back of the door. This I did with the poker, and closing the flap, gratefully sat down and enjoyed the last few miles down into Newcastle. Steam pressure had come back to about 230 lbs but was holding there and as we slid down through Heaton station, I shut the injector. We ground down past a signal cabin I was amused to see named Argyle Street, and swung through Manors station before crashing our way across the biggest diamond crossing in the world and coming to a stand, on time, in Newcastle Central station. No time to waste as we were coupled off (at Newcastle, for safety reasons, Haymarket Firemen generally did not couple and uncouple because of the presence of the electrified third rail) and as we pulled away on to the King Edward Bridge we passed the grimy Gateshead A1 which was waiting to work the train right through to Kings Cross. At that point, I certainly did not envy the Gateshead Fireman his night's work. We entered Gateshead shed where a relief crew were waiting to coal and prepare '162 for our return journey, whilst we went to have a well earned, and much needed cup of tea or six. I did however, take some time to have a look around Gateshead shed and was fascinated by the roundhouse construction. I was also amazed to learn that one could obtain a hot meal in the canteen, round the clock.

We worked the 20.20 ex-Kings Cross to Edinburgh back and were due away from Newcastle at 02.31. At our booked time we ran out to the shed exit in preparation for running to the station. At Gateshead, there was a one-way system which meant that on arrival from Edinburgh, there was no need for a turntable as the engine just ran through Gateshead nose first and reversed over the High Level Bridge to access the station at the north end. We duly backed on to the High Level bridge where we were held, waiting the arrival of the train from the south. This was extremely convenient as it was possible to watch for the incoming train as it passed over the King Edward Bridge up river. In waiting, all the activity on the Tyne below was there to interest and amuse.

Before long, we saw the lights of our train move slowly across the King Edward Bridge upstream and I bent to put some coal behind the doors, into the back corners and down each side while Willie gave a touch of the blower. The fire leapt into life changing from languid orange flames to a yellow glare and with a roar of some urgency. I put on the live steam injector to get the boiler nicely filled, giving the footplate a wash down at the same time. Outside, the signal came off and with cylinder cocks roaring in the darkness, we slid backwards towards the station. As we did so, the incoming engine slipped past us, the crew giving an acknowledging wave as we passed. Again, the Shunter was waiting to couple on for me and whilst he attended to that job, I turned again to my fire. I knew from listening to the regular Firemen that the lift up to Forest Hall was the big hurdle with a 'cold' engine and had also noted the gradient which we had recently descended. I got a big fire in and watched as pressure increased. The boiler was sitting nicely about ¾ full and pressure was around 220 lbs and rising. We had a much lighter train and a much easier set of timings and, according to Willie, it would be 'a dawdle.' Whistles pierced the night shadows of the station and slowly SAINT JOHNSTOUN moved the train out into the night. We banged and crashed across the big diamond crossing which was in fact a whole series of diamonds in multiple and swung round through the platforms at Manors. As we cleared the speed restriction through that station, '162 gave voice at the chimney as Willie lengthened the cut-off for the climb up to Heaton and on beyond. I started firing and had pressure sitting nicely on the red mark. As we cleared Heaton station, '162 started to blow off and I hurriedly slammed on the exhaust injector, knowing that I would not be popular with any sleepers in the surrounding properties. We swung away to the left passing Heaton engine sheds on the right. In the smoky gloom, I could just make out silhouettes of locomotives slumbering, waiting their next turn of duty.

The remainder of the trip was uneventful and again, I coped with the scoop at Lucker. I was, however, pleased to see the outline of 'Auld Reekie' and home, as we cleared Cockburnspath and raced down to the East Lothian plain. I reckoned that, overall, I had probably shovelled around seven or eight tons of coal, and my arms were feeling it. Without doubt, firing on the 'coast' put trips to Dundee, Perth and Glasgow into perspective, in terms of firing. I could only think just what seven nights on these jobs were like, for that was the diagrammed work in both Nos.1 and 2 links. The rewards were a result of the fact that Newcastle was a mileage job, in that over the first 140 miles, the crew received another 60 minutes payment for every 15 miles run. On a round trip of 265 miles, this was a worthwhile bonus and, of course, there was the night duty enhancement on top. A week of seven nights on the 'coast, which included a full Sunday, brought the participants money that I certainly could only dream of, but money which was earned at a price. Nevertheless, when I received my week's wages for this particular week, I was well pleased with the additional money.

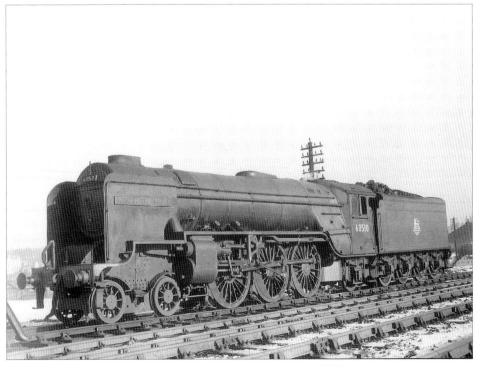

A2/1 60510 ROBERT THE BRUCE stands up at the buffer stops at the west end of the shed on a wintry day in February, 1955. (J. Robertson/ Transport Treasury)

N15 69220 ambles off the 'Sub' at Haymarket Central Junction with the return working of the 'Sub goods' on 5th November 1955. The train is a light one and I wonder if the Fireman had to resort to one-handed firing as I was required to do some two years later. (J. Robertson/Transport Treasury)

24. SOME CHARACTERS

Like every establishment where a large number of people were to be found at any given time, Haymarket had a more than a fair share of real characters and there was always some fun or other entertainment. Indeed, with so many young men together at any one time in the winter months, there was always some mischief afoot, mischief which then sometimes gave hours of merriment to others. Take the case of the disappearing pianos for instance.

Immediately opposite the shed, on the south side of the main lines, was the Russell Road depot of the Edinburgh Corporation Cleansing Department. Now, in those days, and with people being allocated new council houses, many had pianos which were old-fashioned and which were never going to sit comfortably in the modern housing of the day even if they could be got through the doors, which many could not. There was, however, no market for second-hand pianos, and thus Edinburgh Corporation started a collection process for discarded pianos, and they were brought to Russell Road depot and stored, for what eventuality I know not. Anyway, in the fullness of time, it was discovered by the staff at the Cleansing depot that some pianos had gone walkabouts. Suspicion immediately fell upon, where else, but Haymarket and the Cleaners. The police were involved and the depot was searched. The Shed Master steadfastly supported his staff and stated that he would never believe that his men had been involved. In any case how could heavy pianos be carried across four sets of main running lines and indeed, who would even contemplate such a thing and for what purpose? No, it was impossible!

Nothing was found and apologies were made, and accepted, but the pianos were still missing. Time went past and the uproar has been all but forgotten when the Shed Master decided that the old air raid shelters standing near the shed exit should be pressed into use as additional storage space for such items as firelighters, bales of cotton waste and the like which were bulky and took up valuable space in the material stores. The air raid shelters were the standard square brick buildings with a flat concrete roof and no windows, and had been long unused. The Labourers were sent to clear out and stock the shelters, and lo and behold, what did they find but several pianos gathering dust in the gloom. This of course gave rise to much hilarity and became a main topic of discussion in the Drivers' bothy for weeks.

One old Thornton Driver happened to be in the bothy when the story was being related for the umpteenth time. He listened closely and then said to the assembled company, 'you dinnae ken jist hoo relieved I am tae hear what ye are sayin'. Ye see, I wis comin' in throught the toon wi' a freight early in the morning some weeks ago and we were jist approaching Haymarket Central Box when my mate says, 'here, will ye come ower and see this silly bugger! I crossed the cab and looked oot, and dae ye ken, there was someone sitting in atween the lines playin' a piano. We were gaun tae report it at Waverley but efter some discussion, we thocht, wha' the hell will believe us an'so we jist said naethin', but man, I've been sair worried ever since an' thinkin' I wis beginning' tae see things.' This revelation set the bothy off once more.

Amongst my fellow Cleaners I had quickly found out those I could relate to and those who were just never going to be anything other than people I had to work with. As it turned out, I gravitated towards those who, like myself, were on the railway because it was in the blood, as it were. Others were there because it was a job and had neither interest nor indeed much loyalty. They just turned up, did the job and drew their money at the end of the week. Now, in retrospect, perhaps they could not be faulted because very few of the Cleaners I worked with, myself included, were ever likely to become registered Firemen, and the senior ones who did so must have asked themselves, why? The diesels were coming and coming fast. At this time it was mainly DMU railcars but Haymarket was losing steam work and in the very near future, Cleaners and Firemen were to be asked, and indeed paid, to leave the industry.

However, back the characters. One who stood out larger than life was a country lad who hailed from Bonnyrigg to the south of Edinburgh. His name was Willie Titzell and he did have a full career. He transferred to Corkerhill for his appointment as Fireman, and whilst there, excelled himself by falling out the engine when uplifting the train staff for the Renfrew branch. In fact, he was very lucky to escape serious injury and it was not in any way his fault. He had been holding on to the cab handrail as he leant out, when it gave way. It was afterwards said, perhaps unkindly, that only he could have fallen on his head and broken a leg. He then moved south to get married, finishing up as an electric Driver at, I think, Slade Green on the Southern Region. He did, I know, act as a Locomotive Inspector on the Southern although I do not know if he was ever appointed as such.

Willie was good bit senior to me and spent a lot of time firing. He had a great capacity for hard work and could he shovel coal. He fired a lot on the main line and encouraged the younger Drivers who were about as daft as he was, to have a go, and noise, plus lots of black smoke, generally accompanied his progress. He had, in a previous summer, spent a lot of time firing to Driver George Elliot in No.2 link. Now, Driver Elliot had suffered some serious personal trauma, and these were the days when counselling was just unheard of. In more enlightened times, Driver Elliot would have been afforded a significant degree of assistance, attention and support in coming to terms with his problems. Instead, he was left to soldier on, and in this he was aided and abetted by Willie. The upshot was that Driver Elliot was taken down from No.2 link, and confined to shed duties (the turntable as it turned out) because of persistent speeding. It was a tragedy which just should never have happened.

Another character, but for other reasons, was an older lad, one George K*** and even yet I will not identify him further. He was deep thinking, educated man who was well read and with whom real intellectual conversations were possible. George, in my last year on the footplate, became the official Call Boy, taking telegrams round to men advising of changes of duty etc. He was married to a young French lass and they had a baby daughter. When I transferred on to the clerical side of the depot and covered for Roster Clerk, I had close contact with George and we became friendly. I was appalled to read in the paper, some time after I had left Haymarket that he had been arrested for murder and indeed pleaded guilty to, and was eventually jailed for what turned out to be a bizarre and most brutal, pre-meditated crime. The details are not for this book, but I realised then that one could never be sure about people.

I think one of the saddest incidents involving a Haymarket Cleaner, apart from the fatality described in an earlier chapter, centred around another fairly senior Cleaner, named James Marshall. James came from the village of Dalmeny, just at the south end of the Forth Bridge. When Cleaners and Firemen were being offered financial 'carrots' to leave the service as the diesels came in, James applied for a transfer to the Painting Squad on the Forth Bridge, where his father was employed. The transfer came through and James joined his father on the bridge. I was horrified to learn some time later that James had fallen from the bridge at the North Queensferry end, on to the road below, and had been killed instantly. The tragedy was compounded several years later, and indeed almost to the day, when his

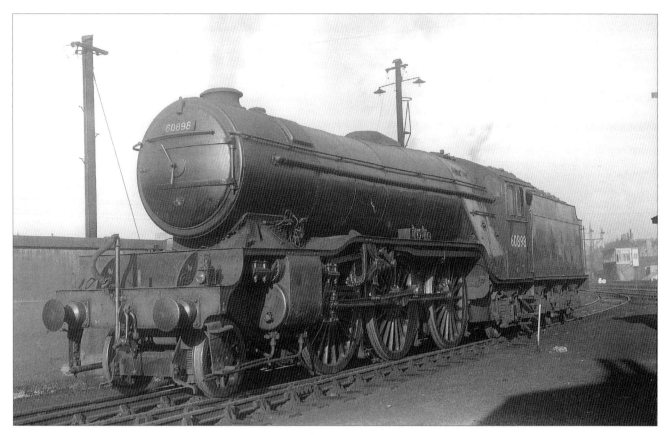

An Aberdeen Ferryhill V2, 60898, at the Haymarket exit points at on 28th March 1959. Having almost wrecked the turntable at Dundee Tay Bridge in 1957 with A2 60535 HORNET'S BEAUTY and there being no other suitable engine to work a heavy passenger train from Aberdeen southwards, my mate, Driver W. Donaldson agreed to work the incoming engine onwards and this was it. On the journey from Dundee I cleared the tender of coal and had it swept and washed out when we arrived on shed. (M. Robertson/Transport Treasury)

father fell from the bridge into the River Forth. His body was never recovered. Later, much later, I came to know James's mother who kept the Post Office in Dalmeny village, and she was a lovely, elderly lady who had little reason to like the Forth Bridge.

Other Cleaners there were, characters in their own right. There was David Whitelaw, railway daft, who transferred to the Midland shed at Birmingham Saltley and found that, because of his age, he was eligible to be passed out for driving. I understand that he declined to do so and went to the Post Office instead. He and his ilk were a sad loss to the industry in these trying times. Then there were the others who were no great loss to the industry. One Cleaner, a fairly senior Cleaner named Diamond, did not cover himself with glory one night when firing on the 17.15 Glasgow Queen Street, but he did cover the detraining passengers with soot and dirty water when he allowed No.60012 to blow off as it stood under the big, low, soot-encrusted beam at the buffer-end of Queen Street Station. That cost BR big money in compensation.

It was, as I started to pen these lines, a sad reflection that I could not recall any other Cleaner with whom I worked at Haymarket, and who continued in railway service and made a career, as I did, other than Willie Titzell. There may have been one or two but, in my 38 years with British Rail and twelve subsequent years in railway consultancy, I have never, ever, come

across an ex-colleague from those cleaning days, in any part of the railway in Scotland. This, I think, is the biggest indicator of how the rail industry became less and less labour intensive as steam was worked out. It is also very much a personal opinion, but I do honestly feel that the loss of a whole generation of footplatemen who were serving the long apprenticeship on the road to becoming Drivers was very much to the detriment of the railway and was very much a factor in the increasing rate of signals being passed at danger, a situation which later reached almost epidemic proportions. It was caused, I suspect, mainly by wholly inexperienced (in terms of railway knowledge) people being recruited and trained as Drivers, straight from the streets. Youngsters, like myself, who started cleaning and went on to do many years 'on the shovel', and over all routes worked from the depot, gained an in-depth level of route knowledge which could not be taught in a classroom.

The Firemen and Passed Firemen at Haymarket were all experienced men who had put in a fair bit of railway service. At that time, the senior un-appointed (to Driver) Passed Fireman was Jock Grieve who had started away back in 1935. Some 27 years later, he was still a Fireman although, in reality, he was driving most of the time. But he was not an 'appointed' Driver. Younger Firemen who had transferred away to become Drivers at other depots could

in fact, by application of the 'first preference' clause in the Promotion, Transfer & Redundancy Agreement (PT&R), come back to Haymarket as Drivers, although few ever did. But had they done so, they would have been senior to Jock until such times as he was appointed; then, and only then, would he take his proper place in seniority in the driving roster. The reason for staying at Haymarket was the mileage money and the ability to earn what at that time was, in anyone's books, good money. Yet the reality was that pay packets could be, and generally were, much larger at depots like St. Margarets, where freight was the primary traffic and overtime was the norm on many of the freight turns.

The younger Passed Firemen at Haymarket during my time were also very experienced men and, generally, very competent Drivers. Many had started in the early war years and were almost immediately out firing, never to return to cleaning. Accordingly, by having been brought up in such a hard school, they were immensely experienced and by the time most were passed for driving, they could sign a route card which was impressive in the extreme, especially for such young men. They could also competently take over an A3 or A4 and run with the hardest of the experienced Drivers. These Passed Firemen were, collectively, the most likely to hand over the controls of an engine to us young Cleaners and guide and encourage us to have a go. And yet, many of these same Passed Firemen went back firing in the top links over the winter, every winter. It has to be said that my path crossed with many of these younger Drivers and Passed Firemen over the years, as they went on to drive on all forms of modern traction, and to good effect.

And so there was 'Hamish', a.k.a Jimmy Horsburgh, a larger than life character who was often heard before being seen, and was always laughing. Ike Colgan, another comedian, was a man with a flair for writing. His reports were a joy to read, grammatically correct, spelling impeccable and beautifully written in flowing copperplate. It was he who had the turn with *'the most outstanding debutante of the season'* described earlier on in this book. There was 'Blondie', one Alex McLean who, like Hamish, was also often heard before he was seen. Men like Alec Gunn, Tommy Glass, Angus Wylie, Gus McDonald, Willie Inglis, George Paterson, Jimmy McCallum and many, many others, far too numerous to mention, were all outstanding mates and mentors to us younger Cleaners and to them and the others, I owe a debt of gratitude for the guidance, knowledge and support given. This was all to stand me in such good stead as I progressed up through the management ranks in my later years. There of course, were some black sheep. Some, well one or two, were downright unpleasant, and poor mates, whilst others were still in their daft days.

Passed Fireman Bob Johnstone No.2 (to distinguish him from Bob Johnstone No.1, an older hand and a junior Driver) was one such character. He rejoiced in the nickname of 'Tulips', I know not why, and I fired to him quite a bit. Overweight, a fondness for beer was his distinguishing characteristic and at that time (1958) when not driving, he was booked firing in the top link with George Spilsbury and A4 Pacific 'No.12' during the summer timetable period. I recall one day cadging a lift back to Haymarket on the footplate of an A3 which he and his mate, another but younger Passed Cleaner, had just relieved at Waverley. He handed over the regulator not to his mate, but to me. As we came up through the Gardens, the discussion turned to detonators and their use. His young mate admitted that he had never actually looked inside the tin to see what a detonator looked like and had never heard one being exploded. Bob went into great detail about the explosive force of detonators and how they must be treated with extreme care. I was having a hard time concentrating on driving the engine whilst trying to follow Bob's words of wisdom. It was then that some imp of mischief caused his young mate to speculate on what might happen if, say, a detonator accidentally got into the firebox. 'Let's find oot,' says the bold Bob and in a

wink, into the firebox went the full canister of detonators, and he shut the flap. Instantly, expecting the obvious, I leant as far out of the cab window as possible, when there was a muffled 'whump' followed by a sheet of flame, cinders and dust, hitting the tender end. As we ran into the shed I was still in shock, but not quite so shocked as 'Tulips' and his mate, and I was relieved when we stopped on the turntable. I secured the engine and had a quick look in the firebox. The brick arch was on top of the fire or what was left of it. I climbed down and left Bob and his mate to explain that little lot away.

There was Alec Gunn, a really nice man, a good mate and with a wicked sense of humour. I fired to Alec several times, and even after my footplate days were behind me, travelled with him on the footplate on several occasions. Alec transferred to York as a Driver after I had left Haymarket. Whilst still at 64B and in a response to a 'time lost' report, he claimed the lost time was due to low steam and an inexperienced Fireman, or as he succinctly put it, 'I doubt if he could have fired s***e at his Mother-in-law's photograph.' Oh, the penmanship at Haymarket in those days.

Yes, there were the moaners and poor mates, but they were, thankfully, in the minority and, as Cleaners, we were being trained to act and think as footplatemen. That was, always to be unpredictable and never react the in same way twice to any given situation. Yes, we were taught by masters and by their example.

For instance, I was booked firing all of one week, 6.00pm relief and ECS working. My mate was one of the Campbell brothers at 64B, Freddie it was. Towards the latter part of our shift each evening we went down light engine to Craigentinny and brought up a massive lift of empty coaches to be split and set for the morning services. Now this lift consisted of some 22 or 23 coaches and all week, we had been allocated a B1. Freddie let me do a lot of the driving during the shift, but not when we were bringing up that big train. On the first night, whilst shunting at the east end of Waverley, we had to run down to the Limit of Shunt (LOS) inside the North Calton Tunnel and then come back across the station throat. I had taken 61245 into the tunnel and stopped at the LOS. Whilst I was reversing her, the fire screen on the Driver's side swung across and the top edge caught my inner arm at wrist level. Now these screens were provided to reduce glare and heat for the Driver, and were made of thin sheet metal. The corner edge entered my arm just above the wrist and because of the winding movement of my arm, tore a deep cut right up my arm to just below my elbow. I got the engine out the tunnel and then had a look at the damage, which was, surprisingly, not very painful. However, it was spectacular and

blood was flowing everywhere. Freddie was appalled. Quick as flash, he secured the engine and shot off to 'phone the Signalman. That done, he sought out the shift first-aid man in the station, and soon I had the wound dressed and bandaged. Indeed, the first aid man was of the opinion that I should go to Edinburgh Royal Infirmary to have the gash stitched, but he dressed it nevertheless, and most efficiently. Freddie then telephoned the Signalman again, who then, in conjunction with the District Control at Waverley, made arrangements for the last part of our diagram to be carried out by someone else. We then got the road back to the shed. Freddie could not have been more caring, nor could the Signalmen in Waverley West and District Control been more accommodating.

The next night, we brought our big lift up to Nos.1 and 19 platforms, the North Main, and we got a green right out into the Mound Tunnel. The Shunter joined us at the west end of the platform and gave us our instructions about the shunts required. Now, there were two West End Waverley pilots to do all the shunting, but after all, everyone had pulled out the stops for us the previous evening, so we set to and shunted until all coaches were placed. As we did so, we saw the Pilot crews, sitting in the Shunters' bothy playing dominoes, but Freddie said nothing. The next evening was a repeat and again we did all the shunting without comment.

The following evening, when coming up the North Main, we received the green signal but Freddie stopped and told me to couple off. This was done and we pulled forward to the west end. The signal went to red in our face. The Signalman and the Shunter were going ballistic. 'Why had we coupled off?' they howled. 'Because we are only booked to bring the coaches into the station,' my mate shouted back. 'Go back, couple up and bring them out to shunt them,' was the instruction. 'Not our job. That's whit you've got two pilots for. We're gaun tae the shed,' he shouted back. 'But you've shunted the coaches for the last two nights,' the Shunter pleaded. 'Tough, it's no on oor diagram,' replied Freddie. The Signalman re-joined the fray. 'You'll sit there all night or until you do the shunt, Driver, for your not getting the road to the shed,' he shouted. Freddie turned to me and said, 'take doon the clinker shovel from the tender end mate, and pit it in the fire.' I obeyed, fascinated by this power play. Freddie shouted back to the Signalman 'that's OK! We're short of water so I'll jist drop the fire here.' My supposed activity with the clinker shovel showed we were serious. There was an anguished howl from the box followed by language which even yet, is unprintable and would have had even a navvy blushing. There was just no way the Signalman could permit a Driver to drop his fire on top of the

West End points, crossings and cable runs and so we had won the war of nerves. The road came off and we went to the shed. 'The lesson is, son, always keep the b******s guessing and never do the same thing twice,' said Freddie as we rumbled our way homewards. 'Now what really was the point of all that?' I pondered later, but nevertheless tucked that experience away into the inner recesses of my mind for future use.

Then there were the other brother acts at Haymarket, as well as the father and son acts. There were two brothers who even yet I will decline to identify further, and who just never saw eye to eye. Things were so bad that on one occasion, the older of the two, on holiday and bent on taking his wife and youngsters to the seaside on the Fife coast, was standing on the platform at Haymarket station, waiting for the train. As it ran in, he saw that it was his younger brother at the controls. He would not let his family join the train, but sought a refund of fare and denied the children their day's outing, all because he did not think his brother was up to the job.

There were another two at 64B, the Redden brothers; Alex, a Passed man and Walter (Wattie), the younger. It was, I think, Wattie, who was the unofficial 'visitor' on the footplate of A3 60066 MERRY HAMPTON on that fateful Sunday 26th October 1947. On that day, when working the 11.15 Edinburgh to London Kings Cross passenger train, the Driver, Tom Begbie, had failed to read the Late Notice case at the shed and was thus unaware of re-scheduled bridge work requiring a diversion to the Goods line at Goswick. The train consisted of 15 coaches all heavily laden and on approach to Goswick the Driver failed to observe the sequence of the signals and entered Goswick loop at a speed of 60 mph instead of 15 mph. The engine and nine coaches turned over into a deep ditch which ran parallel to the loop and 28 people were killed, with a high number of seriously injured.

Wattie Redden was, at that time, a National Service Naval Rating who had the intention to follow his brother to railway (footplate) service and was unofficially riding on the footplate that day. He was also badly hurt in the accident but at the Inquiry which followed there was no evidence presented to suggest that his presence on the footplate, irregular although it was, had any bearing on the accident. Tom Begbie's grandson was a Cleaner at Haymarket and was a bit senior to myself.

Some Firemen deserve a mention for other reasons. Jimmy Hogg was one of the younger Passed Firemen and Jimmy was, well, rotund to say the least and rejoiced in the nickname 'Podge'. Despite his girth, and on one occasion whilst firing on the Carlisle road on, I think, 60097 HUMORIST, the vacuum brake cylinder underneath the engine came adrift and dropped down, fouling the track. Jimmy crawled underneath, no mean feat for a big man, and secured the cylinder safely clear of the track, and the train continued to the first point where '97 could be replaced. He received, quite properly, a commendation for this action. Jimmy, as a Driver in the late 1980s, was frequently to be seen at the controls of the preserved A4 60009 UNION OF SOUTH AFRICA on her main line running. Jimmy was also an outstanding ice skater and played ice hockey, I believe. He was also, like many other Drivers and Firemen, a member of the Royal Engineers (Territorial Army) Railways and Ports Squadron and later Royal Corps of Transport (275 Squadron), for many years.

It was, however, the Drivers at Haymarket who topped the bill. In No.1 link, as we have already discussed, there was 'the Undertaker', well named and fitting the role to a 'T'. But then there was 'the Iron Man'. This was Jimmy Laird who ran No.9 with Bob Gemmell, an ex-Bathgate man. I once saw Jimmy fall from the running plate of No.60009 while preparing her for the 'Early Aberdeen'. At that time he was certainly in his sixties and he fell from a kneeling

Driver Peter Robertson and Passed Fireman J. Wilson pose in front of immaculate A1 60161 NORTH BRITISH, at the east end of the shed in April 1956. At this time, No.3 link worked the Up *QUEEN OF SCOTS* Pullman south from Waverley and it is thought that this is the allocated locomotive for this working. The headlamps and headboard will be uplifted at the kit store when the engine pulls forward to the shed exit. (J. Robertson/Transport Treasury)

position on the running plate to the shed floor, landing on his back, a fall of nearly seven feet. Now, I do not think that, at 18, I would have got up from such a fall, at least not quickly, but Jimmy leapt to his feet, and, with a string of oaths, drew back his foot and kicked a can of engine oil, a nearly full 8 pint can of engine oil, across four roads of the shed. Iron Man indeed!

Of the others in No.1 link, well there was Bill Nairn, fully described in Norman McKillop's book *Enginemen Elite*, as was Tommy Smith, both legends in their own right. Dickie Bell was a short man who could drive fast and furiously, as required, as could his mate, Tom Fell. Tom became a Locomotive Inspector during my time at 64B and was a first class engineman. Two of his sons followed in his footsteps, Ronnie who was a Passed Fireman when I joined, and Donald, who was passed out, again during my time at Haymarket.

Indeed, there was only one real discord in No.1 link at that time, and that was Bob Porteous. He was just basically a poor Driver, was in the link purely because of his seniority and failed entirely to uphold the otherwise high driving performance of the link. He just could not run to time. When he was working on other than the Newcastle road, he drove erratically and at a speed which was generally too fast for the road concerned. On the Newcastle turns he just did not run and keep time and indeed was known on occasions to drop time for no good reason. Why he was not just taken off I will never know, but even the union representative complained about how he let the top link down.

In No.2 link the Drivers were all competent hands who could run the diagrammed jobs to perfection with, perhaps, the exception of Peter Motion, who could also, on occasions, drive somewhat erratically and in the mode 'a la Porteous'.

No.3 link was much the same with many hard runners, but one Driver stood out head and shoulders above the rest when it came to having a go. I refer to Driver Peter B. Robertson, a man to whom I had the opportunity to fire to only once (officially) and with whom I became friendly, long after I had left Haymarket. Peter set up some remarkable times, especially on the East Coast and his performances have been widely recorded in both magazines such as the *Trains Illustrated* by recorders like C.J. Allen, and also in books, by O.S. Nock.

To quote an example, Peter loved nothing more than the challenge of a late start from Newcastle and I treasure the extract from the Control Log in Edinburgh Control, in respect of such a run. This was obtained for me by a good friend, Fergus Gibson, who was Traffic Apprentice at the time. Peter had worked the morning 'Talisman' to Newcastle and was working the Down train back. The date was Tuesday 17th November 1959. The down 'Talisman' from Kings Cross had been worked to Newcastle by Kings Cross Top Shed Driver Newlands, with A4 60019. The train consisted of nine coaches only, 307 tons tare. Driver Newlands had had a miserable run and had passed into the North Eastern Region at Shaftholme Junction some 17 minutes late. From there north, partly due to signals, and some poor running, he dropped another three minutes by Northallerton. However, things then improved and he eventually arrived into Newcastle Central only 16 minutes adrift.

A further two minutes delay was incurred in the engine changeover because of a vacuum problem as Peter, with 60031 GOLDEN PLOVER, took over. He set out northwards, 18 minutes late. The intermediate running details are scanty but the control log shows Peter passing Marshall Meadows Signal Box (entering the Scottish Region) only 8 minutes adrift, and by Dunbar he was 6 minutes late. By Monktonhall Junction, he was only 4 minutes late and drew to a stand in Waverley only 3 minutes down. Even with a limited load train fitted with roller bearings, to pick up 15 minutes on an already tightly timed train over the 125 miles between Newcastle and Edinburgh was a feat of the utmost skill, yet Peter could repeat this time after time. In the course of that run, I think that 60031 must have reached close to, if not exceeded, the magic 100 mph down Christon Bank. Peter had been timed (and documented by other respected recorders) as regularly reaching the nineties over this stretch whilst recovering a lesser amount of lost time.

Peter was, as they say, worth the watching and was an undoubted thorn in the side of management. The late Charlie Meacher wrote of Peter's almost absolute lack of respect for his superiors as a young Driver and he certainly did not improve with age. Despite being on good terms with him, he slipped a fast one over me one Saturday, long after I had left the footplate ranks, and that will be related later on. Peter was also a bit of an amateur journalist/writer and wrote articles for *The Scotsman* newspaper, the *Sunday Post* and, on occasions, slipped 'inside' stories to the *Daily Express*. Many of these stories embarrassed and annoyed management.

For example, Peter was at the controls of a Goucester Twin DMU on a North Berwick turn soon after their introduction. The set became derailed at the famous curved crossover between the platforms for some now forgotten reason, but the first the Station Master and District Control knew of the incident was when the *Daily Express* photographer and a journalist turned up and started asking questions. Peter had seized the moment to make a bob or two on the side by contacting the press, at the same time failing to advise the powers that be.

However, his real moment of notoriety came about 1960/61, when he had 60031 GOLDEN PLOVER (again) on the backshift 'Talisman'. Now '31 had been prepared by Willie Inglis, one of the better and more conscientious senior Passed Firemen at Haymarket. Some time after the engine had gone off shed and indeed after the train had left Waverley, Willie went into the bothy for his break. He washed his hands and feeling for a cloth to dry them, came across a cork in his jacket pocket. It was the cork out of the oil reservoir on the middle big end of '31. Willie lost no time in alerting the Running Foreman who, in turn, immediately advised Control to have train stopped and '31 taken off for examination at the first suitable point, since there was the very real risk that she would be throwing oil out of the reservoir.

The scene changes to Berwick where at this very time, Peter was running off the Royal Border Bridge in preparation for accelerating away south, but the signals at Tweedmouth were set against him. The 'Talisman' was brought to a stand opposite Tweedmouth shed and the Running Foremen there instructed that '31 was to come off the train as a failure. When told the reason, Peter offered to squeeze underneath, fill up the middle big end, replace the cork and go forward but no, the engine had to come off. Peter was given a rather down-at-the-mouth Tweedmouth V2 and went on to lose a packet of time to Newcastle more, I think, out of spite than necessity. There, on the front page of the Daily Express the following day was an article headed *Just Fancy! Main Line Express Train Delayed By a Missing Cork*. Peter had had his revenge.

I do know that Peter had started putting together an autobiographical book after he retired, and it also must be said that he did have a considerable talent for writing, a talent which I considered, vastly exceeded that of an earlier Haymarket author. He showed me a rough draft, along with many of the photographs with which he intended to illustrate it, and quite a well-written and valuable documentary on a footplate career, which commenced away back on the NBR, it would have been. Sadly, Peter died very shortly thereafter and on making inquiries of his wife some time after his funeral, I discovered that the draft of his book and photographs had been destroyed.

In the Goods link, the real character was Peter Bowie or, to use his nickname, Davy Crockett. This was after the popular TV series of the time and because Peter turned up to work of an evening wearing a real coonskin hat Davy Crockett style. Peter had also another claim to fame (or notoriety). In the brewing industry, in particular the bottling process, any spillage was run off through drains in the conveyor or whatever, and collected in a spillage container. The spilled, and collected, beer was known locally, I am led to believe, as 'pundy' and was collected in big containers. Now, what happened to the 'pundy' I know not, but there were 23 Breweries in Edinburgh at this time, and at least three lay in close proximity to 64B. Indeed, there might have been more. Peter had a key for one of these Brewery 'pundy houses' and was reputed to take an ample fill each time he passed going to and from work. Now, Drivers and Firemen coming on duty having had a beer or two was not unusual, as was the practice of dropping in for a quick one when walking to and from the depot on relief turns, and management did not actively discourage this practice, but Peter, in the Goods link, and in the wee sma' hours often appeared to have partaken generously. Small wonder he was also known, sometimes, as 'Pundy Pete'.

Amongst the running Fitters there were some real characters. The 'crème de la crème' were the Examination Fitters. This fine body of men were responsible for carrying out an almost microscopic examination of each locomotive before it entered traffic, and this they did with the assistance of a helmet mounted miner's lamp and a long shafted hammer, similar to that used by wheel-tappers. They would go round each engine, peering into the dark recesses, and tapping this and tapping that. This they would then repeat under each engine before signing the engine off as fit for traffic. Now these Fitters did a great job and found faults which would see a locomotive failed on occasion.

One of their number was a man called Alex Barrowman, who had been a Doctor, a GP, before being struck off the Register for some infringement or other. Now, how a Doctor of Medicine came to have qualifications which allowed him to be a railway Fitter, and an Examining Fitter to boot, I never, ever, did find out but, in the course of time, and certainly after I joined the Clerical ranks at Haymarket, one day the morning tabloids were full of the fact that Fitter Barrowman had finally, after many years, succeeded in getting himself re-instated on the register as a Doctor, a GP and a fully qualified medical person. And so he left 64B to take up medicine again and I have often had the vision since, of this newly re-appointed Doctor, sitting his patients down on a bed and slowly going around them, with miner's light illuminated, peering into their dark recesses and tapping them here and there with his long shafted hammer.

The Running Fitters and their mates were a unique breed and, as already described, spent a lot of their time in petty arguments, arguments which sometimes led to drastic actions in order to prove a point. On one occasion, a row raged about the steam passages from the cylinders to the blast pipe of a locomotive. This was during a nightshift and the sight of several Fitters, all grown men, red in the face and howling at each other like spoilt children, provided a bit of light relief for us Cleaners. Then, quite dramatically, one of the Fitter's mates climbed up into the open smokebox of one of our A4s waiting preparation. Taking a bolt from his pocket, he dropped it down the blastpipe. Hardly had he done so when the enormity of the action struck home to the more learned of the group. Whilst he was listening to hear where the bolt might be going, the rest were just going, and very fast! 60024 was immediately stopped and of course, had to have all piston and valves stripped down for the offending bolt to be removed. The nut with the bolt got several days in the house to reflect on his actions.

We had but one Joiner at Haymarket whose main employment was the renewal of engine floor boards. These suffered from wear and tear, not to mention the effects of hot coals, and thus required renewal or partial replacement at fairly regular intervals. This Stewart did, armed only with an axe and a saw. He was never seen with any other tools, just an axe and a saw. One day he was called to the General Office to attend to the door which was fouling the floor and sticking. Bets were taken as to what Stewart could do with his axe and saw to cure this. Wonder of wonders, he turned up with a *plane* and proceeded to plane the floorboards down. Everyone took great care where exactly they put their feet when entering or leaving the office thereafter.

The Running Foremen were also a breed apart. The senior Running Foreman was Ross Dougan, an NB man and a man who received very full coverage in Norman McKillop's *Enginemen Elite*. Ross was one of the old school and a martinet. The Cleaners, indeed everyone, walked softly on Ross's shift. However, while a man who worked 'by the book' he was also scrupulously fair, and it must be said that he backed many of us Cleaners when booked out firing, when the Driver did not want to take us. Quite simply, if you did your job, Ross never bothered you.

It was during one night shift in the early part of 1958 that we Cleaners had been mucking around between engines and someone had picked up a big brass nut and tossed it into the group. The nut was then thrown from hand to hand until the Gaffer shouted the number of the next engine to be cleaned. Someone then tossed the nut away, just as an Examining Fitter stepped out of the fitting shop door. The bolt hit him on the forehead and down he went. Ross came storming up the shed seeking the culprit but no one would own up, and no one would tell tales. The upshot was that the whole squad were booked off duty and told to go home. However,

before we could all do so, the Fitter who had been injured made it quite clear that it had been a pure accident and was not the intentional act Ross believed it to be, and so we were put back to work. However, the full squad were disciplined and as result, I got the only black mark I ever had in the whole of my railway career, on my service history card, thanks to someone else.

Charlie Scott was the next senior and he was, in every way, a gentleman. I do not think I ever heard Charlie raise his voice all the time I was at Haymarket, but he ruled his shift with a rod of iron nevertheless.

Willie Elder was the youngest Running Foreman and had been a Fireman and young Driver at the shed. He was excitable in the extreme. He flew about the place and could curse and swear with best of them, and frequently did.

Willie however, had a gift for developing situations into full blown comedy acts, especially when it came to Peter Gibson, the Chargehand Labourer. Every morning, the Shed Master would hold a morning conference at around 10.00 to which the Mechanical Foreman, shift Running Foreman, Roster Clerk and Chargehand Labourer would be invited, to give a run-down on the previous 24 hours performance at the depot, and any problems dealt with or anticipated. Now Peter was a rotund man who had a slight lisp and a penchant for using big words, always in the wrong context. He was, unconsciously, a master of the malapropism, and this is where Willie came into his own on the weeks he attended the conference.

He would, in a lull in the proceedings, or when tea was being served, innocently ask Peter a question, generally unrelated to work, and Peter could not help but respond, with the gems coming thick and fast. One morning, Willie asked about an ex-member of Peter's staff who had passed away and Peter confirmed that yes, he would be going to the funeral which was to take place at 'Warriston Creamery'. Of course he meant Crematorium. With the conversation up and running, Peter then asked if the assembled group thought it would be OK for him to attend a funeral 'headless' as he did not possess a hat. The meeting dissolved into hysterics, hidden behind hankies, papers or whatever came to hand whilst Peter would look on, wondering what was so amusing. I think his real *piece de resistance* came when discussing attending a function held on the previous evening, with his wife. He remarked to the gathered audience on the length of time it took women to get ready. His wife had been upstairs for a while and Peter had been getting impatient. 'I shouted up the stair and asked what was taking so long, and, do you know what, she was manuring her nails!'

25. RAILWAY TERMINOLOGY

On the railway, in and around Edinburgh, we spoke 'railway speak' and used terms which were double Dutch to the average man in the street. Now this is the case railway-wide, but the Edinburgh version was poles apart from the Glasgow version, for instance. At Haymarket, we 'piloted' a train if assistance was required. In Glasgow, and in particular on the old G&SW, they 'coupled' when providing a second locomotive. We did not 'couple on' or 'couple off', we 'tied on' and 'tied off'. Sixteen ton mineral wagons were 'bogies'. In the West they were 'end doors'. In Waverley station we had the 'Klondyke' which was, in official speak, the South Main siding. At St. Margarets, they had a 'Burma Road'; indeed, I have encountered many 'Burma Roads' throughout the Scottish railway system over the years. Generally a 'Burma Road' was an escape line when other routes became congested, and was so named after the road built by General Stilwell and British soldiers, assisted by Chinese labour between British-held Burma and Free China (Kunming) to circumvent the Japanese blockade of China.

At Haymarket, we never referred to trains by either their official name (if named) or indeed the timetable reporting number. Trains had their own peculiar identity amongst the footplatemen (and indeed the general railwaymen in and around the city). For instance, mention the 'Dog and Monkey' to any Haymarket man and he would

immediately know that you were referring to the 23.50 Parcels train from Edinburgh to the south, the last parcels train out of Waverley nightly. Now do not ask me how or when it got this particular nickname. I have, during all my railway career, asked that question and have never been given any inkling as to why it was so named. The 'Dog and Monkey' was worked out of Edinburgh by Heaton men but we Haymarket men took the engine down to the station each night to be relieved there and I personally have received some very peculiar looks from late night passengers waiting on the platform at Haymarket station as they overhead me using the signal telephone (located in a wooden box actually on the platform) and telling the Signalman at Waverley West that the engine standing at the signal was the engine for the 'Dog and Monkey'.

We had 'the Diners' already referred to which, in reality, was 'The Heart of Midlothian'. The 'Non-Stop' was the 'Elizabethan' and the 'Pullman', quite obviously, was 'The Queen of Scots'. Then we had the 'Colchester', the 'Leeds', the 'Early Aberdeen' the 'Junior Scotsman', the 'Mail', the 'Papers' and so on. Goods trains, too, were known by a name, generally pertinent to destination or origin; so we had 'The Leith Walk' the 20.35 ex-Leith Walk East while the 'Stobs Camp' was the 02.30 ex-Haymarket Yard to Carlisle. On this the No.5 link crew were relieved at, and worked back from, Stobs Camp, just

south of Hawick.Recalling nicknames and railway jargon brings back to mind a comedy played out on a light engine going from the shed to Waverley involving one man's personal 'jargon'. A Locomotive Inspector, one no less than Chief Locomotive Inspector Cunningham, was riding in the cab back down to the station after a visit to the shed and the crew, a young Passed Fireman and a very junior Passed Cleaner, were on their best behaviour. The Cleaner was calling signal aspects to his mate and approaching Haymarket tunnel mouth, he shouted 'ye've got twa broons at the tunnel.' Now the signal was displaying a double amber aspect (being a four aspect signal) but while 'yellow' or 'amber' would have been a perfectly acceptable description, 'broon' (for 'brown') certainly was not, and the Cleaner found himself confined to shed pending a full eyesight examination. He left the service shortly afterwards without it ever being determined if he suffered from a colour defect in his vision or if he really did think the aspect was 'broon'. It has to be said that the ex-LNER colour light signals did display a very strong, almost orange, aspect instead of the much lighter BR yellow and care had to be taken, especially at night and if one had been attending the fire, when held at a red signal. At first glance it could be mistakenly assumed that the signal had cleared to yellow, such was the proximity of the two colours in the spectrum.

Stranger in the camp! St. Margaret's J88 68320 stands in exalted company in No.1 road at the top end of Haymarket, probably on loan to cover a trip to Cowlairs works by one or other of the regular Haymarket J88 duo. (Transport Treasury)

On 4th May 1957, Haymarket V2 60927 lifts a passenger train up the climb past Niddrie North Junction and on the Waverley route proper. It is thought that the train is the 2.33pm Edinburgh/Carlisle which was a No.4 link turn although it has not been possible to identify the Driver. (J. Robertson/Transport Treasury)

26. HOLIDAY FUN

The height of the 1958 summer was upon us and the Trade holidays loomed. Now in Scotland, each city or indeed large town had their own holiday fortnight. The two biggest Trade holidays were the Edinburgh holidays, traditionally the first fortnight in July, when most of the bigger employers shut down for the two weeks, immediately followed by the Glasgow 'Trades' in the second fortnight in July. Each weekend was a challenge for the railways throughout the holiday period, and Haymarket got more than it's fair share of the additional working. By this time, too, the 'Starlight Specials' were all the rage. These were special excursion trains between Edinburgh or Glasgow and London which ran overnight, composed of open tourist stock or whatever came to hand. They ran to no fixed timings but offered a return journey to London and back for the princely sum of 21 shillings – a guinea of old. Even in those good old days this was a bargain.

On the Friday evening of the 1958 holiday weekend, at the finish of the Edinburgh fortnight and the beginning of the Glasgow Trade holidays (the infamous 'Glasgow Fair') the Starlight Specials ran south as eight full trains, most to be engined and crewed by 64B. It was a case of all hands to the pumps. I was actually dayshift on that weekend, but on the late shift and night shift, everyone was being pressed into service, with unfortunate results, as it transpired. One young Cleaner who had only started on the Monday of that week found himself on the wrong end of a firing shovel on a V2, working one of these specials. This was his first firing turn since there was absolutely no one else available. He reached Berwick, thought it was Newcastle and on being told there was still a wee bit to go, stepped off the engine and resigned the service, there and then. This was the sort of calamity that could arise when the depot was scraping the barrel for train crews.

The extraordinary circumstances of this particular weekend were compounded by the fact that there was a bus strike involving Scottish Omnibuses. I was booked 07.00 'relieving' on the Saturday and when my mate and I went down to Waverley to relieve our first incoming train, I could hardly believe my eyes. The queues of people stretched away up the carriageways and the incoming locals literally had passengers falling from the coaches when the doors were opened. It was, in short, complete mayhem. My mate was Alec Gunn and we were due

to relieve an incoming Starlight and take the empty stock to Hardengreen Junction, out on the south side of the city, via the 'Sub'. The train, well a train, arrived in the suburban platforms in Waverley, in Platform 20. There was a procession of trains coming in from the south and Locomotive Inspectors were on the platform to ensure that all was going as well as could be expected. Our train (or so we had been told) arrived behind a Gateshead A3 No. 60070 GLADIATEUR and, as it came to a stand, I climbed up on the tender to check the water level whilst my mate relieved the Gateshead crew. The water in the tank was very low and so I swung the bag on the water column across and Alec turned on the water. Just at that, an Inspector came rushing up and shouted that we should get the train on the move, pronto. With just over half a tank, we agreed to move and, having put up the empty coaching stock headcode with the lamps, we set off through the Gardens. I fired round the box and, on regaining my seat, saw we had the road on to the 'Sub' at Haymarket Central Junction. We ambled round without any great hurry but as we approached Niddrie West Signal Box the home signal was thrown back to danger in our face and we were brought to a stand. I went forward to see what was amiss and to sign the Train Register Book as required by Rule 55. 'Where were we bound for?' asked the Signalman. 'Empty coaches for Hardengreen Junction,' I replied. 'Well son, you better go back and tell your Driver that you have a full train of passengers who do not, I think, want to go to the sidings at Hardengreen Junction, and I think that he might want to come up and speak to Control,' he said.

I went back and informed Alec accordingly. By this time the Guard had come along to see what was what. Alec explained. 'But we're booked for Glasgow Queen Street,' said the Guard, who had not, I suspect, realised just where we were. Alec then spoke to Control who confirmed that we had relieved the wrong train and that the train *we* were on should now be winging its way westwards to Glasgow and not southwards to Hardengreen. We were then instructed to stay with the train and work it forward and that we would not require to call once more, at Waverley. The road re-set, we swung down to Portobello East Junction where we rejoined the East Coast main line and, for the second time that morning, the passengers were taken through Edinburgh Waverley and we then

worked the train through to Glasgow, arriving there with very little water to spare. We were relieved by Eastfield men at Queen Street and dispatched home to Edinburgh by the first train. We had lost a good part of our planned work because of the morning chaos at Waverley, but arrived home at Haymarket around 13.30, where Jimmy Austin, the Running Foreman, met us. 'I'm looking for a wee favour,' says he. 'I have an engine here for a relief to the 14.00 Kings Cross but the Tweedmouth crew are at Waverley. I want you to take this engine doon to the station.'

Alec looked at me and nodded. 'That's fair enough,' I said, so we went and sought out the Heaton A1, 60116 HAL O' THE WYND. She had been prepared and so I just made up the fire for the men who would be relieving us at Edinburgh, and off we set. We arrived in Waverley and the madness was still in progress. We coupled on to a very full train load of passengers on the 14.05 relief to 'the Diners' and waited our relief. The Guard came forward and gave us the train details, 13 on, 440 tons. We were not in fact working the train we told him, we were waiting relief, but this fell on deaf ears. The Guard could not care less who was working the train and the road was off before the Tweedmouth crew finally relieved us. We both heaved a sigh of relief since we would have had no real option but to work the train forward and hope for relief en route. Since our bits and pieces were still at the depot, we crossed the Station to get a lift to Haymarket Station. Alec decided to go for the 14.40 Dundee and we joined the train with time to spare and settled back. Off we set, dead on time and it was only as we were in Haymarket Tunnel that I suddenly thought that this train, which I had previously worked, was one of the few Dundee services which did not actually stop at Haymarket. I was right, and we had to sit still until the Dalmeny stop. There we were faced with a bit of a wait for a train back to Haymarket. It was some time before I let Alec forget that particular day!

An interesting view of the east end of Haymarket shed taken from the shed exit area on 15th September 1938. From left to right in the middle foreground are the General Offices with the 70ft. turntable and the coaling plant to the rear. The only engine in sight is an ex-NER Atlantic, one of a few allocated here and a reminder of the pre-grouping days when the NER had the sole right to work the Edinburgh/Newcastle passenger trains. Nos.7 and 8 roads were allocated to the NE engines and the Atlantic here is standing in No.8 road. The new Fitting Shop has not yet been built but will be located immediately to the left and slightly behind the running shed. The oil and general stores (not in view) will also be extended in the area where the oil barrels are lying; the new messroom only being constructed later. It is unusual to see Haymarket shed yard quite so quiet. (Philip Fox/Transport Treasury)

27. AN EXPERIMENT

I had, since my firing turn on the Suburban Goods with 'Matha' Brand, pondered many times about the perceived need for one-handed firing on our older, non-superheated NB locomotives. Indeed the thought of being required to so haunted me a bit, for I found it awkward and very difficult. Towards the end of July, I found that I had been 'red-inked' and was to be the Fireman on the 16.00 'Prestonpans Stone', a late shift equivalent of the 'Sub' Goods, but with a wee bit further to run, for a full week.

I booked on in plenty of time on the Monday afternoon to find the old faithful, N15 69220 was the booked engine. My mate was to be Driver A. B. Inglis who was neither sick, lame nor lazy but was, nevertheless, accommodated in this link. This was because, as a main line Driver, he could never memorise the timetable for the trains he was required to work, over the Dundee road in particular. Now, the timetable was not easy, for a lot of the Dundee passenger trains had a stopping pattern designed to accommodate market days in the farming community along the Howe of Fife and so, a train would have 'Tuesdays Only' stop at, say, Springfield and a 'Thursdays Only' stop at Kingskettle. Poor old A.B. He just never got the stops right and either stopped on non-stop days or just ran through. In the event, the patience of management wore thin and off main line duties he had to come.

69220 was already prepared when we joined the engine and I slipped up on to the top of the side tank to check the water level. This was down so I shouted that we should top it up. A.B. got down to turn the water on as I put the bag into the tank. Now, the bag had recently been renewed and was stiff (they were leather bags). I pushed it in as far as it would go but as the water was turned on, it started to spurt up and over my feet, as well as going into the tank. 'Sod that' I thought and stood up on the top of the boiler out of the way, as the tank filled. It was almost full when I stepped down. Disaster. A combination of the curve of the boiler and nailed boots meant that I slid helplessly onto the tank top and one leg went down the filler hole. Water was now flying everywhere and I was well and truly soaked to the skin. A.B. had taken himself off to a safe distance at the first hint that all was not well, and stood there shouting instructions which included 'get oot that bloody tank and get that bag back ower the side so I can get the watter turned aff.' There was little sympathy there for my predicament, I thought. At last, the bag out and water turned 'aff', I made my sorry way back to the cab.

The benefit of a tank engine quickly became apparent, being warm and cosy and with a greater degree of privacy with the doors shut. I telephoned off shed and we slipped down to Haymarket Yard for the first part of our working. This was to take empty vans and containers to Corstorphine, shunt there and bring back any loaded vans etc. I put on a big fire and filled the boiler. I then stripped off my overalls and shirt and draped them over the boiler end. The outer clothes were soon steaming away whilst I hid in the corner of the cab dressed only in boots, socks and light trousers. A.B. was highly amused but, full marks, he concentrated on what was happening outside to let me lie low inside. By the time we arrived at Corstorphine I was again dressed and reasonably dry and ready for the fray.

After shunting for a bit, we coupled up to our short train and worked the wagons back to Haymarket yard. There, after setting the vans, we coupled on to our brake van and set off on the next part of the job, the bit I was eager to see. With a light fire and a full head of steam, we ambled our way on to the 'Sub' and ran round to Niddrie West. There we took the Lothian lines past Wanton Walls junction and came out at Monktonhall junction on the East Coast main line. We sat waiting the passage of the 20.35 Leith Walk East to Newcastle Class C freight, the 'Leith Walk'. This was a high priority express freight worked by our No.5 link. With whistle shrieking, the long train leant in to the curve, the K3 in charge giving voice to the summer evening. A quick wave to the Fireman and the train was passed, the vans rocking and rolling over the junction. We then got the road to follow and set off for Prestonpans. This was a glorious part of the journey. As we cleared the short but dangerous tunnel at Morrison's Haven (express trains often encountered blowbacks there owing to the combination of speed and low tunnel roof) we trundled on our way while I enjoyed the view over the wide expanse of the Forth Estuary to the hills of Fife and beyond. It is a view I have, even yet, never tired of. All too soon we passed through Prestonpans station and came to a stand at the signal box beyond. There, we were shunted through the road and back into the down sidings. Coupling off our brake van, we coupled to our waiting train and then set back once more on to the van.

As we had our sandwiches and tea, A.B. explained the working. The train consisted of 16 ton mineral wagons, all unfitted, loaded with stone (I think from the Dunbar/Oxwellmans area). We nearly always had a big load of twenty or more wagons, the maximum load being 26, and the Driver could choose to return to Haymarket yard either by going back round the 'Sub' or by going directly 'through the town'. This latter move meant that the train would be worked through the Waverley. The difference? Well, if the 'Sub' was the chosen route we got away from Prestonpans quickly, but the gradients of the 'Sub' had to be negotiated including the steep falling grade down through Craiglockhart to Gorgie East, with a non-fitted and heavy train. If Waverley was chosen, we were held at Prestonpans until the down 'Talisman' passed clear around 22.20, with a corresponding later arrival at Haymarket. A.B. chose the 'Sub' on that first night. We had a load of 21 wagons on and then he dropped the bombshell. 'Going roond the Sub, son, you'll need tae fire one-handed if I've tae hae the steam I need,' he said. 'Oh, great,' I thought, but nodded in agreement.

I began to prepare the fire, setting a good charge of coal down behind the door and opening the blower. I dropped the door and set the injector. With a full boiler and the safety valves beginning to lift, the exit signal cleared and we were off. A.B. had the lever right down as he pulled the regulator into first valve. 69220 got hold of the heavy train without a slip, although there were several 'rugs' as the couplings were taken up, and we slowly accelerated the train down through the station. I opened the firedoor and threw a dozen shovelsfull round the box. With door closed, pressure sat on the red line so the injector was set. At Monktonhall, we were signalled back on to the Lothian lines and soon were dropping down to Niddrie West, where we were checked by signals. I took the opportunity to open the doors and put another good round on. Off came the signal and we set sail for Duddingston. At this point, we were not on the hill proper so again I fired little and often, keeping pressure up to the mark. As we cleared Duddingston and swung round on to the climb, A.B. gave me the nod and the dreaded one-handed firing began. It really was very difficult to place the coal with any precision and was merely a case of pushing the shovel as far in as possible with one hand, the blast on the fire doing the rest. The fire was an incandescent white for we were now in big valve and the lever right forward. Open the door with the right hand, push coal into the box with left, drop the door with the right, so the firing of 69220 went on as we blasted up the 'Sub' and through the leafy glades of the south side. I had little chance to look out and my left arm was aching. However, 69220 was steaming well and the injector was keeping pace with the drain on the boiler. As a bonus, there was no 'gi'en it a guid stir up' with the poker. I put the shovel down as we blasted up the last few yards to Morningside Road and the top of the hill. Back came the regulator to first valve, then with a quick pull back into big valve, A.B. shut it completely. The lever was pulled back two or three notches and a strange quiet descended on the footplate. We could now feel the weight of the train push against the engine as the gradient fell away. Soon, speed was increasing and A.B. was 'jagging' the steam brake handle. The grind of brake blocks on the driving wheels and the smell of hot, nay burning, metal assailed my nose and ears. A.B., still jagging the brake handle, looked across and shouted 'weel, that's it, we're away so hope we've got the road at Gorgie!' We were, I then realised, running away, with the train now controlling us...

Whilst we hurtled, well it seemed like hurtling, down towards Gorgie I thought 'what now?' but strangely, felt no fear. Gorgie East Junction distant came into sight and... it was ON.

Whistling loudly we approached the junction and the signal box. I could see the Signalman at the window now as we screamed towards him. The home signal loomed near and, at the last minute off it came. We were off the worst of the gradient now as we passed the box and swung down towards the junction at Haymarket Central. The Central's distant was off as was Gorgie's starter, as we rattled across the junction, still at a fair lick, and swung left from the South to the North Lines and then right again to cross to the yard entrance. I was much relieved to see Haymarket Yard and was trembling with the excitement of the past several minutes.

As we ran light back to the shed, I had a look in my fire. Things were not as I would have liked and there was far too much unburned coal still in the box. The Firedroppers, once more, were not going to be pleased with this I thought and, as before, pondered the whole question of this one-handed firing. I did not in my heart of hearts believe for one minute that this was necessary, even though the Drivers who demanded it were long experienced hands and had fired on these engines in their younger days. I was just not convinced, and the

opportunity to do something about it arose later in the week.

The Tuesday was a repeat of Monday with A.B. but on the Wednesday, he was rest day and I was delighted to see on the daily roster that a young Passed Fireman, Joe Cummings was to be my mate. Now Joe was one of two brothers firing at Haymarket. His older brother, Andrew, was a senior Passed Fireman but I never did fire to him. Joe hailed from close by my part of the country, Uphall and, I have to say, he was a first class mate always, and a gentleman. He took a great interest in my career both then when I fired to him and afterwards, as I climbed the promotional ladder to become a senior operating officer in Glasgow HQ. Joe was a political animal although this interest never interfered with the duties or his relationships with his workmates. Nevertheless, I was absolutely delighted when, years later, Joe became Convenor of West Lothian District Council, a worthy achievement. It was also fitting that, during his tenure in office, he attended the ceremony to welcome passenger trains back to Bathgate.

But I digress. Joe and I joined 69220 on that Wednesday afternoon and the

first part of the diagram passed as normal. We eventually arrived, engine and van, at Prestonpans and coupled on to a full load of 26 wagons. Joe opted for through the town and we settled down to wait for the passage of the 'Talisman'. Bang on time she ran past, behind A3 Pacific 60043 BROWN JACK. With an exchange of waves with the crew, I turned to give the fire some attention. I had mentally prepared a plan, hoping that Joe would not interfere. I placed a few shovels of coal into the box to stir up the partly dead fire, and closed the door. Blower on, I waited as the chimney cleared and then shot another round all around the box, then began filling up the back of the door. Door shut again, I set the injector and as the pressure rose to just short of the red line, the signal dropped and we were off. Joe took her easily out of the sidings and on to the main line. As the rear of the train cleared the points, and with a wave from the Guard, he pulled her across into big valve but with the lever in notch four. The blast really stirred up the fire, and when the chimney was clear again, I opened the door and fired a dozen shovelsful all round the box. The valves were

beginning to lift as we plunged into, then out of Morrison's Haven tunnel accompanied by the inevitable blow back and with the flames hitting the bunker. This was expected, so we were both pressed in to our respective cab corners. The Monktonhall Junction distant was off for us and Joe let her out a notch. Speed increased and 69220 was giving voice now as we ran up towards Newhailes Junction. I had the door open and was firing light and often. I dropped the door and 69220 began to blow off against the injector. I re-opened the door and thought, since the door was curved and thus formed the equivalent of a deflector plate when open, there was little chance of too much cold air striking the tubeplate. I decided to leave the door open. Round the curves and through Portobello station we ran, the cab now brightly illuminated by the intense white heat of the firebox. Joe looked across at me several times but said nothing, and we proceeded with the needle right on the red line and a pleasingly full boiler of water.

At Piershill Junction we were diverted to the Granton Line, off the main line and then on to the left-hand chord at Lochend Junction, to be brought to a stand at London Road Junction. I had a job keeping 69220 quiet as we stood, for we were in an area of tenement housing and it was just after 23.00. However, I also had to try and keep a good fire and head of steam for we were still faced with a curving climb from rest. We stood for about fifteen minutes before the road cleared and we were able to swing left through Abbeyhill station and rejoin the main line at Abbeyhill junction. Now, this part of the road was on a 1 in 70 rising gradient through the Calton tunnel. The firelight illuminated the tunnel walls as we blasted our way up through till at last we burst out into the evening sky at Waverley East. We had the road right up the North Main and made our passage known as we crashed through the station. Out through the Mound Tunnel and into the Gardens, and then back into the darkness, turned to day by our passage, of the Haymarket North tunnel. I had left off firing as we ran into the Waverley and now closed the door. Pressure was still sitting high but was now beginning to come back as we ran into the reception loop at Haymarket Yard. We shunted our train and ran light to the shed. I had a look in my fire and was delighted to see the bars clear over much of the grate. The Firedroppers would have an easy time with this one.

As we walked across to the booking off point, Joe said, 'you've enjoyed yourself today, haven't you'. I told him of my wish to try out my ideas and the problems I had with one-handed firing. He told me that a lot of the old Drivers had fired in the really hard school of late NB days when continued employment rested on good

performance and therefore no chances were taken. 'Auld habits die hard, son, he said, but it's good that you're prepared to question things and try things out for yourself. We had plenty of steam today, so your wee experiment did work.' I was happy with what had transpired. Things reverted to the old ways again on the Thursday and the rest of the week. I tried to discuss what I had tried with A.B. but his way was best, and that was that.

On the Saturday, there was no goods and we were booked, as part of the diagram, for empty coach working instead. We came on duty to find we had a 'Director', 62690 LADY OF THE LAKE. Now these engines were right hand drive engines which put me in an awkward position, in more ways than one. I am naturally left-handed and fired that way. This went down well with Drivers since very few liked the Fireman firing with his back to them but on this engine, that is where I found myself, and I do not think A.B. liked it. However, if he wanted steam, then that was the way it had to be. Now, I do not know if this set him off, but he turned decidedly funny and started to moan. The main thrust of this was that he should not be employed on ECS working since, on his punishment form from way back, it was stated that he should not work vacuum-fitted stock. I think that someone had not properly thought out the wording used since it was obvious that he was not to be allowed to work passenger trains but the terms were quite clear, so I egged him on a bit to see what might happen. Sure enough, after a lengthy diatribe, he set of for the Running Foreman's office, while I settled back to enjoy the fun. Well, very few ever won an argument with Ross Dougan and A.B. was back in no minutes flat totally defeated. We spent a pleasant afternoon thereafter working coaches to and from the Waverley and Craigentinny, me firing the Director from the right hand (wrong) side of the cab, and A.B. moaning to high heaven. At least I did not have to look at him!

I had enjoyed my week firing on the 'Prestonpans' despite all the wee problems, but I was destined to have an even better week in the near future.

A2 60530 SAYAJIRAO is not in steam and is perhaps being moved by the shed shunt J88. The Running Foreman's office window can be seen in the left background. This was the locomotive involved in the tragic derailment at Longniddry on the late evening of 17th December 1953 whilst working a special Christmas parcels train south, leaving the Fireman dead and the Driver seriously injured. The engine, though badly damaged, was repaired at Doncaster and put back into traffic in a relatively short space of time, returning to Haymarket in February 1954. (J. Robertson/ Transport Treasury)

A2/1 60507 HIGHLAND CHIEFTAIN 'dead' in Haymarket yard on 6th May 1956, probably waiting attention in the Fitting Shop. It was quite normal for engines waiting repair to be stabled in the west sidings in Haymarket yard nearest the shed proper. This was one engine of the four ordered as V2s but subsequently built as Pacifics by Edward Thomson, and Haymarket had three of the four. This engine was also paired with the tender (No.5672) originally carried by A4 4469 SIR RALPH WEDGWOOD which was destroyed during the bombing raid which so badly damaged York shed on 29th April 1942. The tender carried the stainless steel strip along the bottom edge to the end, but this was kept painted over. (J. Robertson/Transport Treasury)

28. THE 'LARBERT'

A week or so after my Prestonpans adventure I swapped a dayshift week of relieving turns for the backshift Larbert. Now this was a wee passenger job allocated to the Control link and involved going out with an engine which had been prepared for us, working the 15.43 all stops to Larbert and returning with the 17.39 to Waverley, again all stops. This was not the easiest of jobs since we ran in front of the 16.00 Waverley Glasgow express, which was one of the important commuter services, as far as Polmont Junction with stops at Linlithgow and Polmont, before we got clear. After arrival at Waverley, we then ran down to Craigentinny and worked at least one big rake of empty coaches up to Waverley.

I was really looking forward to this job since it was another new road for me and we ran over the ex-LMS lines from Carmuirs East to Larbert station. I booked on at 15.00 and looked out for my mate, a young Driver that I only knew by sight and name, one Willie Bowman. Now Willie was not the most silent of men at the best of times and generally one knew if he was on duty because he often could be heard before he was seen. He also revelled in the use of adjectives, in fact, one adjective, with which he adorned nearly every second word he uttered and was thus known in the shed as Willie F*****g Bowman. I had been assured by his regular Fireman with whom I had exchanged duties that he was all bark and no bite, and was, essentially a very good mate.

I joined him as he booked on and we had a look at the notices before checking what engine we had. This, it turned out, was to be B1 61007 KLIPSPRINGER, one of our own, and in apparently good condition. She had been well prepared with a nice fire, heavy behind the door and a tender of nice hard coal. The tank was full and I had little to do before it was time to 'phone 'off shed'. It is true to say that the devil finds work for idle hands, for having tested both injectors, I then tried a few shovels of coal down the length of the long firebox. I was not happy and looking in, found 1007 had a new, long deflector plate which hindered my ability to shoot coal to the front of the box. At this juncture, Willie was looking around the outside of the engine or else he might have cautioned me, but left to my own devices I shot off and came back with a shorter, well-burned deflector plate which I transferred to the firebox. My big mistake!

We phoned off shed and soon had the road to the station. When we had backed on and coupled up to our train of six coaches, I turned to getting ready for the 'off'. Another Driver had joined

us on road learning and he placed himself well behind the Driver's seat out of my way. I filled up the back of the box. The grate on a B1 was level at the rear half and then sloped away to the fore-end. Willie said, 'fire at the back of the door and doon the sides but go sparingly on the front end. These engines shake the fire furrit themselves and dinnae like too much doon the front.' I took this in and shaped up the fire at the back of the box accordingly. Injector on, I filled the boiler and just before time we were sitting with a full head of steam and the valves just sizzling.

At 15.43 a whistle blew. I looked back and shouted across to Willie that we were right away. A shriek on the whistle and he lifted the regulator handle and we were off. I closed the cylinder cocks as we plunged into the Mound tunnel. Green signals took us through the Gardens and all was well on the footplate. Pressure was still on the red line and the boiler sitting nicely ¾ full. The B1 was fairly smooth and since I had never fired one on anything other than ECS workings, I was looking forward to seeing what she could do with a train, though admittedly a light one. We shuddered to a halt at Haymarket, where the usual passengers were waiting to join. Many of them were the schoolboys and girls from the many Edinburgh Merchant (private) Schools, who commuted from the Central Belt. With all safely aboard, we got a green flag and were on our way again. I waited until we had passed the shed before getting off my seat and picking up the shovel. I speared a dozen or so shovelsful down each side and fired another six or eight to the fore-end. Putting the last four just inside the firedoor, I shut the flap and set the exhaust injector. By this time we were past Saughton Junction and running for Gogar when I became aware that pressure was slipping back. Picking up the shovel, I fired another round and shut the door. Pressure continued to slip back and was just sitting under 200 lbs, and by this time I had shut off the exhaust injector, but to no avail. Now Willie had realised that all was not well and was looking at me, as was the other Driver. Passing Queensferry Junction, he motioned me into his seat and took the firing shovel. Another round of coal was shot into the box but again with no success and by now we had 180 lbs and it was still falling. Willie was really looking concerned since we were reaching the point where the ejector might not continue to maintain vacuum and the brakes would go on, and the faster '16.00' would be closing in behind us. We were past Winchburgh Junction and I had the exhaust injector on once

more to keep some water in the boiler. At about 175 lbs the gauge stopped falling but remained unmoveable. I heaved a wee sigh of relief and fired in just a few shovels at a time, closing the flap in between firing bouts. We were through Philpstoun and approaching Linlithgow, still fairly well on time. At last the brakes went on and we drew to a stand in the platform. I opened the big firedoor and, using the shovel, had a look at the fire. There it was, a great haycock right in the centre on the change of grate levels, about halfway down the long firebox. Willie had a look as I reached for the poker, and watched as I pushed the fire right forward to the fore-end. The effect was instantaneous. Pressure started rising and was above 200 lbs as I returned the poker to the tender-end. Whilst waiting for the right-away, Willie, in his forthright manner, told me to keep my left hand up when I was firing, since it appeared I had been striking the brick arch with the coal when trying to fire it forward, causing the hump to develop. Had I left the long deflector plate in situ at the shed, this would have forced me to take more care when firing. We barked our way out of Linlithgow and, very carefully, I started to fire again. Injector on, flap almost closed and '1007 started to blow off. I held the pressure on the red line as we stopped at Polmont, then we swung to the right at Polmont Junction to clear the main line and dropped down to Falkirk Grahamston. I could now relax and take in this strange road and soon, after we left our Grahamston stop, we ran across the swingbridge over the Forth and Clyde Canal and approached Falkirk Camelon station. There, Willie motioned for me to close the flap and let the fire burn down. This I did, shutting off the injector as we swung to the right over the tight, curving junction at Carmuirs and joined the Scottish Central main line at Larbert Junction for the last mile or so to our destination at Larbert.

At Larbert, I coupled off and we ran round our coaches in preparation for propelling them back into the bay platform. This done, I uncoupled again and we ran all the way back to the Carmuirs triangle to turn. There, we were brought to a stand on the chord, waiting the passage of a West Coast main line express. This hove into view hauled by a Crewe North 'Princess Coronation' and was, I think, a Crewe to Perth express with through coaches from Manchester to Aberdeen. It was a heavy train by any standards and was noteworthy, as I observed during the remainder of the week, for having a former Pullman car and a 12 wheel diner. We followed this train back to Larbert, where I coupled on to our own

91

modest train in the bay, and then had our sandwiches.

The inner man satisfied, I set about preparing for the return journey and fired to the fore-end with the big door open, before closing it and concentrating on the rear half of the firebox as instructed. Willie, I must say, watched but said nothing, so I assumed all was well. The return journey passed without any problem and with enough steam, and I did enjoy the high speeds attained through the Winchburgh cutting before we had to slow for the 35 arch Almond viaduct. On arrival at Waverley at 18.29, Willie told me to keep a good bright fire in her in preparation for the next part of the adventure. When our train had been lifted and shunted, we reversed out into the Mound Tunnel before reversing again and proceeding through the station and on down to Craigentinny. There we were met by a Shunter who guided us on to the heavy lift of empty coaches bound for Waverley. We had 22 coaches on, about 720 tons and faced a rising gradient from St. Margaret's shed of 1 in 75 right to the platform end at Waverley but, as Willie explained when he saw the look of horror on my face, we were piloted by a St. Margaret's engine on the rear.

I made up my fire and filled the boiler as we were waiting for the Guard to come along. When he had given us the train details and joined the coaches I went to the phone. 'Hae ye got the pilot oan?' asked the Signalman in Craigentinny

Junction Box. I replied in the affirmative. 'Wait for the signal then,' came the reply. I rejoined '1007 which, by this time, was blowing off strongly. Off came the signal. Willie gave a cock-crow on the whistle and away back the train came the answering call. He did not open the regulator immediately but waited until we felt the pilot buffer up against the train behind us, then up into first valve went the regulator and as we passed on to the main line, into big valve it went. The big train was accelerating as the banker dug in behind. Willie let her out a turn and the roars were almost continuous at the chimney. I set to firing and the blast whipped the coal off the shovel immediately the blade entered the door. It was just a matter of deflecting the shovel this way and that, and the blast did the rest. We thundered through the middle of St. Margaret's shed, men pausing to watch our passing. The safety valves were sizzling and I banged on the second injector as our tender pointed up the hill. Willie let her out a bit further and the noise was ear splitting. Children in the back courts paused in their play to watch us and here and there, a head appeared out of a tenement window to watch the pyrotechnics. Up the North Main with brakes now going on, we slid to a halt at the west end where the Shunter was waiting to uncouple us. This done, we were given the road out through the Gardens and we waved as we passed under the two latticed footbridges to the

usual summer's evening's audience of Mums, Dads and bairns, all enjoying the free entertainment of railway operation at its best.

After we booked off, I walked across the 'Sub' with Willie to catch a bus home from Gorgie Road. As we walked, Willie raised the matter of the deflector plate and the hump on the fire. His words had me thinking for a long time to come. 'You see, son, he said, I dinnae think it's all your fault. I jist think it all wrang that you Cleaners are taken oot on a Pacific that your mither could fire, tae be passed oot. You should be taken oot on a B1 or a Director or something else that jist isnae plain sailin.' I ken you've had some main line turns but you were caught oot the day, jist because naebody prepared ye fur the problems you can encounter firing a B1, but I also think you've learned a lesson you'll no likely forget.' All this was punctuated by his favourite adjective and having said all that, we finished our journey in silence. As I say, I pondered these words going home that night, again and again. He was just so right.

On the Tuesday we had another B1, 61244 and on the Wednesday we were booked to have yet another, 61076. She was not on shed when we went to look for her and Willie Elder explained that she had been used to turn a spare Royal Mail coach on the Gorgie triangle and was on her way back from Waverley. She ran into the shed and we joined her on the turntable. The Passed

Ivatt 4MT 2-6-0 43135 at Craigentinny in the usual queue of engines waiting to go on shed at St. Margaret's in the late 1950s, probably on a Saturday afternoon. It was this locomotive, then allocated to Polmont, which provided us with the exhilarating return journey from Larbert described in the text. (W. Hermiston/Transport Treasury)

Fireman we were relieving said 'I don't think she'll be going on the Larbert the day for she might hae a hot driving box.' Right enough, the middle left-hand driving wheel was very warm indicating the possible development of a hot axlebox. Willie Elder came across with the Leading Fitter. They threw a pail of cold water over the box and the Fitter said he thought that it was just the newness easing off and 'she'll be fine.' Willie, my mate, looked dubious about the whole thing. 'Are you gaun tae take her or will you fail her?' Willie Elder asked. Willie B. pondered a moment, obviously a bit unhappy. The Fitter chipped in, 'it'll be a' right noo. The Larbert's an easy wee job and the box will soon ease off.' Willie said, 'well, if you'll go underneath and dose the box with oil, I'll take it.' The Fitter grumbled but did so and we were soon phoning off shed and on the way to Waverley. There, as I prepared the fire and filled the boiler, Willie went out and had a look round, feeling the wheel centre with his hand. 'Well, she isnae any hotter', he observed when he climbed back into the cab.

We were soon underway, and having cracked the method of firing B1s (with a new deflector plate in place) we galloped along to our first stop at Linlithgow. As we drew to a halt, the pungent smell of hot metal assailed our nostrils. Willie shot off and was back in a flash. 'I'm gaun tae hae tae fail her, he said, but I think we'll manage to get to Larbert.'

I had been a wee bit careless with the injector since the engine was not being worked over-hard after Linlithgow. When running into our Polmont stop, Willie was a bit fierce with the brake since he wanted to speak to Control, and we stopped with a jerk. A woman, obviously waiting for a passenger in the car park across on the up side of the station, was standing by the door of her car. As we ground to a stand, the water in the boiler had obviously surged and some had been drawn into the vacuum ejector. A gout of sooty water shot out the chimney and fell about her. Poor soul, she looked up, she looked down, she even looked across at me, but could neither figure where this unexpected downpour had come from, nor why her car had suddenly changed colour.

We got down to Larbert without further ado, except for a driving axlebox that was now well ablaze. We docked our coaches and then, without turning the engine, we waited to see just what Polmont shed was turning out to replace '1076. We did not have long to wait. A single-chimney Ivatt 2-6-0 'doodlebug', 43135 running tender-first, drew to a stand on the main platform across from us and we were hailed by the Polmont Driver. 'This is your replacement engine, he shouted, we'll bring it through the road.' Willie's response was pungent in the extreme, but we duly exchanged

footplates with the Polmont crew. The Driver was in fact very apologetic, explaining that 43135 had just come on shed from a freight working when our call was received, and was immediately about turned and sent down to us. I had a look in the firebox. The fire was a dull red mass with blue flame playing on the surface, but the boiler was half filled and steam pressure was sitting well up. However, a look at the tender did nothing to raise my spirits for there was a mix of small coal and ovoid briquettes spilling from the shovel plate. This was exactly the scenario I had dreaded, knowing that I just was not experienced enough to be sure of coping with this unexpected turn-up. Nevertheless, we requested the signal to allow us to run forward on the Up Main before setting back into the bay and coupling to our train. This done and time marching on, sandwiches and teas forgotten, Willie went out to have a look around the engine, and I set about the fire. I took down the poker and ran it through the fire. There was no sign of any serious clinkering, despite the briquettes, and I was able to bare the bars. Although the engine was fitted with a rocker grate, given the short time now at my disposal, and in terror of decanting all the fire into the ashpan (it had happened to better Firemen than me) I chose not to go down that road. Instead I fired round the box and into the back corners, before closing the firedoors and setting the blower. Steam pressure started to rise slowly as Willie rejoined the footplate. 'Have you ever driven or worked on one of these engines?' I enquired. 'No, but its only anither ingine,' he replied. Had he any ideas about how it should be fired, I asked? 'Little and often roond the box, wi' a big back of the door should dae it,' he responded.

I opened the firedoors and was pleased to see that the fire had brightened up considerably and was burning through nicely. I fired another round and then began to fill the back corners, scrabbling in the tender for the largest pieces of coal I could find. Departure time was almost upon us but I had 220 lbs of steam on the gauge and a full boiler of water. I looked out and back, waiting for the Guard's signal. The green flag was waving way down the train. 'Right away mate', I called out. Willie opened the regulator and with a slight slip, 43135 got hold of the train. With 5ft 3in driving wheels, she accelerated away quickly with our short train, and Willie had to steady her for the swing left at Larbert Junction on to the Carmuirs chord line. 43135 rode somewhat harshly, even at those low speeds, but there was no opportunity for anything faster as we took up our Camelon stop, followed by the stop at Falkirk Grahamston. As we stood at Grahamston, I fired another round down each side of the box and across the fore-end, finishing with a few

shovelsful into the back corners. She was sizzling at the safety valves and I set the right-hand injector. The line out of Grahamston climbed away up past Grangemouth Junction and across a high embankment to enter the cutting up round Laurieston towards Polmont Junction, still climbing all the way. 43135 took this in her stride and steam pressure held rock steady at around 210 lbs. I was now relaxing and thinking to myself that this was not a bad little engine at all. On regaining the E&G main line at Polmont junction we took up our Polmont stop. Getting away from Polmont on what was, by and large, a level main line, 43135 picked up speed quickly, and as she did so, so the footplate suddenly became a lively cakewalk. Sitting on what passed for seats became distinctly uncomfortable. However, we were approaching Linlithgow and another station call.

On leaving Linlithgow, we were on a very fast piece of splendidly engineered railway and off we went as Willie opened her up. All hell was let loose. I could hardly stand to fire her and the floor was bouncing up and down under my feet. As we swept along past Philpstoun and on through the Winchburgh cutting, the floorboards started rising up and a couple slid down and disappeared through the hole in the floor. I was holding on like grim death as 43135 swayed and bucked. I picked up the shovel again and, balancing on what flooring was actually left, I fired another round in the box. She was steaming well and the injector was holding the water level up against the thrashing she was taking. As we crashed across the pointwork at Winchburgh Junction, an injector steam valve flew off and went out over the side before I could catch it. Coal and briquettes were shaking down and filling what was left of the floor, much of it disappearing through the holes and down onto the track. The pail was next to go over the side, accompanied by the footplate brush. I stood back, braced against the tender end and watched this madness in awe. Willie was grinning like a madman as he stood, one hand gripping the regulator and the other the cab sheets. We crashed and banged our way through Gogar and shot past Saughton Junction. An Edinburgh-bound train was coming off the north lines and drew alongside and the crew, fellow members of 64B, on seeing us appeared to be in hysterics. Rude signs were exchanged and then – silence, as Willie shut the regulator and wound the reverser back. We coasted down past the shed and drew to a stand in Haymarket, with a fair proportion of 43135 now missing. The peace and calm was wonderful after these last hectic minutes.

As we slid down through the Gardens, 43135 generated a fair excitement amongst the regular enthusiasts who haunted the overbridges there and who knew the

Edinburgh engine working arrangements like the back of their hands. This was a very unusual event. We drew to a stand in Waverley and our passengers walked by, wholly unaware of the mayhem recently enacted on the footplate of 43135, whilst we tried to establish some semblance of order in the cab. The floor was re-laid but with a hole or two and the spillage was cleaned up simply by the expedient of just tossing it into the firebox. We duly ran to Craigentinny and worked our empty coaches back to Waverley, tender-first as usual and with our pilot in attendance at the back end of the train. I have to say that, with the smaller driving wheels, 43135 performed admirably on the climb up to the station. We were, nevertheless, very pleased to abandon 43135 on the turntable at Haymarket, its arrival an unwelcome shock for the Running Foreman.

On the Saturday which, sadly, was to be the very last day of steam working on this train, we booked on to find not a B1 as we had expected, but a D49, 62705 LANARKSHIRE prepared for the job. I had fired these 4-4-0s on ECS workings but, up until that time, never on a main line train working, and I was curious to see just what the experience would be like. 62705 steamed like dream and was particularly easy to fire. I had, as instructed, filled up the back half of the grate to the flame plate, and in running, all I had to do was slide the coal along the sides and back of this heap of fire. Gravity, and the motion of the engine, did the rest by shaking the fire forward. However, in running, whilst I had thought 43135 had been rough, this engine tossed me all over the place and even when seated on the generous seats formed by large tool boxes, my ribs were being smashed against the cab sides as she rolled, pitched and hunted her way to Larbert and back.

That, as it turned out, had been the easy part. After our train had been pulled off at Waverley, we proceeded as normal down to Craigentinny. I coupled to the train of empty coaches, again as I had done all week, and then went and phoned the Signalman at Craigentinny Junction Box. 'Had we our pilot?' I was asked. Well, since a pilot was booked, and had been provided all week, I said, yes. 'Now son, said the Signalman, the Pullman's running a wee bit down so if you've got your pilot, and your Driver disnae hang about, I will let you out now, but tell him he's got to run.' I gave an assurance in the affirmative and went back to tell Willie. 'OK, no a big problem,' says he, and blows up the brake. He gave the cock crow on the whistle as the road came off and pulled open the regulator. 62705 got hold of the train but, try as I might, I was unable to hear the response to our whistle from the pilot. Willie gave a frown as we slid out on to the main line, then let the reverser full out. 62705 gave roar at the chimney and we began to accelerate the train. 'That's more like it, shouted Willie, now that bugger is beginning to give us some help.' Since we were running tender-first and I was on the inside of the curve as we swung out of Craigentinny Yard, I looked back and just caught a glimpse of the end of our train as we went under the road bridge. Horrors of horrors, there was no pilot at the back end. Here we were,

some twenty coaches or so on, a Shire with 6ft 8in driving wheels running tender-first, the prospect of a 1 in 70 rising gradient from St. Margaret's to the end of the platform at Waverley and running in front of the 'Queen of Scots' Pullman. I crossed the cab and shouted the bad news to Willie. He reacted as if he had received an electric shock instead of just an ordinary sort of shock, and then gave vent. The air was pure 'Billingsgate' as he questioned the birthright of the St. Margaret's Running Foreman, the Drivers there, Edinburgh Control and the stupid B******d of a Signalman for giving us the road. Everyone, it seemed, was to blame, except us, the heroes from Haymarket who had been betrayed and left to face the music, music which was sounding dreadfully like a Funeral March to my mind, for had not I assured the Signalman that we did indeed have a pilot.

I returned to the shovel as we rolled past Piershill Junction on the main line and our one hope of salvation, being turned onto the Abbeyhill loop. 62705 was blasting away at the chimney and

accelerating the train quite nicely. Willie came across and shouted that we would be OK if it did not start to rain, at least he thought so. Thus assured, I fired another round into the white hot inferno and checked the water level. The pressure was on the red line and we were in fact blowing off as we thundered through St. Margaret's loco and turned on to the climb. Willie looked across and just shrugged. The reverser was full out, the regulator out at the stop and we had more than enough steam and water. It was now in the lap of the Gods. We crashed our way into Calton Tunnel South and inched our way up through the darkness. Out into the daylight again and we could see the Signalman in Waverley East box hanging out the window and waving us on. At that, we felt a smattering of rain and almost immediately, 62705 started to slip violently.

Willie closed and then snapped open the regulator. Another slip and again the regulator was immediately closed and opened. Giving a fair imitation of a volcano in full eruption, we clawed our way over the top of the 1 in 70 gradient and into Nos.10 and 11 platforms. As we ran to a stand at the platform starting signal at the west end of No.11, across the station, we saw the engine at the head of the Pullman draw to a stand in Nos.1 and 19, the North Main. It had been a close run thing, and Shires went up a notch or two in my estimation. In retrospect, so did my estimation of the Signalmen in Waverley East Box since, because we were occupying the main line up through Calton Tunnel South and not moving too quickly, they immediately set the route behind us as we cleared Abbeyhill Junction and swung the incoming Pullman across on to the line through Calton Tunnel North and up the north side of the station, thus preventing any further delay. This had the result of the Pullman being on the other side of the station from normal but since an engine change had to be effected, there was no problem in getting intending passengers, not that there were usually many, from No.11 to No.19 in the available time.

So ended another interesting week, with other lessons learned, and experience gained on different engines. It was also the end of an era. The 'Larbert' had been a long established train working from Waverley, dating away back to the 1920s at least, but now, the new, clean diesel multiple unit trains were taking over and steam would soon be nothing more than a memory.

I have to say that I did again have the opportunity to fire both a Director and a Shire on the main line, albeit on work which was not in any way onerous. The northbound expresses from London carried through coaches to destinations such as Glasgow, Aberdeen and Perth. The 10.00 'Flying Scotsman' conveyed through coaches to Glasgow Queen Street which were

booked to be transferred to and run forward on the 18.30 from Waverley. The 'Junior Scotsman' conveyed through coaches for both Aberdeen and Perth and these went forward on the 18.45 Aberdeen and 18.55 Perth respectively. These through coaches were detached by the station pilots and transferred to the appropriate forward service from Edinburgh. However, as most of these main line departures from Waverley services were important and busy trains in their own right, there was a finite delay tolerated to ensure incoming connections were met and if, as happened fairly frequently, the northbound trains were late, the outgoing train would be dispatched on time. When this happened, Control was quickly on to the Running Foreman at Haymarket to provide engine power and a crew to work the portions forward as a special service. Haymarket, in the summer months and in the late afternoon, was never awash with spare engines and anything that was immediately available was pressed into service, including foreign engines if necessary. So, in the summer months particularly, it was not unusual to see a two or three coach train headed north or westwards from Waverley by a real mish-mash of locomotive power, and our own B1s, Shires and Directors were usually to the fore. However, I have seen Thornton 'Scotts' and 'Glens' purloined for this purpose. Indeed, on one summer afternoon in mid-1958, our own 62690 LADY OF THE LAKE worked the through coaches off the Down 'Flying Scotsman' right through to Aberdeen, being re-manned, of course, at Dundee.

Now, these special workings had to be manned and again, in the summer months, spare crews were not exactly clogging up the system at 64B, so the young bloods were often given their chance to shine. Younger Passed Firemen with one or two driving turns would often be lifted from main line link firing turns to drive these trains, accompanied by Passed Cleaners. Sometimes, the very youngest and least experienced were pressed into service for these trains. I fired a Director to Dundee on the Aberdeen portion off the 'Flying Scotsman' on one occasion, and went out to Glasgow on a Shire on another. The trains were light, but tightly timed, and some very slick working was involved.

B1 61076 was the engine which ran hot whilst working the Edinburgh/Larbert on one of the days I fired on the working. Her failure gave us the doubtful pleasure of becoming acquainted with the Ivatt 2-6-0. (J. Robertson/ Transport Treasury)

V1 67610, one of the three Gresley passenger 2-6-2Ts allocated to Haymarket, standing in full reverse gear in the shed loop, apparently abandoned. These engines gave good work and were used on both passenger trains and latterly on empty coach working and I had the opportunity of firing '7610 and her two sisters in my time at 64B. Indeed, I had the great pleasure in firing 67615 over the Galashiels via Peebles road on one day when we were required to stand in for a failed DMU. (J. Robertson/Transport Treasury)

29. THE 'FAIR MAID'

A couple of weeks later, after exchanging my booked turn for a full week, I was firing in the Junior Spare link at 07.00. On the Monday and Tuesday, I had been lifted for various relieving and ECS jobs, interesting enough in their own right. However, on the Friday daily working sheet I had been elevated to 07.30 Senior spare and, on taking duty on the Friday morning Jimmy Austin, the Running Foreman, was on the lookout for me. 'Come on across to 60090 with me,' he said. Puzzled, I walked across the shed with him, sensing that there was yet another panic, not at all unusual for Haymarket in summer.

We approached A3 60090 GRAND PARADE standing gleaming in the morning sunshine just back from Doncaster after a general repair and sporting a new double chimney. She was booked for the 'Fair Maid', at that time running from Perth to Kings Cross and due out of Edinburgh at 08.30. This train was soon to become the morning 'Talisman' starting from Waverley and with an earlier departure. The regular crew had just joined the loco and the Driver was Norman Taylor, to whom I had fired on the 10.00 Glasgow many months before. This was a No.3 link turn and there was a younger Passed Fireman booked as his mate. It was he to whom Jimmy Austin addressed himself: 'We're lifting you for a driving turn, Jock, he said. I've no spare Drivers around so you get the driving turn.' To Norman, he said, 'this is the Spare Fireman today, Norman, so he'll be your mate.' Norman looked at me and said, 'oh, we've met somewhere afore. This laddie has been oot wi' me before, I think.' I nodded and said 'the 10.00 clock Glasgow some time ago.' 'Weel Jimmy, I've nae doot we'll dae jist fine,' said Norman. I climbed aboard and stowed my jacket and satchel. Pulling on my gloves, I picked up the shovel and had a look round the fire. The engine had been prepared for us and had a good fire, well burned through, around the box. Pressure was sitting just below 200 lbs and there was half a glass of water. Everything was just fine. I then checked the tender for water, but again the preparation crew had filled the tank for us.

Meanwhile, Norman had gone for a walk around the engine. I climbed off and checked the lamps, noting that the 'Fair Maid' headboard had been set in place on the centre lamp iron on the buffer beam. Time was marching on and Norman, after calling a warning around the A3 climbed aboard and blew off the brakes. I unscrewed the tender handbrake and with a warning screech on the whistle we moved off to the shed points, where I 'phoned out. A few minutes later, we were slipping down through Haymarket station to the Waverley. Being ex-works, '90 moved almost silently with no appreciable Gresley ring from the connecting rods. Indeed, the most obtrusive noise was the peculiar 'frying bacon' sizzle from the exhaust ejector at the double chimney. This was to become a common feature of the double chimney A3s and A4s. We slipped down the South Loop to come to a stand at the east end, awaiting the arrival of the train from Perth. There was quite a crowd of passengers waiting on No.10 platform for the train, and '90 drew many admiring glances as she stood, shining like a new pin, in the loop.

At about 08.15 our train ran in, hauled by 60534 IRISH ELEGANCE and worked by Perth men. After she had coupled off, we slipped out of the loop and backed on to the train. I went in between to couple up as the Guard came forward and gave Norman details of the loading. Now this train, with its afternoon sister working, 'The Talisman' was of a 'limited load' formation of nine BR MkI coaches, all fitted with roller bearings. The train, if I remember correctly, in the up direction, was as follows: BSK, FK, CK, RFO, RK, SO, SK, SK and BSK. Tare weight was 307 tons.

We departed on time and after the usual PW slows through to Monktonhall Junction, '90' accelerated this train very quickly and without any of the fuss associated with my first trip on the coast. Being just ex-works, she steamed like a dream and the double chimney was a vast improvement. I ran with a very light fire just covering the bars at the fore-end, but with a full fire behind the doors. This the Gresley's liked and I can say that I never was, at any point, in trouble for steam. Indeed, I sat down and enjoyed the scenery for much longer spells than before and we ran into Newcastle Central, a few minutes early, at 10.33 and were quickly uncoupled and away across the King Edward Bridge to Gateshead.

The return trip was a repeat of the outward journey with similar loadings. The Kings Cross men brought the down train into Newcastle spot on time and we were away at 12.36. The A3 accelerated like lightning up the hill, after we cleared Manors and we were doing at least 60mph as we cleared the top of the climb at Forest Hall. From there, running was hard to maintain the 126 minute timing for the 125 miles, but '90 was never fully stretched although Norman did give her a bit of stick on the climb from Alnmouth up to Little Mill. We streaked down Christon Bank with speed touching the high eighties, and we passed into the Scottish Region at Marshall Meadows, two minutes early. Norman did not push her further and we eventually arrived in Waverley still with a couple of minutes in hand.

On the journey back to the shed, Norman was quick to acknowledge a job well done. We put '90 on the turntable and I had a look at the fire as Norman dropped down and walked around feeling the bearings. The firebars were showing through in the centre of the box and there was very little fire in front of the box. A good day with a great engine, and experience of what a transformation the double chimney made to what were already very fine locomotives.

67620, the only V3 2-6-2T at Haymarket, passing the shed on an Edinburgh Waverley to Stirling train running via the Forth Bridge. On the right can be seen the 'Caledonian' link line from Edinburgh Princes Street via Dalry Middle Junction to Haymarket West Junction whence the 'Caley' had running powers over the Edinburgh & Glasgow Railway to Polmont Junction and on to the former Scottish Central Railway. (J. Robertson/Transport Treasury)

30. THE BACK END OF 1958

Before the big shift back at the end of the Summer Timetable, I did get out on passenger trains once or twice more. I had another run to Dundee and then, unexpectedly, a run to Galashiels via Peebles with V1 2-6-2T 67615 on the 13.18 ex-Waverley and back with the 16.05 from 'Gala' – Galashiels – in lieu of a DMU which had failed. It was the first and only time I had the experience of exchanging tokens on a single line of railway. The Peebles road was absolutely breathtaking as we meandered down through the round Border hills, following the River Tweed for much of the journey. The V1 was a delight to work on and fire and again, steam was not a problem.

At New Year, I was again booked firing on Hogmanay (31st December) but was booked off on both the 1st and 2nd January 1959. I had once more changed duties with another, more senior Passed Cleaner, to fire to Peter Motion in No.2 link, working the 07.30 Edinburgh to Aberdeen and returning with the 09.18 from Aberdeen. Both were heavy trains, strengthened for the holiday traffic and the 09.18 conveyed through coaches to Kings Cross and had a restaurant car.

I booked on at 06.40 and checked on the booked engine. This turned out to be the A2/1 60507 HIGHLAND CHIEFTAIN. I had never fired this particular engine before but was acquainted with sister 60510, so did not feel any anxiety at all. My mate for the day, Peter Motion, I knew by sight and indeed how could one miss him. He had the name of being a poor runner but was quite definitely a character, and larger than life.

To digress for a moment, Peter had been driving on one of the usual No.2 link Dundee turns, I forget which and it matters not in any case. Some days afterwards, the Station Master at Tay Bridge station had been out on routine signal box visitations and in the course of this task, on cross-checking Train Register Books for Tay Bridge Central and Tay Bridge South boxes, discovered that Peter had made a somewhat speedy crossing of the Tay Bridge to the point where the Permanent Speed Restriction of 25 mph over the bridge had been exceeded by a goodly amount. A report was duly sent to the District Operating Manager who then sent it to the Motive Power Superintendent, Edinburgh, who duly required the Shed Master at Haymarket to get a full report from the errant Driver Motion. Now by this time Peter was on nights, but a letter in the form of a 'PLEASE EXPLAIN' was duly sent out for his attention. Nothing more was heard. Peter just ignored it. A reminder was sent out. No reply. A

third and strongly worded letter threatening all sorts of retribution if a reply was not forthcoming by return was sent out. Peter was not impressed. Mr. Cherry, the Shed Master, was also neither impressed nor amused. 'Send for Motion,' came the cry. 'Motion's again on nights,' was the reply. Mr. Cherry, thwarted yet unbeaten, tried another tack. 'Who was Motion's Firemen on the day in question?' he asked. The Passed Fireman was duly identified. 'Ah, said Mr. Cherry, a Passed Fireman. Has he signed for the Dundee road?' 'Yes, he has'. 'Is he on days?' he asked. Once more the reply was in the affirmative. 'Wheel him in,' ordered the Boss.

The Passed Fireman duly reported to the General Office as requested and was ushered in to the Inner Sanctum and was sat down opposite Mr. Cherry across the desk, with John Thomson, the Chief Clerk as witness and referee. 'Now', began Mr. Cherry, 'this is a matter of some importance. I believe you were firing to Peter Motion on this given date.' 'That's right, I was,' replied the Fireman. 'Well', said the Boss, it has been claimed that your Driver exceeded the speed limit over the Tay Bridge by quite a margin.' 'That's quite right,' came the reply, the honesty of which took the Boss by surprise. 'OK', said Mr. Cherry. Now you are a 'passed' man and have signed the road for Dundee. What is the speed limit on the Bridge?' '25 mph,' was the response. 'Good', says the Boss, 'you do know the road. Now as a passed man and knowing what you know, did you not think that you might just have had a responsibility to draw your Driver's attention to this speeding?' 'Oh yes, said the Fireman, I did. I said to him as we crossed the Bridge and entered the High Girders, I said, here Peter, do you no think your going just a wee bit fast ower this bridge?'. 'And what did your Driver say to that?' asked Mr. Cherry 'Weel, he just looked across at me and said, do you no mind this f*****g bridge fell doon once afore!'

The Passed Fireman was excused. Mr Cherry rolled round on the floor with laughter. John Thomson nearly choked on his false teeth (he did at a later date but that's another story) and the office just shook with merriment. Motion had put another one over on authority. The chapter was closed there and then.

This then was the man to whom I was to fire that morning. I was on '507 and checking around before he joined the engine. Now Peter was a big man and yes, he could only be described as fat. He had several chins, all of which wobbled, and almost piggy-like eyes. He muttered something about it being

'a no bad morning,' adding after a few seconds 'fur a funeral.' I greeted him in a more traditional fashion and told him that I had checked the tank, set the lamps and everything appeared OK, the engine having been prepared for us. 'Great, he said. we'll jist bugger off oot o' it then'. A blast on the whistle, cocks roaring, we slid forward in the winter darkness to the outlet signal. Down to the 'phone, '507 for the 07.30 Aberdeen,' I said. 'Righty-oh, wait for the signal,' came the response. We waited for around five minutes during which time I had a closer look at my fire. There was a big back of the door in and well burned through fire around the rest of the box. Pressure was on the mark and the safety valves were sizzling. While we were waiting, another crew on relieving duties climbed up to travel down to Waverley with us and the Fireman was a Cleaner who was just senior to me, Ronnie Drummond. Now I got on well with Ronnie although, he, for some unknown reason suffered a fair bit at the hands of his peer group when cleaning. Off came the disc and again with cocks hissing we slid, in a vast cloud of steam, out on to the main line. The signal box lights of Haymarket Central Box glimmered weakly through the mist before I shut the cocks and visibility was restored. We clanked our way through the almost deserted platforms at Haymarket station and entered the South tunnel on a yellow.

As always, I was fascinated by the firelight on the tunnel roof and walls as we slowly moved through the darkness. Out into the Gardens and a double yellow took us through the Mound Tunnel to platform 16 and on to our train. Our Guard was already up and waiting for us. We came against the buffers and Ronnie dropped down and coupled on for me. Checking that all was well, I thanked him and as he and his mate went off, I set the lamps and rejoined the cab. The Guard had come up for a heat since it was indeed a bitterly cold morning. We had 12 on for 420 tons tare. Not a lightweight train by any means. 'An' she's gey busy this morning,' said the Guard. He and Peter compared stops, Haymarket, Inverkeithing, Kirkcaldy, Cupar, Leuchars and Dundee Tay Bridge, due in Dundee at 09.19. I have no idea if the Guard confirmed the going speed over the Tay Bridge that morning.

I turned to my fire and setting the exhaust injector to keep her quiet, filled up around the back of the box and fired a few shovelsful down each side of the box. Peter had blown up the brake and the brake test had been completed. Off with the injector, pressure just off the red line and a nice grey haze at the chimney, just waiting for the 'off'. I was now surprised at just how calm I was. The apprehensions of my first main line days had gone. This, I thought, is what experience is. I'd had good days, I'd had my disasters, I'd had a cold run with a B1 but I was now just able to take what comes. It was a great feeling. Whistles blew. The Guard's light winked at the back of the train and with a blast on the whistle, Peter had the regulator open and we were moving. After confirming that the train was following, I crossed back to my seat and settled down to observe signals. We picked up speed through the Gardens and plunged into Haymarket North tunnel. After a brief stop at Haymarket to pick up another surprisingly large number of passengers, we got the 'off' and were soon underway again and roaring past the shed. I commenced firing and '507 responded by blowing off. I eased my firing after that and was totally surprised at just how little coal was being fed to the firebox, yet with the exhaust injector on and the pressure on the red line. Over the Forth Bridge we rumbled and I made sure that I had room in the boiler for more water as we dipped down through the North Queensferry tunnel and Inverkeithing. As we stood at Inverkeithing, I was aware of Peter eating his sandwiches. I thought that he might have skipped breakfast. Away from Inverkeithing and we were soon on the switchback that was the East Coast main line through the Kingdom of Fife. As we dropped down to Kirkcaldy and entered the outskirts of the town, Peter beckoned me across the cab. 'See there,' he said, pointing to the graveyard we were passing. 'They hivnae got a care in the world.' Well, probably not I mused, considering they are hardly in the world. He nodded and resumed his deliberations outside the cab window.

Away we went again, blasting our way up to Dysart and over the top of the hill. Down through Thornton we rumbled at a suitably low speed then away up the hill to Markinch and Falkland Road. Little time to waste here as I fired round the box and '507 lifted this heavy train over the shoulder of Falkland Hill. Then it was along the level and past Lochmuir cabin towards our next stop. At Cupar, he looked across and asked 'hiv ye ever been ower the Tay Bridge?' I nodded that I had. 'I jist dinnae like that brig at a', he shouted back, 'it's been in the watter once before.'

Away from Cupar we sped, making for Leuchars Junction. Leuchars came and went and soon we were racing through St. Fort and Wormit. The Tay Bridge loomed. 'He's got me as bad as himself,' I thought. 'What is this with the Tay Bridge?' We slid round the curve past Tay Bridge South Signal box and then we were on the bridge proper. The mid-winter sun was just showing signs of struggling above the eastern horizon

and, as always, I revelled in the panoramic views up the firth towards Perth and down and out to the North Sea. I also had another look at my fire since '507 was going through to Aberdeen on this train. As we ran off the bridge, without incident it has to be said, I filled up the back corners and generally made sure the fire was in good order. As we ground to a halt at Tay Bridge station, the Aberdeen crew, who were going forward, jumped up. The Fireman had a quick look at the fire. 'A nice fire, son, thanks', he said. I nodded then slipped off and up on to the tank as he swung the water column bag across. I slipped the bag into the filler and the water was turned on. Dundee Tay Bridge station sat below sea level and water pressure was poor. It took an age to fill a tender and that is one of the reasons that Edinburgh engines used to come off at Dundee. It was quicker to change engines than fill up depleted tenders.

We made our way to the Porters' messroom on the platform to have our break. 'I've nae piece left', says Peter, 'I just couldnae wait an' I've feenished it.' I offered him a sandwich from my box. 'Naw, I think I'll go an' look for a pie somewhere,' he replied, and off he trotted. He was soon back with not one but three meat pies which then disappeared with amazing rapidity. After several cups of tea, he declared himself 'human' once more and began to be quite chatty. After a time he went along to the Inspector's Office to find out how the 09.18 from Aberdeen was doing.

He returned and announced that the Aberdeen was on time and that we would have A2 60531 BAHRAM as our steed for the return journey. '531 was a Ferryhill engine with a wicked reputation as a rough rider. Peter confirmed this, saying, 'these fly Aiberdonians always roster this engine so that their ain men dinnae hae tae work the bloody thing. She's a richt bitch o' an engine.' That did nothing to cheer me up at all.

At 11.06 on the dot, '531 ran in at the head of a big train and stopped with the tender conveniently at the water column. I threw my bag up on the footplate and climbed on to the tender. The bag was swung across and we began to fill the tank. The Aberdeen Driver (because despite what Peter had said, the Ferryhill men did of course, on occasions, work '531) stood chatting to Peter. I gave a shout as the water welled up and overflowed. At least we had plenty of water.

I rejoined the engine. The Aberdeen Fireman had a big fire in behind the doors and classic saucer shaped fire. The footplate was washed down and immaculate, there was just over half a glass of water and pressure was sitting nicely just around the 240 lbs mark. 'She's a'richt, son', the Fireman said, 'but sarry aboot the coal'. I looked at the shovel plate and was surprised to see

the coal was in large lumps and a hard grey colour. It was a hard splint coal and since Ferryhill did not have a coaling plant, and there was thus little breakage, the coal had been loaded into the tender in the lumps as it had arrived at the depot. 'You'll hiv to breck ivery piece', said the Fireman in the broad Doric tongue of the North-East, 'but it burns weel an' ye'll hiv nae bother wi' steam.' They took their leave and the Guard came up and gave us our load. '13 on, for 435 tons, and she's weel loaded this morning,' he shouted. As he made his way to the rear of the train, I slipped a dozen shovelsfull round the box and set the exhaust injector. I now knew the hard grind we faced to climb up out of this subterranean hole and on to the Bridge. It was an unremitting slog all the way to the High Girders although we had the benefit of an engine which was already well heated up. I climbed on to my seat and looked back, for the platform was on my side of the cab. Whistles blew, and a Porter relayed the Guard's 'right away', promptly at 11.15. Peter had let the reverser down to around 50% and tugged the regulator into first valve. Cylinder cocks roared as '531 got hold of the train without any slip or fuss. This was where the 6ft 2in driving wheels came into their own. A Gresley might just have been skittering and slipping at this point. I slammed the cylinder cocks closed and '531 began to give a healthy roar at the chimney. We had the train clear of the platform and clear signals all the way up to the bridge. I turned to the tender end and picked up the coal hammer.

I began to break up what looked almost like slate; when struck on the seam, it broke easily enough but with splinters flying everywhere. Peter looked at what I was doing. He just shook his head and then removed it from the shrapnel which was flying around the cab. With a good pile of broken coal, I started firing. The heat from the firebox was incredible. This coal obviously had a high calorific value. I cooled things down for myself by putting the first two or three shovels just inside the door, and then began firing round the box. Peter had pulled the reverser up to around 35% and BAHRAM was rousing the neighbourhood of the Esplanade as we clawed our way round the curving climb to the bridge proper. I partially closed the firedoor flap and climbed back on to my seat. In the cold morning air, '531 was spewing out a healthy dark grey exhaust which streamed away behind the train and hung in the frosty morning sky. Pressure up on the red line and ¾ of a glass of water. Everything was fine so far. We rumbled across the bridge at the required 25 mph with the regulator back in first valve. As we curved off the bridge and passed Tay Bridge South signal box, Peter left the reverser where it was and pulled the regulator out to the stop. '531 surged forward and I began firing to counter this drain on the boiler. The heavy train was accelerated away and the reverser was gradually being pulled up as we began our headlong rush through St. Fort and over one of the fastest pieces of railway on this line. BAHRAM was steaming like a dream but, oh, was she rough. She developed a nose to tail sideways swing and we banged and crashed our way along with the cab floor shaking and rolling. Even in my seat, I was being banged up against the cab side. This was not funny, I thought. No wonder the Ferryhill men tried to avoid her.

With a loud hiss of air, Peter applied the brakes for our Leuchars stop and we slid to a stand at the long island platform. Being the eve of a National holiday, the platform was busy and we were two minutes down by the time the 'right away' came. We blasted away from the station and I fired another round. The firing was easy but breaking up the lumps of coal was becoming a real bind and a hazard to boot, since small splinters flew everywhere and I was afraid I might just be struck in the eyes. '531 was a pleasure to fire and along the stretch to Cupar and our next stop, the speed was not high and the riding bearable, just! Cupar came and went. We sped along the Howe of Fife, glittering with rime in the cold frosty air, over Bow of Fife level crossing and soon we were swinging round the left-hand curve and through Ladybank Station. I picked up the shovel for, once

more, we were faced with another stiff climb, up through Kingskettle to Falkland Road. Peter had her out in around 35% and as we blasted up past the recently closed station at Falkland Road, '531 started to blow off against the injector. This coal was good, but if only it had come in a smaller size. Over the top, regulator closed, we ran quietly down through Markinch and on to Thornton. Here we were booked to run through and, so, with the climb up to Randolph Siding ahead, it was back to the coal hole for me.

Soon, with the regulator all but closed once more and the reverser set in the coasting position, we slipped down through Sinclairtown and drew to a stand at Kirkcaldy still two minutes down. Again, there was a large crowd of intending passengers and further time was lost as they joined the train despite a five minute station duty time being allowed. The green flag waved and away we went, hell for leather, along the switchback of the Fife coast. Our next stop was Waverley and Peter was out to claw back all the lost time. We ambled through Inverkeithing, respecting the permanent speed restriction in place here, and then on to the 1 in 78 climb up through the tunnels and the Forth Bridge. As we hit the bottom of the climb I began firing and by the time we had cleared the North Queensferry tunnel, I had a full head of steam and a full boiler of water. We rumbled over the bridge and I now sat

back in my seat, enjoying the never failing views up river from our lofty domain. As we ran off through Dalmeny, I had a look in the fire. Peter shouted to put the poker in behind the door and shove the fire forward. This I did, and closed the flap. We were once more hitting the high spots for speed as we tore down the hill to Turnhouse and over the River Almond. The speed had risen to the seventies here and it was exhilarating as we rushed up round the curving approach to Saughton Junction with '531 banging, crashing, rocking and rolling all over the place, and joined the lines from Glasgow. As we ran up to the junction we caught up with, then overhauled, a passenger train on the South Main lines and I waved to the passengers who were looking out at this high speed express train overtaking them. We steadied for the approach to Haymarket station and the tunnels and as we ran through the Gardens I opened the flap and looked again at the fire. The firebars were showing through in places and yet, boiler pressure still sat above 225 lbs, but with enough water space to keep her quiet in the station. We ran in to platform 19 at 13.08, exactly one minute early with our relief standing on the platform. The relief crew would work the empty coaches down to Craigentinny whilst we walked round and cadged a lift to the shed on a light engine going that way. As we booked off, Peter said, 'well, we've survived another day son!'

From the sublime to the ridiculous at Haymarket. The second of the allocated J88s, 68339, is the 'shed shunt' locomotive and remains largely as built by the NBR way back in 1904. It is standing on the ash pits at the top end of the shed. This engine was three-shifted and was often to be seen at the head of a line of dead engines, making spectacularly long shunts. (J. Robertson/Transport Treasury)

For me, this is one of the saddest sights. J83 68481, in fully lined BR black, had for many years been the No.1 Waverley West Pilot engine and was kept by her regular crews in a highly polished condition. Superseded in March 1959 by an EE 350hp diesel shunter, 68481 is still in steam and working as a shed coal pilot, but her days are numbered. (J. Robertson/Transport Treasury)

31. CHANGING LANDSCAPES

As 1959 dawned, so dawned another most peculiarly bizarre period in my footplate career. I have said that I had availed myself of the self-study courses ran by BR Scottish Region and had attained passes in the Basic Railway Induction course and First and Second Year Rules and Regulations course. During the winter of 1958/59, I had enrolled in the Railway Operating Practices course, a series of lectures given by the then Chief H.Q. Operating Inspector, Bill Hinam, in Glasgow. I had accepted that I could only attend, shifts permitting, and that I might have to do a lot of self study to keep up. I was, however, back cleaning on regular three shifts and could therefore arrange the nights on which it was possible to attend.

The year 1959 was only a few weeks old when, one morning on the dayshift, I was instructed by the Chargehand Cleaner to make my way to the General Office and report to Mr Cherry, the Shed Master. Somewhat puzzled, and not a little concerned, for Mr Cherry was exalted at 64B, I made my way across to the General Office and knocked on the Inquiry window. It was answered by David Galbraith, the Staff Clerk. Recognising me, he said, 'come away in.' I entered the holy of holies, cap in hand. John Thomson, the Chief Clerk said 'come in and have a seat. Mr. Cherry is on the telephone but we'll go in and see him when he's free. Would you like a cup of tea?' Now this was a turn up for the books but it could not be trouble if I were being offered tea, so I accepted, and sat amongst the Clerks and with Mrs Williamson the typist smiling at me, sipped my tea. Soon the summons came and through to the inner sanctum John Thomson and myself, passed.

George Cherry thanked me for coming in. He then went on to explain what he had in mind. I was being offered the opportunity to become a temporary (unpaid) member of the clerical staff on a co-opted basis designated 'office boy', until I was required for firing duties. But there was more. The most difficult clerical job on the depot was that of Sandy Mercer's, the Roster Clerk. None of the other lower-graded Clerks at Haymarket were apparently willing to learn the job, and the problem was compounded by the fact that the District Motive Power Relief Clerk, Grade 2, had never mastered the Haymarket roster although it was on his duty list for coverage. This post was held by David Masterton, who hailed from Carnwath, was Carstairs trained and thus was a Caley man, and Caley (ex-LMS) rostering and NB (ex-LNER) rostering

were poles apart in practice, even in these days of British Railways. David was quite simply terrified of the prospect of having to cover the Haymarket rosters post with all the inherent problems they posed.

The offer before me was, quite simply, that I went in as Office Boy, on pay based on the average earnings over the three week cleaning cycle. I would train alongside Sandy Mercer in the roster job during the early part of the year, and cover his leave as Roster Clerk. For that, I would be paid for any lost firing turns and would go back firing as required in the summer other than when Sandy went on holiday. This resolved, at a stroke, all the problems I had in attending my night classes in Glasgow and also meant an end to the drudgery of cleaning through the long winter days and nights and I accepted straight away.

On the next Monday morning, in sartorial circumstances far removed from the cleaning gangs, I reported to the General Office at 08.30. I was allocated the desk nearest the Inquiry window and shown my expected duties. I had to prepare and sign all the authority forms requested in the written applications for privilege travel and also write out, record and issue free passes. I was expected to prepare some weekly statements of failures for the DMPS Office at Waverley, and also to sort out all repair cards submitted by Drivers in respect of 'foreign' engines, and send them forward to the owning shed. I was expected to make the tea for the office (and morning conference) requiring a visit to the kit store (described at the beginning of this book) to fill the teapot from the ever-boiling kettle on the open hearth. I also had to do all the filing of correspondence and assist as required or as otherwise directed.

The administration at Haymarket was undertaken by a fairly small workforce relative to the overall number of staff. In overall charge was George Cherry, the Shed Master who had come to Haymarket via Carlisle Canal and who was, during my time there, to go on to become the District Motive Power Superintendent in the Fife district. He was in every way a Company man and operated by the book but he was always fair and honest in his dealings with the men and their Trade Union representatives. The bulk of Drivers, Firemen and Cleaners belonged to ASLEF with only a few being members of the NUR. The shed staff, labourers and others, excluding the craftsmen, were also represented by the NUR; crafts were represented by their respective unions. All clerical staff belonged to the TSSA. George Cherry dealt with all in

an even handed manner. He was, at that time, graded Special Class 'B'.

His immediate Assistant was the Mechanical Foreman and during my time this post was held firstly by John Banks who then succeeded Mr Cherry as Shed Master, and then by the man who replaced him, George Russell, formerly Shed Master at Polmont. John Banks was a real character. A Yorkshireman, he had come up through the fitting ranks at Botanic Gardens shed, Dairycoates and Starbeck, and he stood all of about 5 feet 3 inches tall. He did, however, have large feet for his size and wore huge boots and inevitably was known by his nickname of 'Noddy' though never to his face. He was graded Special Class 'A'. John was also, in his spare time, a Scout Master in the city and one fine evening, took his troop down to Leith Central Diesel Depot for a 'look round'. Now imagine John, 5 feet 3 inches, in big boots and shorts, amongst a company of teenage scouts, some, if not all, taller than he. Inevitably the group were confronted by Running Foreman Dick Marshall ('the Bat') and asked what the 'blankety blank' they thought they were doing. John spoke up and said he was the Shed Master at Haymarket and was just taking his lads for a look round. 'Nane o' your cheek, son, said Dick, 'and get tae f*** oot ma depot.' Short shrift indeed! Dick Marshall gained his nickname by virtue of his favourite saying to his staff: 'if anyone's looking fur me a'll be hinging aboot the tap o' the shed!' Bat indeed.

There was a (permanent) night shift Mechanical Foreman, Grade 1 and this covered by Alec Berry, a young man who was seldom seen during office hours, for obvious reasons.

The Class 1 Chief Clerk was John Thomson, one of the old school, who had started way back with the NB Railway. John was always a gentleman though he must have found it difficult to remain calm when confronted by some of the other larger than life characters who comprised the clerical staff. John was also, to say the least, parsimonious in the extreme when it came to distributing railway property. If say, you went and asked for a new pencil, you first had to show the old one and if, in John's eyes it could stand another sharpening then so be it. If it truly was beyond use, he would unlock the big drawer in the front of his desk, take out a new pencil from the hundreds he had in there, and break it in half. All we ever could get were half pencils! I just went out and bought my own. He also employed a similar approach to a request for a new piece of carbon paper. He would examine the old piece, have you hold it in front of the fire so that the remaining carbon ran, and then suggested that it would do for perhaps another fortnight. An interesting insight into just how he had been brought up on the NBR.

The second in command was the aforementioned David Galbraith, the Class 2 Staff Clerk. David was always the inveterate worrier and took himself, and his work, far too seriously. David was responsible for making up the wages each week and paying out the staff, assisted by Mark Wright

The other class 2 Clerk was Sandy Mercer, the Roster Clerk, who, as I have said, had, without a shadow of a doubt, the hardest and most responsible task at 64B for it was he who covered all the

booked diagrams every day of the week and found staff to cover holidays, sickness, courses and all the special working which was thrown at Haymarket all through the summer months. This job was not made any easier when all the mileage turns were thrown in to the equation and it was his job to ensure that the men who (under the provisions of the National Agreements) were entitled to the mileage turns, did in fact get them. Any slip up in the rostering and a claim for payment of the mileage would follow, as sure as night follows day. This then was the job that George Cherry wanted me to learn. The remaining Clerks at Haymarket were graded Class 4 and

were, in order of seniority, Mark Wright, M.C.M Wright, the Availability Clerk and a leading light in the Railway Staff Association (Scotland) West Edinburgh Club. Mark, a pipe smoker, purveyor of risqué stories and no respecter of rank or position, was a man who went his own way, took time off as it suited him and generally was a law unto himself. In many ways, John Thomson was too nice when it came to dealing with the likes of Mark as I later realised when, at the tender age of 21 years, I was appointed a Relief Station Master in the Glasgow South District and had to make many difficult, and unpopular decisions. The next senior clerk was Bill Hastie, a rotund figure of a man who

was the Punctuality Clerk. Bill, a very experienced railwayman, was one of the very few Haymarket colleagues who went on to finish his time with British Rail, at Millerhill Traction Depot.

Then there was Eric Caw who looked after stores and consumables like loco coal. Eric was recently returned from national service with the RAF and shared an office with, and was driven mad on occasions by, the aforesaid Mark Wright.

Joe Wise was the junior of the class 4 Clerks and covered the Mechanical Foreman's Clerk's post. He worked with the Mechanical Foreman in the wee office upstairs in the new Fitting Shed. Joe was an accomplished junior football player

and he and I became good friends, both of us going through, and comparing, the tangled love lives of teenagers. Joe also completed a lifetime with BR, ending up in the Area Manager's organisation, firstly at Dundee Tay Bridge and then Perth.

The remaining member of staff in the General Office was Mrs Williamson, the Typist. She was a widow of indeterminate age but must have been in her fifties at that time. She was a short, plump lady who did not suffer the younger Clerks gladly and who was not beyond carrying stories to John Thomson. To be fair, she did suffer at the hands of some as will be revealed later in this story. These persons then, formed the administrative backbone of 64B.

I settled in very quickly to my new role and was made very welcome by all concerned. The pace of life was very relaxed, except for David Galbraith who always appeared under extreme pressure and never had time to enter into the general banter of the office. Indeed, within a couple of weeks of joining the office, David passed me the weekly Staff Utilisation Return to do, claiming pressure of his other work. Now this was a weekly return whereby every member of footplate staff had to be accounted for, on a day by day basis in the work he carried out on the day. So, for example, Cleaners firing had to be split from Cleaners cleaning or Cleaners carrying out special duties .The same applied to Passed Firemen and the available staff each week, plus those on holiday, sick etc. had to equate to the total number of staff allocated to the depot. In short, the return had to balance each week.

To do this meant scrutinising the daily worksheets compiled by each Driver, the time office records and the weekly and daily rosters. I quickly realised though, that this return appeared to have a much lesser significance at the office of the DMPS Edinburgh District at 23, Waterloo Place, to where it was consigned. To compile this return, since it was not my responsibility, I was given three hours overtime each week. I quickly found out that, if the return for a previous month was just manipulated and balanced, then HQ were completely satisfied, as was Mr Galbraith. Why a class 2 Clerk had not thought of that surprised me. Indeed, Alec Croy, who was to follow me later, resorted to copying out old returns for previous years, thus short-cutting the process even further!

When covering for Joe Wise I had to compile a weekly return of locomotives using the wheel drop pit; when the blank return sheets ran out and new ones were requested from the DMPS I discovered that this form had been discontinued some time after the end of the war! Yet, here at Haymarket, people had been religiously preparing and submitting them certainly up until the early part of

1959. Yes, it was a funny old railway back then!

One of the more important duties which fell to me was the making of the mid-morning and mid-afternoon tea. Now back in this book, I described how, every morning, there was a 10.00 conference in the Shed Master's office regarding the general working of the depot for the previous 24 hours, any problems arising and any issues anticipated in the current days operation. This group generally numbered between 6 and 10 people and of course, the hospitality was extended to them as well. This involved preparing some 16/17 cups of tea AND remembering who took what in the way of milk and sugar. We did not run to self-service in that department. The tea was made in a huge teapot and water was drawn from the big iron kettle which sat permanently steaming in the next door kit store. Some funny things happened to that kettle over time! I remember making the tea one morning and serving the office. Mrs Williamson, having half consumed her cup of tea, then complained about a funny taste and the fact that there was a black ring around the inside of the cup. Nobody else appeared to notice but, on investigation, I found that the kettle contained a few small lumps of coal, which, by the time it was discovered, were extremely clean and, I suspect, totally germ-free. In retrospect, I cannot understand why she complained for did we not, on the footplate, consume fairly large quantities of coal dust with our sandwiches, over a period of time?

It has to be said that I quickly became bored with the routine clerical work in which I was involved, for there was no real challenge. I think John Thomson sensed my frustration for, after a few weeks familiarisation in the General Office, I was instructed to report to Sandy Mercer in the roster office, located at the rear of the Running Foreman's office across the shed. So started another most interesting, challenging and instructional period of my railway career, a period where time just flew by and where at least one different problem confronted us each day. I took great delight in the challenge and also derived much satisfaction from the solution of these problems.

In better condition and, at this time still employed as No.2 Waverley West Station Pilot, J83 68470 comes on shed for coal, fire cleaning and preparation before running back down to the station to commence work once more. 68470 was replaced by a diesel shunter at the same time as the No.1 West End Pilot, 68481, (see p.104) in 1959. (M. Robertson/Transport Treasury)

On 28th June 1959, Aberdeen Ferryhill's A2 60531 BAHRAM runs off the 'table after being turned to face home and is proceeding to the coaling plant, although the tender is still well loaded. This engine had a reputation for the roughest riding of the Scottish A2s and it was reputed that Ferryhill only rostered her on turns worked by other than Aberdeen Drivers! Whilst not strictly true, I can certainly attest to her rough riding qualities since I had worked her back from Dundee just six months earlier, on 31st December 1958. (J. Robertson/Transport Treasury)

32. FIRING DAYS ARE HERE AGAIN!

It was clear by the start of the summer diagrams that I was likely to be firing as a red ink Fireman, that is on a full week basis, most weeks and so I was returned to the footplate. My departure would leave the office without a boy, but this was soon filled by another senior Cleaner who had to be accommodated on ill-health grounds, and we spent two or three weeks together as he learned the ropes. His name was David Swan, a nice lad, who had recently been married and worried a great deal about the future. Now this was around the time when the Salk vaccine for poliomyelitis had been introduced and all young people were being urged to be immunised. This led to some discussions and David, a new husband with imminent fatherhood looming and the new responsibilities that would bring, thought that he should have the vaccine, but only if someone would go with him, for he was desperately 'feart' of needles. Needless to say, Joe Soap here agreed to accompany him to the clinic in the High Street one lunch time and an appointment was duly made. It was the idea that I would sit with him but when his name was called, he suggested that I should go first so that he could see what was what. I bared my upper arm and at that point was aware of a nurse shouting, 'Mr. Swan. Come back, Mr. Swan!' Jim had watched the needle go in, and took off down the High Street like a shot. It was me who returned to Haymarket with a sore arm. David never did go back!

Back I went to the relentless grind of preparation and relief. I also spent some further days on the Haymarket pilot, a job which I really enjoyed since I was permitted to drive for a part of each day on most days. I tended to swop turns for late shifts as this made travel to and from home easier and of course, since day turns were popular amongst the younger Firemen, I found it easy to pick and choose jobs. I swapped into the Junior Spare link quite a lot and early in June I was, for one day only, booked firing on the 12.00 'Carlisle' over the Waverley route. This turn was allocated to No.4 link and my Driver was Faber Dewar, a small, lean man with a great sense of the ridiculous. The 12 noon Carlisle was the not quite all stops, mid-day passenger service to Carlisle and on the day in question consisted of only four coaches and a BG, totalling 170 tons, not a heavy load in any book. We returned with the 15.33 ex-Carlisle, this time an all stops passenger with a similarly light load.

I joined the allocated engine, A3 60057 ORMONDE which had been outshopped in September 1958 with a double chimney. This had been one of the Doncaster-built A1s of 1925, converted to A3 in 1946, and had been a Scottish Area engine from 1928 and a Haymarket engine since 1943. So '57 had been duly prepared and the preparation Fireman had left a full fire in behind the doors and back corners of the firebox. I quickly shot a round of coal down each side of the box and along the fore-end, closing the flap to allow this to catch alight in its own time. By the time my mate joined the engine, I had checked the tender, tested both injectors and set the lamps. After he had a quick look around, he blew off the brakes and we went forward to the shed exit points where I 'phoned out. We were soon on our way down to Waverley and '57 showed that she was in first class fettle. She rode smoothly with only barely perceptible clicks as the rear wheels rode over the rail joints. The boiler was nicely filled and pressure was rising very slowly as my fire caught alight. We slid down through the station and reversed on to our small train in platform No.9. At 12.00 on the dot, we received the 'right away' and, with consummate ease, '57 had the light train on the move and into the South Calton Tunnel with a mere sigh of steam at the chimney.

This journey down over the Carlisle road was, at least to Hawick, a much easier trip than my previous exploit on the 'Waverley'; our first stop was at Galashiels where we were due at 12.53. Now 53 minutes for the 45½ miles, the first 14 miles on an average rising gradient of 1 in 70 was no sinecure even with a light train and we could not hang about, especially on the long climb. At no time however, was '57 thrashed quite like SPEARMINT on my one previous trip over this road, but we did have a much lighter load. However, the difference the double chimney made was obvious and although ORMONDE was being worked on full regulator and with the reverser out around the 30% mark, this had little effect on boiler pressure or water level. Both were easily maintained at respectable levels throughout the climb, with no hint of any breathlessness, and I was shovelling somewhat less coal. Not quite a fair comparison given the 10 coach load with a single chimney A3 on my last trip, but an eye-opener nevertheless, regarding the benefits of the Kylchap arrangement.

We took up all our stops on time and ran into Hawick dead on time at 13.28. Here, sitting high above the town and the River Teviot, I questioned Faber about what lay ahead since I had never been south of here. This he described as 'more of the same, son, another 15½ miles o' hard slogging up tae Whitrope but the saving grace is that we dinnae stop until were over the top.' He was right of course and from the platform end at Hawick the line climbed up the valley of the Slitrig Water on just a slightly easier rising gradient than that up to Falahill, averaging around 1 in 85 rising, but with a final three mile stretch at 1 in 75 up over the summit, deep in the folds of the Cheviot hills. I had three minutes to get my fire in order at Hawick and I filled up the back corners and under the door finishing with a dozen or so shovels down the sides and across the fore-end. With exhaust injector set, and '57 deafening the good citizens of Hawick as she blew off, at 13.31 we got the green flag.

Faber opened the regulator to first valve until the drivers caught the rails on the severe curving climb out of the platform and then pulled it right back into big valve. The reverser was set at 25% but was soon being eased out as we hit the short 1 in 90 and then on to a 1 in 70 gradient. The safety valves had shut with the distinctive 'pop' as the demand for steam was increased. As we climbed away from the town I started firing again, little and often and pressure sat easily on the red mark. Round the reverse curves and over the viaduct crossing Slitrig Water at Lynnwood, we headed up into the barren hill country, and the long slog up through the lonely settlements of Stobs and Shankend. Slowly we wound our short train up through the curves in the hills, with our exhaust darkening the summer skies. Over the long 15 arch Shankend viaduct we climbed, and blasted through the lonely station. We were soon up on the higher slopes and running across bleak moorland with the distinctive top of Leap Hill clearly visible on the right-hand side. Under a cattle creep bridge, then we plunged into the 1,208 yard long tunnel immediately on the approach to the summit. Out of the tunnel and soon the lonely signal box at Whitrope summit came into view. Here, with a wave to the Signalman, we went over the top. The regulator was closed and the reverser wound into 25% in preparation for coasting down to our next stop at the extremely remote station at Riccarton Junction. Riccarton Junction was a lonely and small, mainly railway community which was wholly dependant on the railway since there was no road at all into the village. Indeed the village shop, the Riccarton branch of Hawick Co-operative Society, stood on the platform as part of the station buildings. Riccarton was the junction for the Border Counties railway, the old NB road into Northumberland and on into Newcastle and as such, supported a small engine shed, a sub-shed of Hawick, and now maintained to provide banking assistance on the long and steep climbs up to Whitrope Summit which lay at a height of 1,008 feet above sea level.

On leaving Riccarton, the line now descended in long curving loops, almost as steeply as it had climbed, down through the Cheviots and under the looming shoulder of Arnton Fell, on the long 10 mile falling gradient down through upper Liddelsdale to Newcastleton. In just six minutes for the six miles after leaving Riccarton Junction, we stopped at lonely Steele Road before setting off again downhill to Newcastleton, one of the larger communities on the southern edges of the Cheviot hills. We rattled over the short Sandholme viaduct crossing Hermitage Water and ran into Newcastleton station on time at 14.15. Now, no one at Haymarket ever referred to Newcastleton by that name and it was always called 'Coppshiehome' (spelt, I think, as pronounced) and indeed I pondered over maps trying to identify where this Coppshiehome was, or why it was so called. The reason for this was never really explained to me. Away from Newcastleton and over the Liddel Water we crossed the Border and into England just before Kershopefoot station. We were non-stop into Carlisle now as we ran over the switchback of small ups and downs on the English side of the border and paralleling the actual border with Scotland, through Penton to Riddings Junction where the Langholm branch diverged. We did not dally and, running on now virtually level gradients, passed through Longtown, Lyneside, Harker and Parkhouse, soon passing over the 'Caledonian' main line at Kingmoor before dropping down to Port Carlisle Branch Junction and on into Citadel station, arriving at 14.47 on the dot.

There, we were relieved and made our way to the mess room on the Platform whilst '57 was taken off to Carlisle Canal shed to have the fire cleaned, to be coaled and prepared for a later return to Edinburgh. After our food and a welcome cup of tea, we made our way back through the station to take over a new engine which had been worked down from Carlisle Canal and coupled to the coaches forming the 15.22 Carlisle to Edinburgh passenger train. The engine was another A3, but one of the Carlisle Canal allocation, No.60079 BAYARDO which, at that time, had run a few thousand miles and had not, as yet, received a double chimney (this was fitted in January, 1960). Working the 15.22 departure from Carlisle Citadel, we were confronted with 24 station stops before reaching Waverley at 19.10.

The return journey was a repeat of the outward journey but with an even harder climb up from Newcastleton to Whitrope, and the long 15 mile grind up to Falahill from Galashiels. Our new A3, despite approaching a general repair, was completely on top of the job and I have to say that, overall, I did really enjoy my first (and only) through trip to Carlisle. However, I do also know that the 12.00 and the 14.33 workings to Carlisle were amongst the easier of the turns, and while I had experienced a big heavy train as far as Hawick on a one-off basis, the men who regularly worked these heavy passenger trains and the many heavy through freights were confronted by what must have been one of the most difficult lines of railway anywhere in the country.

A Gateshead visitor; several of which would appear daily. On 30th March 1952 A1 60115 MFG MERRILIES has been coaled, watered, had the fire and ash pan cleaned and is now being taken by the disposal Driver back into the shed Strangely, she has not been turned to face south and perhaps the Haymarket Running Foreman has some agenda of his own! (J. Robertson/Transport Treasury)

33. ANOTHER 'COAST'

Early one afternoon in July, again having changed for spare turns, the Passed Fireman on the 13.30 'Diners' was lifted for driving and I fell to the turn. This train was more properly known as the 'Heart of Midlothian', the 13.30 London Kings Cross which also conveyed through coaches from Perth and Aberdeen. Consequently it was always a big train in the summer time and at the weekends was always supported by at least one relief working. However, on the day in question, a Friday, we were on our own.

After booking on and being given the news about what I was doing, I checked to see who my Driver was to be, fully expecting it to be one of the No.2 link regulars, since this is where the turn was allocated. I was (most) pleasantly surprised to find that my Driver was to be Alec Fisher, also from the Spare link, and covering for the annual leave of the regular Driver. Our engine was A1 60160 AULD REEKIE. Alec arrived just after I had booked on, and immediately recognised me from our week on the Haymarket pilot. We walked to the oil store and drew a bundle of waste and some washed sweat rags before making our way to the front of No.1 road, where '160 sat gleaming in the midday sun. She had been prepared and after checking the tank was full, I walked forward to the kit store to draw the lamps and the nameboard. Alec brought '160' down to the shed exit points where, after setting the lamps and placing the nameboard on the centre lamp iron above the buffer beam, I 'phoned out. On rejoining the cab, Alec indicated that I should take the Driver's seat and drive the engine down to the station. When the disc cleared, I took off the steam brake and pulled on the regulator. Steam roared at the cylinder cocks as we moved off shed and on to the main line. I was concentrating hard on the signals as we slipped down to Haymarket station, and really felt important sitting at the controls as we passed down the length of the fairly busy No.3 platform at Haymarket. The signal at the tunnel mouth cleared to amber and, with a shriek on the whistle, we plunged into the darkness. Soon we were running through the Gardens with the usual group of spotters and visitors standing on the two iron footbridges watching the railway scene below. With a toot on the whistle and a cheery wave, we slipped into the Mound tunnel and ran down through the North mid-road, past the coaches of our train, in Nos.19 and 1 platforms (the North Main). I counted the coaches as we passed and

was not at all surprised to see that we would have fourteen on. Slipping out towards the Calton Tunnel North, we cleared the shunt signal which would take us back on top of our train. The signal cleared and, winding the reverser into back gear, I gently eased the huge locomotive back on to the standing coaches, just kissing the buffers. I opened the regulator again to squeeze up and set the steam brake. This got the nod of approval from my mate.

While so employed, Alec had been attending to the fire and I had paid little attention to what he had being doing. I slipped off and coupled up to the train and then took the tail lamp around to the front and set the express train headcode. On re-joining the engine, I then had a look at Alec's handiwork and was surprised to see a huge fire sloping away from the back of the box towards the fore-end. Alec saw the look on my face. 'I thought ye might want to drive a wee bit, he said, and I was jist intending to make things easy for myself.' I shook my head and shouted back that I had only been over the road twice before and there was no way, with any degree of confidence, that I could take the regulator. He nodded and shouted in my ear that his fire would let me sit until about Longniddry or even further on before I had to fire. 'Jist makin' things easy,' he shouted, and laughed. I later found out that Alec was quite prepared to let his Fireman drive (shades of our days on the Haymarket pilot, I thought) and did indeed make up the fire to give himself an easy time. The fact that I demurred on this occasion, he accepted, for indeed it was the only sensible approach given my lack of experience, and so I was to benefit from his enthusiastic bout of coal-heaving. It has also to be said that, on another occasion, whilst sitting in the cab of an A2, at the head of an empty coach working and waiting to cross from the relief lines to the yard entrance at Craigentinny, I saw the same up 'Diners' come past with a young Fireman at the controls of A1 60161 NORTH BRITISH. There was Alec relaxing in the Fireman's seat, whilst the black smoke just rolled back over the train.

I was concerned about the possibility of blowing off since, with this roaring furnace of a fire, '160 was making steam very quickly now and there was not a lot of space in the boiler. The Guard had given Alec details of the load and had gone back the train. Since the platform was on my side of the engine I sat, leaning out the cab with a weather eye on what was happening back the train, whilst trying to answer all the questions from the small and not so

small boys, gathered about the cab. Glancing at the steam pressure gauge, I saw it was almost on the red line and '160 was sizzling at the valves, an indication that she would blow off quite soon. I banged on the exhaust injector and anxiously watched pressure gauge and water gauge glass.

Back the train, whistles blew and the green flag was waved. 'Right away, mate,' I called and turned off the injector, before again leaning out to watch as the train slid out of the platform. Closing the cocks, I heaved a sigh of relief as the water level was seen bobbing in top of the gauge glass, although this was partly due to the fact that we were on the 1 in 70 falling gradient through the Calton Tunnel North. I opened the damper as we clattered our way out of the tunnel and over Abbeyhill junction points, and blushed as I saw the pall of black smoke being trailed behind us. AULD REEKIE was living up to her name, and how! Alec just looked across the cab, and laughed. Down through St. Margaret's we rushed with whistle shrieking. No doubt all this black smoke would have the men working there think that Haymarket had turned another green Passed Cleaner out to do a man's job. By Craigentinny, the smoke was beginning to clear to a dark grey haze and by Monktonhall junction, the chimney was all but clear. The fire was a white-hot furnace and the reflected heat was incredible even although I was sitting to the side of the backplate. Steam pressure was on the red line and I had the exhaust injector set.

Alec was dead accurate in his prediction and indeed it was only as we were approaching Drem that I had to pick up the shovel and commence firing. The up journey was uneventful with '160 completely on top of the job. I did not fill up the firebox as Alec had done but fired little and often as I had been taught. Nevertheless, I was on the go for the duration whilst, had I followed Alec's lead, I certainly could have had longer spells in my seat. We arrived in Newcastle at 15.48, bang on time, and after we had been coupled off, it was away to Gateshead shed for a welcome break and meal.

We worked back with the down 'Heart of Midlothian' due out of Newcastle at 18.12. Our train ran in on time and we had an on time departure with a similar load as the up train. Again no problems were encountered and we rolled into Waverley on time at 20.25. Another 'coast' job under my belt!

I have already described the Trade Holidays feature of Scottish life in summer and yet again, the Trade Holiday season was in full swing. On the Friday evening of the 'Glasgow Fair' holidays, that is the first Friday of the second fortnight in July, Glasgow was just pandemonium as working people, starting their annual fortnight's holiday, were rushing to leave the city by whatever means at their disposal. In 1959, instead of flocking to the airport to fly to exotic Spanish resorts, the railway was first choice, with the popular destinations being much nearer to home. Little did I think that a mere three years later, I would be a Relief Station Master in Glasgow and experiencing the thrill of the 'Fair' first hand, in charge of a busy suburban station on the Cathcart Circle.

I had booked on at 17.00 and, with my mate Passed Fireman Magnus Clark, having prepared B1 61260, we coupled to the train engine going down to work the 18.30 Edinburgh to Glasgow. Double headed, we worked the train forward to Queen Street, or in our case, Cowlairs. There we uncoupled and ran clear, to allow the train to proceed down the hill to destination. After picking up a Conductor Driver, since my mate had not signed for this particular route, we ran back to Cowlairs Junction box and were then signalled to the line down through Springburn. From there, we proceeded down to Bellgrove Junction and after passing through were directed on to the City Union lines and on to St. Enoch

station. This was totally unknown territory for me and I crossed from side to side taking in all the unfamiliar landmarks of this cross-city rail route. At St. Enoch we were deep in the heart of the old Glasgow & South Western territory. From here, we were booked to work a 'Starlight Special' leaving at 20.50 and going back the way we had come. As we came off the City Union, we were signalled round the left-hand chord of the St. Enoch triangle so that we had to reverse on to the train. This was done in order to turn us, head east and to get us tender-first on to our train. After coupling on, we had our sandwiches and some tea, before I set about getting the fire into shape for our return working.

Away back the platform, the crowds were immense and St. Enoch, like the other three main Glasgow Termini, was just a seething mass of good-natured humanity seeking the Clyde and Ayrshire coast as well as destinations south of the border, like London, where our train would eventually end up. Dead on time, we received the right away and Magnus pulled the regulator out. With a hefty bout of slipping, our B1 got the train on the move round the curving sweep to the left and on to the City Union line. As we ran up past College Goods station we had the signals clear through Bellgrove and on to the Springburn line, and I began firing.

Clear signals again showed ahead and unchecked, we crossed on to the Edinburgh/Glasgow main line at Cowlairs Junction, where we dropped the Conductor and turned our nose to the north-east. We had an uneventful run clear through to Waverley, where we were signalled down the No.20 platform. Here I uncoupled and we ran out into Calton Tunnel South to the 'Limit of Shunt' before being signalled back through the station and back to the shed. These weekend evenings at Trade Holiday times saw Waverley just abuzz with movement and trains, with many special and relief workings to supplement the normal timetable.

On 18th September 1950, not long out of Doncaster works and sporting BR lined-out blue livery, A3 60087 BLENHEIM charges up through North Queensferry station with the Up Aberdeen express fish train before entering the Forth Bridge. She was returned to BR green livery in August 1952. The train will be either the 12.30pm or the 1.32pm Aberdeen Guild Street to London, but is more likely the latter since this was a Top Link turn at Haymarket. (J. Robertson/Transport Treasury)

34. SPEED MERCHANT

At the back end of July, on one very hot summer's afternoon, I was sent as Fireman on the 16.00 London, the afternoon 'Talisman', with no less than a personage than Peter Robertson, and this one trip to me was the pinnacle of my footplate days. On booking on, I found that we had A3 60098 SPION KOP as the booked engine, which within the last week or so had been out-shopped from Doncaster with a double chimney. Peter joined me at the booking-on window and asked if I had read the notices. At that time I had not and said so, adding however that it was my intention to do so since I did know just how important this was. Peter nodded approval and together we went to the 24 hour notice case where all late/urgent notices were posted regarding such items as emergency speed restrictions, temporary non-availability of water columns or indeed the troughs at Lucker, and any other item which could adversely affect the safety of train running. Reading the late notice case was a pre-requisite for all Drivers and Firemen involved in train working and 15 minutes were allowed in each diagrammed turn for this purpose. The dangers of not reading late notices was highlighted in, and was the immediate

cause of, the Goswick derailment, with the grievous loss of life, mentioned earlier in this book.

Notices read, and with nothing of note happening on the east coast, we walked to the stores and collected some washed sponge cloths. Since the afternoon was so warm, almost unseasonably warm for Edinburgh, I also took the opportunity to fill two bottles with cold water to supplement my supply of tea, before joining SPION KOP on No.1 road. The engine, bright in its new paintwork and cleaned to perfection, looked great in the bright sunshine. It had also been prepared and indeed the preparation crew were just putting the finishing touches to the locomotive. I passed the time of day with the Fireman, a fellow cleaning mate, Wattie Mearns, who was a bit senior to me. Wattie was one of the more dedicated Cleaners who always put that additional bit of effort into preparation and had, on this occasion, not only cleaned the faceplate to perfection but had also found time to rub up the tender end so that it gleamed. The cab was spotless and he had a big fire in behind the door. We were assured that the tender had been filled and after the preparation crew left us, I tried each injector in turn, before setting my head

and tail lamp. Peter wound the reverser into full forward and blew up the vacuum. Shouting a warning, he pulled on the regulator and, with steam roaring from the cylinder cocks, we slid slowly forward to the shed exit. Having telephoned out we waited on the signal; while there, I filled the pail with cold water from the tender and set my two bottles of water in the pail, in the corner of the tender end where it would get any benefit of cooling air as we proceeded.

Soon we were backing on to our train in platform No.11 at Waverley, the usual limited load of nine coaches, 307 tons tare/320 gross. Despite the light load, there was little time for hanging about on this turn of duty since we were allowed only 126 minutes for the 125 mile journey to Newcastle, due there at 18.06. This afternoon 'Talisman' was a very popular train and seats had to be reserved. Standing was not permitted and in the public timetable it was clearly spelt out that the number of passengers carried was limited to the number of seats available. Oh that the successors of the east coast services could follow this practice. Ask anyone who has had a miserable journey between Edinburgh and London on a grossly overcrowded Inter City 225 GNER service.

D49/1 62715 ROXBURGHSHIRE on the turntable at Haymarket on 11th November 1958. As the introduction of Diesel Multiple Units on many of the Edinburgh local passenger train services continued apace, the traditional work for these fine engines diminished and by this time they were being largely employed on empty coach stock with the odd forays out on passenger trains and in particular, the forward working of 'portions' of late incoming east coast expresses. (J. Robertson/Transport Treasury)

On the stroke of 16.00 we got the 'right away' and immediately Peter had the train on the move. This man did not hang about and we accelerated away down through Calton tunnel and were hitting 35mph by the time we were approaching the overbridge at St. Margaret's. Peter patted the regulator shut as we swept though the depot area with whistle shrieking. Tugging it open again as we swept past Craigentinny, he wound the reverser back to around 15%. We shimmied round the reverse curves at Portobello on the permitted speed limit or perhaps just a bit above, '98 riding like a dream. Past Newhailes Junction, the regulator was tugged into big valve and we accelerated round the left-hand curve at Monktonhall and over the Esk Viaduct. At this point, we were clear of the restrictive speed restrictions which dogged all east coast trains on the first five miles out of Edinburgh, and now began to run as an express train should. I commenced firing, little and often, with the confidence of now knowing this road somewhat better. All I saw of my mate was his boots as he hung over the side, concentrating on signals. The run was a sinecure. Firing was light although at frequent intervals, steam pressure sat easily between 200 and 225 lbs for the whole trip and the water level was easily kept at a point just above half a glass. I had ample time to make use of my comfortable bucket seat and admire the Scottish lowland and border countryside, the rich farmland with fields of ripening crops and sleek animals grazing. Life could get no better, I thought.

We were soon through Dunbar and after a sprint along the straight and level at Innerwick, '98 set her nose up the hill at Cockburnspath and onto the climb which would take us up through the eastern edge of the Lammermuir hills where the hills literally fell into the North Sea, and over the top at Grantshouse. As I had eased my rate of firing on the later stages of the climb, Peter let out the reverser to 35% to maintain momentum against the lowering boiler pressure. We cleared Grantshouse station with all but a clear chimney and safety valves sizzling. With the regulator all but shut and the reverser wound back into 25%, we swung round the long curving descent towards Reston. Speed was steadied for the Ayton curve and we were soon through Burnmouth station and running down the high cliffs above the North Sea, gleaming blue, in the late afternoon sun and looking very inviting indeed to someone who had sweat pouring down face, neck and back. Through Berwick station we swept with a few waiting passengers stepping back as we approached, and on over the Royal Border Bridge. This was, and indeed still is, something which still thrills me. The long curving progress away high over the mother of all border rivers, the Tweed, and looking down on the hustle and bustle of the busy town of Berwick-upon-Tweed. This indeed was a birds-eye view!

Water was picked up at Lucker troughs and we sped southwards over the rolling Northumberland plain and on towards Newcastle. Soon, having ground our way round the Morpeth curve and the one place where the Civil Engineer was absolutely right to have imposed a 40 mph speed restriction, after another sprint on favourable gradients, we slowed for the run down through Heaton and Manors. Crashing our way over the biggest set of diamond crossings in the world, we ran into No.8 platform at Newcastle Central, some three minutes early at 18.03. As we came to a final halt, I was off and set the lamps; then, with a warning shriek on the whistle, we moved out on to the King Edward Bridge past the Gateshead A1 which was waiting to take the train on to London, whilst we made our way to Gateshead shed for the usual very welcome food.

We were booked to return with the Down 'Talisman' departing Newcastle Central at 20.34 with again, only 126 minutes allowed for the trip to Edinburgh. At about 20.00 we sought out '98 which had been fully prepared for us, and after checking the tender, I 'phoned out at the west end of Gateshead to the Signalman in Greenfields Junction. The signal cleared in a bit and we drew out chimney leading to clear the subsidiary signal which would then take us back on to the High Level Bridge, where we would then be held until our train arrived from the south. When sitting on the High Level Bridge it was possible to see the incoming service approach over the King Edward Bridge which was upstream, and thus we always had due warning when the fire should be built up.

As we sat on the bridge looking out, and observing all the life below us on the River Tyne in the fine summer evening, Peter explained his strategy for punctual running, whilst no doubt secretly hoping for a late arrival from the Kings Cross men. He explained that after the small dip from the Central to Manors we were faced with a continuous climb to Killingsworth, six miles out, at an average rising gradient of about 1 in 270. It was, he said, his practice to have the train up to at least 60 mph by Forest Hall at the five mile mark, and thus '98 would be working 'against the collar' for that first five miles. No other Driver had ever explained in such detail, a plan for what was about to happen, and I was duly impressed to be treated as part of 'the team'. I now knew exactly what was what and just how hard I would have to work with an engine which was still 'cold', even though we again had the limited load. I had a quick look at my fire which had been well made up by the Gateshead preparation crew and decided to leave well alone meantime. There a good fire all around the box and pressure was sitting at about 200 lbs with ¾ of a glass of water showing.

At about 20.38, the down train appeared on the King Edward Bridge and slowly made its way across and into the station. It was about 20.42 when the Kings Cross A4 slid past us en route to Gateshead, and the signal cleared to allow us to back into the station and on to the train. As we were being coupled up, I opened the blower and shot a dozen or so shovels around the firebox. A grey haze hit the station roof. A quick sprint to set the lamps (the headboard was still in place on the centre lower lamp iron) as Peter conducted a brake continuity test and back into the cab as whistles blew away down the platform, and a green flag was waved. With a quick acknowledgement on the whistle, Peter had the regulator open and the train on the move almost instantly. I slammed the cylinder cocks shut and picked up the shovel. We were twelve minutes down and I had a Driver who was now in his element. I fired slowly and precisely as we blasted through Manors Station and on to the rise at Argyle Street Junction. Pressure rose quickly on to the red line and I set the exhaust injector. Watching the chimney, the grey haze cleared and I began firing once more. With the light load and coaches which were roller bearing fitted, '98 accelerated the train in fine style. We finally kicked the junctions, with their associated restricted speeds, behind us at Heaton North Junction and Peter had the regulator full out against the stop and the reverser set at about 30%. We blazed away up the hill through Benton and on to the steepest part of the gradient (1 in 200). I estimated that we were now running at Peter's desired speed of 60 mph and in a minute or so, he drew his head in and shouted across: 'we made it but we now have to keep at it because we're well down'. Over the next twelve miles we sped over the switchback of small ups and downs with speed into the eighties. Then, after the small summit at Stannington, the brakes went on with a vengeance as we slowed for the Morpeth curve.

After Morpeth, and with the regulator back out against the stop, Peter kept SPION KOP hammering away until again we slowed for Alnmouth. The A3 was steaming like a dream and I was not in any way being over-worked, although the firing was light and often. I had also a better knowledge of where we were and what lay ahead. As we swept through Alnmouth, Peter again drew his head in and consulted his watch. He held up two fingers and then pointed up. We were winning. I was filled with a strange excitement being part of this effort to claw back as much of the lost time as possible and doubled to my task as we blasted up the hill through Longhoughton to the first summit at Littlemill. A dip and then '98 dropped her nose down the six mile bank known as Christon Bank to

Chathill. Here Peter set the reverser at about 18% and in big valve, the train began to hurtle at an ever increasing speed – it later transpired that we had topped 90 mph. This man was a real fire-eater. As we passed through Chathill, the train was again steadied, for Lucker troughs lay just two miles ahead. After a strong-arm act with the scoop and a full tender once more, it was back to much of the same. I threw the coal in and Peter blasted it out. Down through the long dip at Beal with Lindesfarne sitting framed in the blue of the sea, we again topped 90 mph This was one of my favourite vistas on the home run. Past Goswick, up the hill through Scremerston, over the top at Spittal and there the whole town of Berwick lay set out before us in glorious panoramic splendour. Again we steadied for the run down and on to the Royal Border Bridge, and as we passed Tweedmouth signal box Peter indicated that we had regained seven minutes of our lost time.

Through the island platform which was Berwick out came the regulator again, and once more it was back to the shovel. We entered the Scottish Region at Marshall Meadows Signal Box just six minutes adrift with all to play for. On the long 1 in 190 rising gradient up along the sea cliffs, Peter dropped the reverser to about 30% and '98 responded like the thoroughbred she was. Easy through the wide sweeping curve at Ayton and again we accelerated towards Reston and the climb up to Grantshouse, although this was in no way as severe as the northern approaches. By the top at Grantshouse, we had gained another two minutes and an 'on time' arrival appeared in the bag, though yet to come was Portobello East Junction, where fate always appeared to conspire against down expresses. We roared down through Penmanshiel tunnel with the regulator only open a crack and the reverser set in 15%. Here I could put down the shovel and enjoy a good drink of tea, and admire the scenery in the deepening shadows as we sped down to our next slow for the Dunbar curve. Along the East Lothian plain we roared

and by Drem we were on time, hitting the eighties in the process.

The remainder of the run was an anti-climax after all our fireworks and we made our sedate way into Edinburgh through the eastern suburbs, and surprise, surprise, got a clear road through Portobello with all distants lying 'off'. A quick wash in the pail and we were entering No.11 platform at Waverley bang on time at 22.40, having run from Newcastle in a time of 114 minutes net. Now, as I have stated before, this run was by no means exceptional and indeed Driver P.B. Robertson repeated, and indeed bettered, this performance on several occasions, as did several other speed merchants from 64B. Nevertheless it was achieved by an A3 and not an A4 and demanded a strenuous effort by the engine. Indeed, it is in retrospect, I think, much to the credit of K.J. Cook who took over as CM&EE at Doncaster, and his use of the Ziess optical equipment for frame and valve setting, that the inherent weaknesses in the Gresley conjugated valve gear were finally laid to rest and that the Gresley Pacifics were given a 'second wind' and a chance to show what they could really do. The down pre-war 'Coronation' service, with fewer coaches (eight) in limited formation, was allowed an even 120 minutes for this run, and even on the much-vaunted test run on 2nd July 1937 with A4 4491 (60012) COMMONWEALTH OF AUSTRALIA with Driver John Binnie of Haymarket at the regulator, a time of 112 minutes was achieved for the up run, with some 114 minutes for the down. Twenty odd years later, Haymarket men were still

putting up similar sparkling performances, but on all service trains, now with 'common user' engines and on a fairly regular basis.

However, it was the fact that Peter had in his mind a plan to suit all eventualities regarding the running of these express trains, as indeed had many other Haymarket Drivers, which impressed me. He knew exactly where, and by how much, time could be regained, timing section by timing section. Of course, he paid scant regard to the laid down maximum speeds in some locations but again he knew where this was possible, and safe. He, and many other Drivers, took a liberal interpretation of the maximum speeds laid down by the Chief Civil Engineer, but did so with the confidence of knowing that the safety of the train was not in any way compromised. They never took liberties with the lower permanent and temporary speed restrictions. That he, as my Driver, took pains to share his intentions with me on the day, and indeed spoke with me at some length, and on a one to one basis, on various subjects and on where I saw my career going, made me feel a real part of a team, rather than just an inexperienced Cleaner who had to be watched carefully. I consider myself privileged to have had such an opportunity and indeed, this one occasion sealed a growing friendship with Peter, as mentioned before. It was also my last turn as a Fireman on the east coast although I made several footplate journeys later not with only Peter but also some other Drivers, and always on the backshift 'Talisman'.

The old order changeth! It is 6th September 1959 and demolition has started in order to create from Nos.7 and 8 roads a new, custom-built repair area for the diesel electric fleet, segregating them from their steam peers. A2 60537 BATCHELOR'S BUTTON, in grimy condition, sits forlornly amongst the carnage. Nos.1 to 6 roads were to remain in use until the final demise of steam at 64B in 1964. (Alec Swain/Transport Treasury)

J83 68481, formerly one of the Waverley West Station Pilots, now covers the coal pilot duties on the shed and is seen here with the wagons brought up to the top end for clearance of ashes, on 6th September 1959. When full, the wagons will be taken back down to Haymarket yard for working forward to the Borthwick Bank tip. This was a regular routine each morning at Haymarket. In the right background, a wagon of coal is just being hoisted up the side of the coaling plant. (Alec Swain/Transport Treasury)

35. FOOTPLATE FINALE

I fired mainly on preparation and empty coach workings through August, and had one final turn out on the main line. This again happened when I was spare and had to stand in for a regular No.4 link Fireman who had gone sick. The turn was the 20.00 Glasgow, better known as 'The Pullman' and was the onward working of the 11.50 'Queen of Scots' Pullman service from Kings Cross. My Driver was Charlie Rankine, the booked man and we had 73108, an Eastfield Standard Five. There was no hanging about on this turn with 55 minutes only allowed for the journey. Again, it was an uneventful run with an engine which was in fine condition. I had a high regard for these particular Standard class engines since they steamed well and were easy to fire, although they did tend to be somewhat draughty and dirty to work on, especially at higher speeds. Our return working was with the 23.00 class E freight from Cadder to Niddrie and at Eastfield we had been given one of our own B1s, 61245.

As the summer timetable drew to a close, it was obvious that my time on the footplate must also follow suit. Main line diesels in the shape of the 1160hp Birmingham RCW Sulzers had been coming on stream from mid-1959 with D5330 and D5331 arriving in September. They were introduced on Aberdeen and Dundee turns although they were also appearing on the Waverley route. DMUs were still arriving and taking over lesser passenger workings in ever increasing numbers, with the work allocated to Leith Central, by now a depot in its own right.

The introduction of the DMU 'twins' around the Edinburgh area was not an unqualified success however, and indeed was, in retrospect, an indictment of the poor decisions made by senior management, since they were now proceeding with the replacement of steam hauled services which had run in 4/5 or even 6 coach formations. Replacement of these trains by two car diesel units, despite the new cleanliness and comfort, did not go down well with the travelling public at large. Sadly, by the time measures were put in place to strengthen these trains, the psychological damage had been done and passengers on the suburban and local urban services had deserted the railway in and around Edinburgh. A general rot had set in which did nothing for morale. Firemen were on the way out and a big freeze on promotions was also on the way since many smaller sheds were closing and the footplate crews there were able to opt for other, bigger and more secure depots, taking their place according to seniority. All this

spelt disaster for Cleaners and indeed there was a move by BR to induce, by a cash payment, junior Firemen and Cleaners to leave the industry all together.

Fortunately, since I had started my railway career as a Clerical Officer, my destiny lay elsewhere. I had toyed with the idea of applying to go as a 'Fireman on loan'. At many depots south of the border, recruitment into the harsh regime of the footplate life was now well nigh impossible, and places like Birmingham Saltley and all the London depots had advertised for men to go 'on loan' as Firemen. I had seriously contemplated Kings Cross Top Shed but was diverted from that line of thinking by another interview with Mr Cherry. Haymarket was short of a Clerk and since I had been groomed for the internal relief unit for the Roster Clerk over the previous winter, and I since had started my railway career in the Clerical grades in any case, now, he suggested, was the time to make the transitional move back to the 'white collar' side. Any firing turns gained or lost now would be irrelevant in any case. In short, I was going nowhere on the footplate. He was of course, absolutely right in what he said, and I did realise that he had my future career, and best interests, in mind when he gave this advice. I accepted and two weeks later bade farewell, not without great regret, to the footplate and my beloved engines. I had accrued in my time just over 230 firing turns, and in doing so had received a good understanding and experience of railway operation at the 'front end'. This experience was to prove invaluable in the years ahead.

I was appointed a Class 4 Clerk at Haymarket MPD and was designated Mechanical Foreman's Clerk. This meant I spent most of my time away from the main office, sitting at a desk in the corner of the small office upstairs in the 'new' maintenance shed. The Mechanical Foreman was, as I have said, John Banks, and a real character. He was a good boss and left me very much to my own devices. Here, I also came in contact with the Leading Fitter (maintenance) Jimmy Johnstone who was a loud, aggressive man, but a first class Fitter and 'engine doctor'. He was ably assisted by another elderly Leading Fitter, Joe Brown, who had lost an eye in an accident and had been accommodated on duties away from the rigours of fitting life. Joe was the Haymarket expert on valve setting and the conjugated motion on the Gresleys and was somewhat of a celebrity in his own right. He had been at 64B for many years and indeed, in 1959, I suspect he was already well over retirement age.

It was a change to work beside, and listen to, the Fitters' view on engines as opposed to the Drivers' and once more I was in a learning curve, taking in as much information as I could. My duties were not in any way hard. I maintained all the maintenance records of the allocated locomotives and prepared Shopping Proposal Forms for engines which were nearing general overhauls. All the Pacifics, V2s and B1s went to Doncaster as a matter of course, and the Shopping Bureau was located there. However, our ex-NB engines went to Cowlairs and the D49s and V1/V3s travelled to Darlington. The Shopping Bureau would not take an engine which had not run at least 90,000 miles since the last general repair. Now our Pacifics, and in particular, the A4s and A1s allocated to regular crews routinely achieved mileages of up to, and indeed exceeding 100,000 miles between shoppings and were generally accepted as soon as the Proposal Form was received, but any attempts to slip an engine in because of rough riding, poor steaming and so on at lower mileages was doomed to fail. As common user practices crept back in during the early 1960s the Drivers and Firemen could be presented with some real 'dogs'.

I compiled the 4.00pm daily Statement of Repairs carried out and also a series of weekly returns for our local DMPS Office at Waverley. One of these, previously described, concerned the strange case of the wheeldrop returns, which had been discontinued *after the war*. It said much about the bureaucracy of the time.

Generally, I made my way across the shed to take morning and afternoon tea with my colleagues in the main office, and in doing so, passed many fellow Cleaners working in the shed. There were more than a few who were very bitter at my change of fortune and ensured that the bitterness showed, but the majority remained friendly and on good terms.

It was just about this time that a new member of staff entered the General Office in the shape of 'Office Boy'. This was another Passed Cleaner, Alec Croy, who brought a great sense, and indeed, several practices, of the ridiculous into the Office. He was a larger than life character who had been 'taken down' temporarily on medical grounds, and was thus being accommodated. Alec could not in any way be described as an academic, nor indeed was he terribly well educated, but he was street-wise, amiable and a real comedian. His stepfather was a fitter in the Maintenance Shed.

As part of his duties Alec was required, as I had been when I covered as Office Boy, to make the morning and afternoon tea. As was explained at an earlier point in this story, the number of teas required for the staff, plus attendees at the morning conference, made for a philosophical/logistics problem; who had ordered what in the way of milk and sugar and in what combination? When I had undertaken this task, I had served the black teas first, then black with sugar, white, then white with sugar. This did require several journeys but made for less confusion. Alec cracked this in the first week. He took the orders, put all the teas on a big tray and then tasted each before serving to ensure the right teas were going to the right consumers. We, my fellow Clerks and I, observed this practice with some incredulity and quickly made it clear that if we ever saw him taste our teas before serving... well the consequences would be dire.

He was always a bit of thorn in the side of Minnie (Mrs Williamson) our typist. She considered herself a lady and did demand some preferential treatment from us all. Blue stories were a 'no-no' and swearing of course was totally out of the question. Alec, a true footplateman who hardly strung two words together without swearing, came in for a lot of flak. However, he always did his best. The office was heated by a coal burning (what else?) 'Courtier' stove, which did, it must be said, give out a lot of heat to the point where the office, in an afternoon, was more like a Turkish Bath. Alec tended the stove as if it were an A3 on the 'coast'. Minnie went out every lunch time and in doing so, went through the same procedure. She had outdoor shoes, and a pair of sandals that she kept for wearing in the office, and these shoes were changed morning, lunchtime and night. As the winter came in and the days got colder, she required that her sandals were placed in front of the stove to heat, for fifteen minutes before she returned from lunch (Minnie was nothing if not punctual) and Alec, of course, was the designated 'sandal heater'. One glorious day he forgot about the sandals until he saw Minnie hove to across the shed front like a galleon in full sail. We waited with bated breath to see how he might cope with this calamity. Nothing daunted, he took the fire tongs and lifted an almost white hot cinder from the stove, and placing it in one sandal, quickly rolled it round and round before decanting it back into the fire. He repeated this with the second sandal, but the minute the cinder hit the sandal, the sandal started to smoulder. We, the audience were rolling about the floor by this time, Minnie was entering the outside door, whilst Alec was waving and blowing on a sandal which was by then, ablaze. Minnie was, in the best Queen Victoria fashion, not amused and although he apologised, explained what had happened and offered to replace the sandals (presumably with fireproof

ones) we all got the impression that Minnie believed that it had been a deliberate act of arson rather than just arsing!

During this time, George Cherry was appointed to DMPS Burntisland, and Johnnie Banks followed him as Haymarket Shed Master. George Russell from Polmont shed came to Haymarket as Mechanical Foreman and thus became my immediate boss. He was an out and out gentleman with a vast knowledge and experience of the steam locomotive.

However it was Mr Banks, with a similarly highly refined sense of the ridiculous, who encouraged Alec in some of his wilder ploys. Now, the office routine was set in tablets of stone. Minnie typed all day and the correspondence which accrued was uplifted from her 'out' tray at 16.00 on the dot, by the Office Boy (Alec) and taken in to the inner sanctum for signature by the Shed Master. Alec religiously complied but in taking the correspondence into the Shed Master, would say 'what should I do with these Mr. Banks?' 'Noddy' would reply 'just throw them on the fire, Alec!' They would then both laugh and Alec would place them on the desk. This banter went on for some time, until one afternoon when Alec went in with the letters and

The final ignominy for D11/2 4-4-0 62685 MALCOLM GRAEME, condemned to act as stationary boiler behind the new Fitting Shed at Haymarket, before finally being sent off for scrapping. 6th September 1959. (Alec Swain/Transport Treasury)

forms and made the usual inquiry. On receiving the usual answer, he did just that, and threw the lot into the open grate. Minnie's work went up in smoke. Mr. Banks came out of the office holding his sides and crying with laughter, but it was no laughing matter when the joke was explained to Minnie. She definitely did not see the funny side of it! Relations between Alec and Minnie were strained for the remainder of his time with us. Sadly, he was another keen young man who then resigned and went, I understand, to the Post Office.

It was during his tenure of office that we discovered that Mr Banks had another attribute, nothing less than an ability to disappear into thin air. This was discovered late one afternoon in late autumn. We were, in the office, winding down towards finishing time. Now, the line to the turntable lay immediately on the south side, parallel to the General Office. Thus, we, the inmates, were used to the movement of engines past the windows, and the thump, thump as the wheels crossed on to the turntable, which lay outside the Shed Master's office window. Mr Banks was in his office and we were getting ready to pack up for the day when a V1, 67615, passed at a fair rate of knots, immediately followed by a thunderous crash which shook the office. We rushed out and there was a 'Shire' sitting half

way round on the turntable, and 67615, bunker first in the turntable pit, chimney to the sky. Now as I have stated earlier, the only ingress/egress from the Shed Master's office was through the General Office and we *knew* that he was there. But when we went to alert him, he quite simply… wasn't. No one had seen him come through the General Office but he had vanished and it was subsequently believed, perhaps unfairly, that, on hearing the crash, he had climbed out the window and made off!

There was a strange sequel to this story in that, during the following week, an early morning train from Perth had worked in to Edinburgh and the engine, Standard Five 73106, had reversed up to the shed for turning and preparation as usual, before working home. There was already an engine on the turntable when 73106 arrived, and the elderly Perth Driver was sitting dozing, waiting his turn, when the coal pilot, propelling a rake of loaded wagons of coal for the coaling plant, took the turntable road (due to the carelessness of the Shunter in not setting the hand points correctly) and gently collided with the Class Five pushing it slowly, tender first, into the turntable pit. One can imagine the surprise of the Perth Driver when he received this bump, came out of his reverie and found himself about fifteen

feet above rail level as the derailed tender lifted the rear end of the locomotive up in to the air. To have two engines in the turntable pit in one week was some sort of a record, I believe, and trust 64B to hold this distinction.

There was also the afternoon, during tea break, when John Thomson bit into a biscuit and broke his false teeth. Bad enough but he then swallowed one of the broken parts with his biscuit. This lodged in his chest and the First Aid men were summoned, as was an Ambulance, and poor old John was carted off the Edinburgh Royal Infirmary for an emergency operation to retrieve the teeth. It was not in any way a pleasant experience for him, but it did give us callous youths some cause for hilarity some time thereafter. However, after a few days (and fitted with a new pair of teeth) John came back to rule the roost.

Just about this time, I was placed with Sandy Mercer permanently to ensure that I learned the rostering job thoroughly and my in-depth training started immediately. Although I had picked up a lot of what was entailed during my previous time with him, this was the real nitty-gritty of the job and so I started on what was yet another fascinating learning experience in my career, and again an experience which was to stand me in good stead long after I had moved on from Haymarket.

A4 60024 KINGFISHER, now with diamond plaques, at Eastfield shed in Glasgow on 9th April 1955, in the more than capable hands of Haymarket top link crew, Driver W (Bill) Macleod and Passed Fireman George O'Hara. 60024 was the regular Top Link engine of Drivers Bill MacLeod and Tony Macleod at this time. (Transport Treasury)

A4 60027 MERLIN in typical Haymarket pose. Now fitted with a double chimney (February 1958) she is in a less than perfect state of cleanliness. The plaque, depicting the badge of HMS Merlin, the naval shore establishment at Donibristle in Fife, was gifted by Officers of that establishment on 26th May 1946. The engine, with her own crew, was actually worked into the Naval Base sidings for the hand-over ceremony. Although undated, the attention to window cleaning at the Fitters' bothy, in the background, might just indicate springtime. (Transport Treasury)

36. ROSTER CLERK IN TRAINING

Sandy Mercer was a tall, white-haired man who lived down in Roseburn Street just below the depot and he just walked the hundred yards or so up to work in his long, blue, dust coat. Sandy was also very much a law unto himself in that, since everyone else gave the rostering job a wide berth, he was left alone and made his own time, although every hour was generally required to ensure that the daily rosters were posted in as accurate a state as possible. Mistakes did occur, but these were few, and almost inevitable, given the demands of the job.

I acquired a spare blue dust coat and joined Sandy at 08.00 on the following Monday morning. Straight off, he was a good tutor and took pains to ensure that I was understanding all I was being shown. The first job on each Monday was to prepare the weekly diagrams for the following week. The rosters were prepared on what was a broadsheet of blue-ish high quality paper. The weekly link workings, when established for a season, altered not, and so all the turns were listed on a Sunday to Saturday basis. The names of the regular Drivers and Firemen (and their allotted locomotives in Nos.1 and 2 links) were listed down the left-hand side of the roster sheet, on loose strips of paper, secured by paper clips. This meant that, at the beginning of each week, all that had to be re-written were new slips with the names against the turns, as the 14 or 12 week cycle progressed. The full roster of all the links was thus prepared in this fashion. Then a separate list (on scrap paper) was compiled with all the men known to be on annual leave, sick or otherwise not available for the full week. These names were then deleted in red ink on the weekly sheets. With all the vacant turns now shown as requiring to be covered, the list of senior spare Drivers was consulted to ascertain which Driver was nearest to the turn to be covered, and this name was entered in the space, again in red ink.

Now this was where a trap lay if the Roster Clerk was not careful or alert. A Spare Driver (or Fireman) was only allocated a 'datum' time in the spare link. He could, under the National Agreements, then be moved forwards or backwards by a maximum of up to two hours only, from that datum time. So, to illustrate, let us consider a vacancy arising in the top link because of holidays, say 15.00 for the 16.00 Newcastle, a mileage turn. Now there could be a 15.00 senior spare Driver, so the job was his. But there might not be a 15.00 Driver but a Driver at 14.00 and a Driver at 16.00, each datum time equidistant from the diagram time. In this case, the Roster Clerk had to know the date each man entered railway service for it was the Driver with the most seniority, even although this might only be as little as one day, who had the right to the job. Now, if the spare Drivers were at datum times of 13.30 and 16.15 and the earlier Driver was the senior man, nevertheless the job rightly went to the 16.15 man since he was nearest the turn. Sounds complicated? Yes it was.

Thus we would then work down through all the links until we came to the two spare links, now further depleted by the stepping up of Drivers to the train running links. There, we had to backfill all the now vacant places in the spare links by stepping up Drivers from the Junior to Senior spare and Drivers from the tank link to Junior Spare, and then, in turn, back filling these vacancies by going back to the top link and allocating the Passed Firemen in order of seniority, driving turns in the tank links and lower links. The only Drivers not 'stepped up' were the sick, lame and lazy.

Then the process was started all over again by covering the vacancies for Firemen and again, the Senior Spare Firemen got first call for the train working links, from No.1 link downwards, and with the same time and seniority conditions being applied. Finally, all the still vacant positions for Firemen were then filled from the cleaning squads, again on a strict seniority basis. That then dealt with the weekly rosters. However, if Passed Firemen were being stepped up from firing duties to driving, and Passed Cleaners stepped from cleaning to firing, they could be swung on to any shift, as required, that is a Passed man on a rostered dayshift turn in his own grade could be allocated late or night turns if he was required for the full week.

But, every member of footplate staff had a rest day once every fortnight and individual members of staff were regularly being taken off for medicals, eyesight testing etc, or being granted lieu leave on a daily basis, so a further roster sheet had to be prepared for each day with all the vacancies on the day being filled again in strict compliance to seniority and time. On these daily sheets were also entered all the special trains that 64B were required to work, so that crews could be set against the turns. Most special working was advised by a Special Traffic Notice published the week prior to taking effect and in Scotland there was a notice SC1 for ex-LNER lines and SC2 for ex-LMS lines. Haymarket was allocated turns in both Notices. However, there were often one-off, special trains required and these were noted on daily 'advices', normally given to depots 24 hours beforehand, or even just telegraphed through in an emergency.

The daily rosters went up two days in advance so that men on shifts or rest day could be given the opportunity of prior advice. If there was any doubt about any particular individual not being able to see the roster, then the Call Boy was dispatched with a telegram to his home, or a telegram sent via the GPO, to men who were out of town.

And so the Roster Clerk's week was taken up until the Thursday when the daily rosters for the Saturday, Sunday and Monday had to be prepared, and in the summer especially, every Saturday was a day when Haymarket was stretched to the absolute limit, to cover all the special workings. It must be said at this point that, in all my time at Haymarket, no Driver, Fireman or Cleaner ever worked a rest day. This just was not done and the Roster Clerk knew better than to ask. There was, as I have already described, the opportunity to have a sixth shift worked by use of the 'Guaranteed Day', to swing men from night shift to either early or late shifts, but it was not at all unknown for some of the preparation and disposal turns to have 'O/D' marked against the Driver and/or Fireman. This was the point at which the Roster Clerk had thrown in the towel, being unable to cover any more turns; O/D meant 'Other Depot'. This saw Drivers and Firemen being brought in from depots like Bathgate, Polmont and indeed, on rare occasions, as far afield as Hawick, for preparation turns or disposal turns while the Haymarket men worked all the train jobs. It was the Running Foreman's job to make the necessary arrangements for this to happen. These other depots were predominantly concerned with freight and so had little or no train working on a Saturday, although staff were booked on duty purely to satisfy the 44 hour week. The men who were drafted in to Haymarket received travelling time which was overtime, something they would not normally have enjoyed. However, it cannot be said that the 'imports' always enjoyed the experience for they were not, on any regular basis, confronted with the need to prepare six or seven Pacifics in a shift at, say, Bathgate! On the Saturday morning, the daily roster for the following Tuesday was prepared and posted and so we then started all over again.

Sunday working which was not otherwise a rostered (diagrammed) turn also had to be shared out equally, and a book was kept recording the number of Sunday turns which each man had worked. This equality was essential since Sunday work was paid at double time, but it was not a simple matter for the Roster Clerk, because footplate staff had to have a clear 12 hours rest between turns of duty. Often, although a man was entitled to a Sunday turn in the general share out, he might well be rendered ineligible because he could not get the required rest period before his booked Monday job. Sunday work was always another headache and a long-standing bone of contention, but as long as the National Agreements were adhered to, the Clerk was home and dry, though not necessarily popular.

This then was the black art that I had been set to learn and soon I was totally absorbed in the challenge. As I said, Sandy was a first class teacher and there was much hands-on work for me, under his eagle eye. I was soon making fewer and fewer errors and gaining in confidence. The one thing I did learn was that I soon recognised every face at 64B and, what's more, I could put a name to the face. Just after Easter weekend, my biggest challenge arose, for Sandy declared his intention to take a week's annual leave.

Just before Sandy went off on his leave, John Thomson called me over to tell me that David Masterton, the Relief Clerk would arrive on Monday morning to nominally take over Sandy's duties for the week. On no account was I to leave his (David's) side during the week and I should scrutinise everything he did. Shades of past experiences with David, I thought to myself.

The Monday dawned and I was in the Roster office by 07.30. David turned up at 09.00 and introduced himself. He was a small, dapper man who, it all too soon became apparent, was in fear of this particular job. As I have indicated, even in 1959, there were significant differences in rostering procedures in ex-LMS and ex-LNER depots and David hailed from Carstairs and the 'Caley'. I had already made a start on the following week's roster and we were soon both hard at work. However, I became aware that David was leaving much of the covering of train working by Spare men to me, since my acquired knowledge of who was who made this an easier task for me than for himself.

The week was a great learning experience for me for suddenly, I was being left, or being asked, to make decisions, something ex-Cleaners were not generally faced with. We enjoyed a good week together and David was the nicest of men to work with. He, without doubt, had a wide knowledge of motive power administration and as a senior DMPS relief clerk, was required to cover many responsible jobs throughout the Edinburgh District, but rostering at Haymarket, and to a lesser degree St. Margarets, was not exactly his forte and we were to work together many times over the rest of my time at 64B.

I also learned some of the other jobs at Haymarket but did not ever become involved in the 'staff job', allotted to David Galbraith. Mark Wright or Bill

Hastie covered this as required, and to good effect. Joe Wise also had a good knowledge of other jobs and work was covered to a considerable degree by overtime and people stepping up. It was not a common event to have one of the DMPS Class 3 relief clerks cover at Haymarket since vacancies because of holidays/leave/sickness were covered internally by overtime.

However, time was moving on and once again, the summer timetable was imminent. It was at this point that I first had experience of revising the link workings to reflect the summer requirements. On a Sunday morning around the middle of May I was invited to join Sandy, Mr Cherry, John Thomson and Angus Gilchrist, a Driver who was also the ASLEF representative at the depot and a member of Sectional Council 'B', to revise the link workings. This, as it turned out, was a long day indeed, but one which was full of interest, and a challenge. The object was to fairly distribute the allocated engine workings for the summer timetable around the links, whilst ensuring that the best paying work went to the senior Drivers.

The base was established by the allocation of the two turns required each week for the non-stop 'Elizabethan'. These went to No.1 link and we built on that. The allocation of work was important in other ways, not least to ensure that there were sufficient jobs allocated to various destinations to

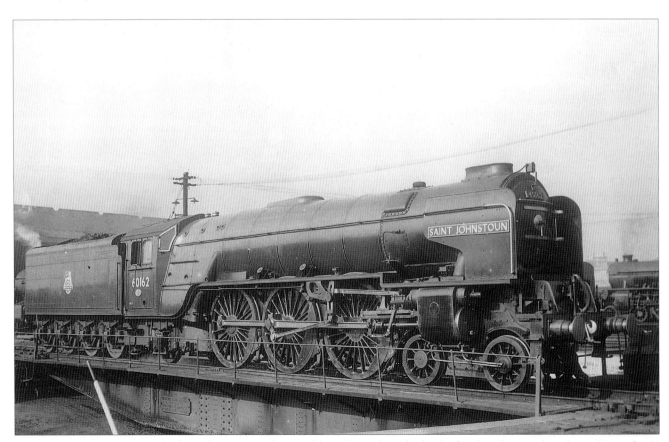

A1 60162 SAINT JOHNSTOUN in the early 1950s, on the turntable at Haymarket. The last in the class, it entered service at Haymarket in December 1949 in BR blue livery and un-named. On return from a Heavy Intermediate repair at Doncaster Works on 21st August, 1951, 60162 sported the new BR lined Brunswick green and the new nameplates so this photograph is after that date. The engine still carries the original 'stovepipe' double chimney, but, like the remainder of the class, had her looks much improved some time later when a rimmed chimney was fitted. (A.A.McLean Collection)

A view inside Haymarket in the dying days of steam, in 1963. A1 Pacifics 60159 BONNIE DUNDEE and 60152 HOLYROOD stand side by side, with a new EE Type 4 just in view. Cleaning had long gone by the board at this time and the two former No.2 link locomotives show nothing of the sparkling finish of earlier and happier days. (Dugald Cameron Collection)

maintain the route knowledge of each Driver in the link. If a Driver had not driven over a route at least once in a six month period, he was entitled to remove the route from his route card (held by the Running Foreman) and request route revision. The maintenance of route knowledge was essential and during the summer months we often had to consult route cards when some strange or exotic special train working was requested. We had Drivers who, even in the late 1950s, could drive over lines such as the Forth and Clyde (Stirling to Jamestown Junction via Buchlyvie) and on to Aberfoyle, even though passenger services has been withdrawn for many years. The Border Counties line from Riccarton Junction to Morpeth and Newcastle was another route that still appeared on several route cards.

And so the links were slowly re-cast and, as stated earlier, this revision could see work which had been in No.1 link, for instance, re-allocated to No.3 link to ensure an equal distribution of mileage work. Indeed, No.3 link did gain the afternoon 'Talisman' the 16.00 Edinburgh to London Kings Cross at this time. The passenger links were the

worst to set up since the freight work tended not to change. The Tank link duties also tended to remain fairly static with little change in preparation diagrams unless there was an amended need for relief/light engine movements.

It was always an event when the summer (and winter) diagrams went up and Passed Firemen saw which Driver they were to be paired with for the whole period, and Cleaners saw who was now being marked up in red ink (though this was now diminishing). Not everyone was happy, and I did know of several instances where a Driver and his Fireman would have no contact with each other on the footplate, other than any communication demanded by the nature of the job. Yes, there was discord at Haymarket.

Rostering was one of the most frustrating yet fruitful and satisfying task I have ever had to undertake and my experiences at Haymarket stood me in good stead for my later life on the railway. I had not lost all contact with my beloved steam locomotives, however, and had the opportunity, almost at will, to make a journey on the footplate and keep my hand in. Alec

Gunn was one Passed Fireman I travelled with on several occasions and he in fact fired to Peter Robertson for a winter, so stolen footplate moments were possible. I also travelled when Willie Titzell was firing, and enjoyed trips on the 16.00 Perth which had been my very first main line turn as a Fireman. It was also at this time that I made many trips on the new EE Type 4s as they took over steam diagrams. I travelled with Peter Robertson to Glasgow and back on the 'North Briton' and was duly given a driving lesson on these locomotives. I also went to Dundee on an EE Type 4 with Andrew Fraser, another No.3 link Driver. This was entirely irregular but I was aided and abetted by Drivers, Firemen and Cleaners with whom I had enjoyed a particularly good working relationship. Because this had to done outwith office hours, I would generally slip down to Newcastle and back on the backshift 'Talisman', or go to Perth and back on the 16.00 Inverness. Indeed, this practice soon resulted in me being 'hoist with my own petard' as it were.

Inside the shed in 1963 with Perth South (63A) Black Five 44722 standing alongside A4 60012 COMMONWEALTH OF AUSTRALIA. Also getting into the picture is EE Diesel Electric Type 4 D279 which was not on the Haymarket allocation. (Dugald Cameron Collection)

37. THE 'CON' ARTIST

We Clerks at Haymarket had significant contacts with the Railway Telegraph Office at Buchanan Street Station in Glasgow. Much of the railway communication back then was conducted over the internal telephone network using both Telegram and direct voice communication, and the Telegraph Office in Glasgow was manned (if indeed I dare use such an expression) by a bevy of girls and women. Most of them were nothing more than disembodied voices at the end of a telephone. However, we came to recognise some of the voices and after some further time, were able to put names to voices. This arose through the inevitable chat between young men and young women, as was ever so, and sometimes the conversations became more personal and serious. I was no exception, being just twenty years old,

and soon had struck up a chatty relationship with one of the girls, which inevitably led to a date. It was agreed that I would travel through to Glasgow, meet said young lady in Queen Street station whence we would repair, perhaps for tea, and then the cinema. And so the arrangements were finalised and the meet was to take place on the next Saturday, a Saturday that was only one week short of Christmas.

It was my Saturday morning 'on' and I intended to travel to Glasgow on the 12.15 Saturdays Only (SO) 'slow', joining the train at Haymarket. Now before I carry on with my story, it must be made clear that the 12.15 SO Glasgow was the booked diagram for the No.3 link men who had worked the 16.00 'Talisman' which ran on Mondays to Fridays only. This Saturday working was one which Angus Gilchrist, the ASLEF rep, watched very carefully since,

if the Friday down 'Talisman' was at all late in arriving, the crew could not have the required 12 hours rest before booking back on duty on the Saturday for the 12.15. It was not at all unknown for a spare crew to have to take the engine to Waverley and work the train back to Haymarket where the No.3 link crew would then take over, having booked on with exactly 12 hours rest and with the requisite 15 minutes for notices before walking down to the station to pick up their train. I had not checked to see who would be working the 12.15 on the day I was travelling.

I walked down to Haymarket station from the depot and stood at the western end of No.4 platform, awaiting arrival of the train. At 12.19 on the dot it ran in, hauled by no less than 60162 SAINT JOHNSTOUN herself, with Peter Robertson and his Fireman, Passed Fireman Charlie Minto, hanging out

A picture that you can almost hear! It shows the daily 'race' between the 4.00pm to Glasgow Queen Street hauled by A4 60011 EMPIRE OF INDIA and the 4.00pm to Perth hauled by A3 60074 HARVESTER of Gateshead shed, in the late 1950s. The use of a foreign engine on a Haymarket No.2 link turn was a somewhat rare event. The 4.00pm Perth always, surprisingly and despite the fact that it contained through coaches for Inverness, ran as Class 'B' stopping passenger as the headcode denotes. The trains, with both locomotives clearly working full out, and with 60011 just ahead, are passing the top end of Haymarket shed and no doubt, money is changing hands amongst some of the Cleaners who will be watching. (Bill Brown collection)

A striking view of V2 60825 standing in platform 17 at a surprisingly quiet Waverley west end, on 17 July 1953. It was not a Haymarket engine but was allocated to sister depot St Margarets, 64A. The photograph shows up well the handsome lines of the V2 class, and the locomotive is at a spot well known to the men of 64B. The clock on the North British Hotel, always kept a few minutes early, shows 2.15pm. The train itself is difficult to identify since the locomotive has only single headlamp up and the coaches are non-corridor. The most likely explanation is that the V2 has brought in and set the empty coaches for a later departure and with Light Engine headlamp now set, is ready to go about the rest of its diagrammed duties. (J. Robertson, The Transport Treasury)

A4 60012 COMMONWEALTH OF AUSTRALIA on the washout road inside Haymarket shed awaiting attention in 1963. The shark's jaws are open as is the smokebox door proper. There is an untidiness in the surrounding area, something which would not have been tolerated just a few years previously. The corrugated asbestos wall behind 60012 separates Nos.7 and 8 roads, by now the domain of diesel electric locomotive maintenance, from roads 1 to 6 in the old steam shed. (Dugald Cameron Collection)

over the cab. Peter saw me before the train was at a stand, and beckoned me up. 'Coming with us', he shouted, 'where's your overalls?' Charlie had the cab doors open and as I tried to explain that I was intending to travel as a passenger, Peter had his overall jacket off, and on my back, before I could draw breath. 'Sit there,' he instructed pointing to the Driver's seat. This I did and turning round to (again) try and explain where I was going and for why, I found that Peter had dropped off and was heading back into the train, or so I thought. Charlie just laughed. Whistles blew and we got the green and Charlie shouted across, 'you're in charge, noo!'

I opened the regulator and got the train on the move, winding back the reverser as speed picked up. I was also concentrating very hard on spotting my signals as speed increased, with all other thoughts well out of mind. As we cleared Saughton Junction and I had '162 back in 15% with the regulator out against the stop, I began to take stock

of my situation. OK, I might get a bit dirty but could always have a quick wash in the gents at Queen Street, I thought. I then turned to my own present situation for here I was, at the controls of an A1, working a passenger train with all stops between Edinburgh and Glasgow, on a day which had started miserable, cold and with a touch of fog, and which appeared to be worsening by the minute. Meanwhile Charlie attended to his fire, apparently quite unconcerned though, in reality, he was keeping a close eye on what was happening on my side of the cab, and on the distant signals. I was now concentrating on spotting signals as we rushed through the cold afternoon. Out of Winchburgh Tunnel, I was struggling to see Winchburgh's home signal which was located high on the embankment on the right-hand side of the line, even although the distant had been clear. Through Philpstoun and I began to check our progress for the Linlithgow stop. I shut the regulator and wound

the reverser out to 25%. Visibility was still fair at this point and, using the Park Farm overbridge as a marker, I started to apply the brakes gently. As we rounded the left-hand corner I could see the platform ahead and, knowing that Linlithgow down platform was short, brought the speed right down and slowly drew along it, stopping with the engine just off the platform. I breathed a wee sigh of relief. Away we went from Linlithgow and again I managed a fair stop at Polmont, and then again at Falkirk High, a station well marked by the tunnel on the approach side. By this point, I knew I just had to hand over to Charlie, knowing I would end up getting twice as dirty.

We changed places and I picked up the shovel. Charlie knew the road like the back of his hand and although I had never fired to him during my time on the footplate, he was a sound Driver. Soon we were through Cowlairs and slipping down the hill to Queen Street. Here, the afternoon was distinctly murky and dull with a real 'pea souper' threatening in the failing light. We ground to a halt at Queen Street and I waited for Peter to re-appear. No sign of him. I looked at the barrier to see if my young lady was waiting but of her there also was no sign, although there was plenty of time for that. What was I to do? Charlie made it quite clear. 'If Peter disnae come', he said, 'you'll hae tae stey on the engine and come to the shed wi' me.' Peter 'didnae' come and off to Eastfield with Charlie and '162, I had no option but to go, now realising that I would be the Fireman on the return journey. Charlie shared his sandwiches with me in the mess room at Eastfield, where my strange attire of overall jacket over collar and tie and tailored slacks drew some strange looks from the locals, who no doubt were thinking 'talk aboot Glamour boys!'

Rejoining '162 I 'phoned off shed and soon we were slipping back down the hill and into the station to couple to the 17.35 'all stops' back to Edinburgh. Previous predictions about deteriorating weather had proved right and this was my first (but not by a long chalk last) experience of a real Glasgow 'pea-souper', a dense, oily, yellow fog that caught your throat and brought visibility down to just a few yards. This was as bad as it could get for steam locomotive men.

The return journey was a nightmare for both of us. After clearing the welcome colour light signals of Cowlairs, Charlie hung out the cab, fighting to catch the dim paraffin lit signal lamps while I tried to help between bouts of firing. With eyes affected by the glare of the fire, this was almost an impossible task. Indeed firing was the easiest part of the journey. We overran Bonnybridge High by three coach lengths and lost time as passengers, the very few passengers, walked back along the train to alight. As we moved eastwards, conditions improved although they were never good but eventually we slid to halt at Haymarket Station. There, waiting on the end of the platform to rejoin us, was the bold Peter. As we ran down into Waverley, he reclaimed his overall jacket and gave us a blow by blow account of the Heart of Midlothian football team victory at Tynecastle, a victory he had witnessed first hand. As I said, Peter was worth the watching, and so ended my romantic outing in Glasgow.

Reflecting on that day afterwards, I realised an important fact. Despite the firing experience I had gained during my time on the footplate, I had never, until that time, experienced footplate work in really adverse weather conditions, simply because we Cleaners never had much, if any, opportunity to go out firing during the winter, and it was a salutary lesson to realise that Drivers and Firemen were working under such extreme weather conditions as a matter of course and as part of their daily job. My respect rose considerably for their professionalism.

Haymarket veteran J36 65234 MAUDE shunting at Kirkliston in July 1958 when working the Haymarket trip E25, better known as the 'Ferry Goods', a double shifted freight working which served the industries around South Queensferry. Neither the Driver nor Fireman can be identified. This engine was normally used on trip working E123, the 'Broxburn Goods'. (Stuart Sellar collection)

Another Haymarket workhorse, J36 0-6-0 65235 GOUGH, was normally the regular engine on the 'Ferry Goods', a daily Monday to Friday double shifted freight working out of Haymarket Yard. Seen here on 13th May 1955 at the top end of the shed, she has been coaled and had her fire cleaned before being set back into the shed. Unusually, she is facing west, since the trip engines all generally worked chimney facing east. Like her sister MAUDE she was one of 25 of the class which saw service in France during the First World War. All, on return from France, were given appropriate 1914/1918 war names to commemorate the event. (Stuart Sellar Collection)

38. FINAL DAYS

During what was to be my final year at Haymarket, we Clerks got the opportunity to assist in the office duties at the new diesel depot at Leith Central, and Joe Wise, Bill Hastie and myself spent one morning each week there, until the office was eventually properly staffed. The new Chief Clerk at Leith Central was Ronnie Gibson, son of the infamous Peter Gibson, Ghargehand Labourer at 64B.

I also had the opportunity to relieve for holidays at other Edinburgh depots during this time and even spent a few

weeks with the 'opposition' at Dalry Road. This was indeed a happy time. The Chief Clerk was one Norman Thorburn and a real character. Travelling to and from Dalry Road from home was a breeze, and since we had to work rostered overtime twice each week, I travelled home to West Calder on the footplate of the 20.00 Slateford/ Buchanan Street freight on these nights, making friends with several of the young Drivers and in particular, one Eddie Blake, whose father was one of the Chargehand Cleaners at Haymarket.

Eddie was a first class Driver and character to boot. On 'normal' evenings I still travelled home on the footplate of the engine, generally a 'Black Five', working the 17.15 Princes Street to Glasgow Central.

It was during this time, in June 1961, that Dalry Road fell heir to a Royal Train working. The Queen came north to open the new permanent home for the Royal Highland Show at Ingliston, near Edinburgh. The train was worked via the west coast main line by two 'Black Fives' immaculately turned out, and set

An old, and somewhat less than perfect photograph, included because it shows most of the Admin staff from the General Office as at April, 1960. From left to right: Joe Wise, Class 4 Clerk, responsible for train delay and failure reports, Eric Caw (head only), Class 4 Clerk responsible for the control of consumables (coal, oil and so on), Alec Croy, Passed Cleaner acting Office Boy, general 'go-for' and the source of much fun and nonsense, R. Herbert, a Traffic Apprentice 'doing' his Motive Power training module at Haymarket, John Banks in the foreground, Yorkshireman, Shed Master and Scout Master extraordinaire, David Galbraith, Class 2 Staff clerk and inveterate worrier, John Thomson, Class 1 Chief Clerk, one of the old school and always the gentleman and finally Mark Wright, Class 4 Clerk responsible for availability returns, collation of information from Drivers tickets and leading light in the West Edinburgh Branch of the Railway Staff Association. The remaining members of staff absent from the photograph are the only female in the Office, Mrs. Williamson (Minnie), Bill Hastie, Class 4 Clerk (who took the photograph), Sandy Mercer, Class 2 Roster Clerk and myself who at this time was assisting Sandy. We were probably up to the eyes in rostering to find time for photographs. In the right background is the one time repository for stolen pianos!

aside for the night on the old Balerno Branch at Ravelrig Junction. To bring the Royal Train into Princes Street the following morning, Dalry Road had asked for the loan of a Class 8 locomotive from Haymarket, confidently expecting an A4. But no, the most suitable available turned out to be A1 60159 BONNIE DUNDEE. It did not work the train but instead languished dead behind the shed at Dalry Road, while 46224 PRINCESS ALEXANDRIA, hastily borrowed from Polmadie, was brought in to work the train. I'm not quite sure why the substitution was made; if 60160 with its obvious Edinburgh connections been available it would likely enough have been used. Instead the decision was taken by the Edinburgh DMPS to obtain a locomotive with 'royal' connotations. I hesitate to use the term 'sour grapes'... Two Locomotive Inspectors and a Running Foreman worked all night cleaning her and she was turned out to perfection on the morning. I had the privilege, quite unofficially and only for a brief time, of firing her back as far as West Calder when she was being returned home to Glasgow on the 17.15 from Princes Street that evening.

In my spare time, through the good offices of a friend I had made at Shotts, I had been able to actually work signal boxes, thus building on the theory learned in the correspondence courses. When I started at Shotts, a young Traffic Apprentice, Hugh Gould, came there to do his small station training. We became friends and Hugh, whose knowledge of railways was encyclopaedic, soon took me in hand and introduced me to that foreign territory which was the Glasgow suburban network and, also, to the West Highland line. On completion of his training he received his first permanent appointment, as Station Master at Burntisland and thereafter I was encouraged by him to get hands on experience 'in the box'. I spent many happy Saturday afternoons working either Newbiggin or Kinghorn signal boxes, with the odd foray into Burntisland Junction.

By the end of my footplate days I had requested an examination by an Operating Inspector on my knowledge of Rules and Regulations, a pre-requisite for anyone wishing to gain promotion in the field of current operations. I was subsequently examined by no less a personage than the Chief District Operating Inspector (Edinburgh) Jimmy Stevens. This oral examination took two days, two days of questions and answers, two days of hypothetical situations and how they should be dealt with. It was a punishing session, but I passed and was delighted, to say the least. I also learned some years later that Chief Inspector Stevens had been so impressed as to append some very complimentary footnotes on my Service Record which did me no harm whatsoever in later years. I was now scanning the Vacancy Lists and applying

for posts both in the clerical field and also, since I now held a rules qualification, in the Station Master grades.

Dieselisation had been in full swing at Haymarket since March 1959, with the shed and fuel storage and fuelling facilities constructed at the 'top end'. The 1160hp Birmingham RCW Sulzer diesel locomotives had appeared in ever increasing numbers and in February 1960 the EE Type 4s arrived, with D256, D259, D260 and D266 replacing Pacifics on the Aberdeen road. Indeed, a Haymarket diagram was now in place for sixteen Type 2s running in multiples of two, working a daily total of eight Aberdeen passenger and freight services. The EE Type 4s were taking over the east coast services as well as being deployed on the Aberdeens. Although they were all crewed by a Driver and Fireman (the latter took charge of the train steam heating boiler, the most temperamental piece of equipment ever designed as it turned out) the writing was now on the wall for Firemen and big changes in the working of the shed were also taking place. Maintenance areas for the diesels were being established, areas where steam was not welcome, areas which were being kept in a state of cleanliness, almost clinical cleanliness, for this new form of traction. On the downside, we also had Traction Electricians appointed to the staff numbers, and with these men came Trade Union problems of catastrophic proportions. This was the time when the ETU was communist-led, and it appeared every revolutionary in the union came on to the payroll at Haymarket. For the very first time in my experience, we were having union disputes at the drop of a hat. They (the electricians) were almost impossible to work with, called each other 'brother', were always making totally unreasonable demands and changed the face of 64B for ever. The term 'lines of demarcation' was being heard, and argued about, for the first time ever.

At about the same time, in March 1959, there came the end, sadly, of another era when the two West End Waverley Pilots, the J83 0-6-0Ts which been part of the scenery there for ever, or so it seemed, were withdrawn and replaced by diesel shunting locomotives, D3558 and D3560. The East End pilots worked by St. Margaret's were also similarly replaced. However, this was not initially the happiest of ventures, since it was soon discovered by the operating authorities that the '350s' were not actuating track circuits in the station environs and each of these locomotives thereafter, and until the re-signalling of the late 1970s, worked permanently coupled to a fully-fitted open wagon. They were also limited to a top speed of 25mph and could not complete some of the complicated shunts required as speedily as the J83s they displaced. However, with the ever-increasing

numbers of DMUs, the amount of shunting required at Waverley was also much diminished.

All in all, morale was in a state of decline. Steam was still to the fore, but was fading as the diesels continued to arrive and take over. Turns were being lost, and worse still for the industry, considerable amounts of traffic, both freight and passenger, were being lost too. The diesels themselves were proving to be unreliable and failure-prone, although how much of this was due to poor maintenance procedures by men who were used to the robust engineering of a steam locomotive, where a blow with a hammer would cure many ills, may never be known.

However, much of the problem could also be laid at the door of poor management at policy decision levels. The lack of standardisation in emerging diesel types, all with different manufacturers, led to enormous quantities of differing spares being required, and traction training for Drivers on each new type. This was a black period, where the left hand appeared to know not what the right was doing. Sadly, even the biggest and most powerful of the diesels proved not wholly capable of working the hardest of the turns which had previously been easily worked by steam, and a great cloud hung over Haymarket. It was a sad time and the mood did not begin to lift until mid-1961 when the EE Type 5s, in the shape of D9000, arrived at Haymarket, the first of the celebrated Deltics. It was followed quickly by D9004, D9006 and then the remaining five. These locomotives went on to prove just how good they really were, working the principal east coast trains with ease, and with significantly accelerated timings. One of my last tasks at Haymarket was to sit down with the Shed Master and devise the cyclic diagrams for the Deltics, diagrams which saw them clock up over 1000 miles, and more, nearly every 24 hours. I saw the first three Deltics arrive, and have on film, the first being shunted into the diesel shed by a diminutive J88. Quite a contrast in both tractive effort and age!

However, my efforts at advancement were eventually rewarded and in December 1961, at the age of 21, I was appointed to the position of a Relief Station Master in Glasgow South District. The promotion came at the right time for me. The Haymarket I had joined was changing out of all recognition. Steam was now being consigned to history, although not before some of our Gresleys were given the opportunity to show, in no small way, just what they could do, in steam's great Indian Summer on the Glasgow/ Aberdeen three hour services.

For myself, I had realised a boyhood ambition. I had actually worked as a member of the crew on the footplate of some of the finest steam locomotives anywhere in the world. I had been privileged to work with men, and alongside men, who were, in every sense, railwaymen. They had been my teachers and mentors and through them, I had gained unquestionable experience which was to stand me in good stead in the years to come. These men I still remember, and I will always be grateful to them. During my time there, I had, in my own small way, even contributed to the administration of one of the most well known locomotive depots within the whole of British Railways, *Haymarket*.

Probably one of the best known Drivers at Haymarket in the 1950s, Willie Bain of No.2 link looks down from the driver's cab window of his beloved A1 60162 SAINT JOHNSTOUN, at the shed exit in June 1954. The cab side is sparkling and gives an indication as to the perfect turn-out of the rest of the locomotive. For the best part of that decade, 60162 was probably the locomotive which set the benchmark for cleanliness anywhere in Scotland and perhaps further afield. The Fireman is not known to the Author but identification would be welcomed. Note that the engine has not yet been fitted with the rubber fairing between tender and cab, something which was to become standard very soon afterwards. (Stuart Sellar collection)

Tailpiece

Waverley No. 1 Pilot, J83 68481 seen propelling an empty coach shunting movement back into Waverley, in Princes Street Gardens. The engine is in its normal pristine state of cleanliness, a state which had nothing to do with the Haymarket Cleaners, all cleaning being undertaken by the three regular Drivers (all over 60 years of age) and their Firemen. (W. Hermiston/Transport Treasury)